RECLAIMING THE ARID WEST

THE AMERICAN WEST IN THE TWENTIETH CENTURY

Martin Ridge and Walter Nugent, editors

Richard Lowitt. *The New Deal and the West.*
William H. Mullins. *Depression and the Urban West Coast, 1929–1933:
Los Angeles, San Francisco, Seattle, and Portland.*
Donald L. Parman. *Indians and the American West in the Twentieth Century.*
William D. Rowley, *Reclaiming the Arid West.*

RECLAIMING THE ARID WEST

The Career of Francis G. Newlands

WILLIAM D. ROWLEY

INDIANA UNIVERSITY PRESS

Bloomington and Indianapolis

The paper used in this publication meets the minimum requirements of
American National Standard for Information Sciences—Permanence of
Paper for Printed Library Materials, ANSI Z39.48-1984.

Manufactured in the United States of America

LIBRARY OF CONGRESS CATALOGING-IN-PUBLICATION DATA

Rowley, William D.
Reclaiming the Arid West : The Career of Francis G. Newlands / William D.
Rowley.
p.   cm. — (American West in the twentieth century)
Includes bibliographical references (p.   ) and index.
ISBN 0-253-33002-5 (cl : alk. paper).
1. Newlands, Francis G. (Francis Griffith), 1848–1917. 2. Water
resources development—West (U.S.)—History. 3. Reclamation of
land—West (U.S.)—History. 4. Irrigation—Nevada—History.
I. Title. II. Series
E664.N4R69   1996
328.73'092—dc20
[B]   95-34788

1   2   3   4   5   01   00   99   98   97   96

to Cette
une jeune fille de l'ouest

CONTENTS

ILLUSTRATIONS

FOREWORD

Francis Newlands is not a forgotten figure in American history. Every textbook mentions him. He was the driving force behind the so-called Newlands Reclamation Act of 1902. The measure established the nation's reclamation policy and had a profound impact on the development of the western economy in the twentieth century. It empowered the Department of the Interior to build reservoirs and reserve public lands for farmers in the arid areas of the West, and it gave the Secretary of the Interior unprecedented administrative authority. It was a radical measure designed both to conserve and utilize resources within the western states. Equally interesting is the fact that the legislation was sponsored not by a Theodore Roosevelt Progressive but by a Democrat at a time when that party was deeply committed to states rights. If Newlands's name is well recognized, much of his personal life and political career have remained somewhat tainted and in the shadows. Stories about fabulous wealth, purchased congressional and senatorial offices, and of using the state of Nevada as a "rotten borough," where corruption was a byword, have helped to create this reputation.

William Rowley's biography presents a very different picture of Newlands and his era. Newlands was a complicated and sophisticated man who not only expressed seemingly contradictory ideas but also lived a dual political life. On the one hand he was an advocate of honest politics and political reform, on the other he managed to "play the game" in Nevada politics. He was a man who welcomed the promise of an enlightened twentieth century, but he believed that African Americans were an inferior race who should be educated to be hewers of wood and drawers of water and certainly denied the franchise. In fact, he went so far as to advocate that the Democratic party in 1912 include a platform plank calling for the repeal of the Fifteenth Amendment. Newlands passionately believed that only the national government could and should control the nation's resources but he balked at the idea that the nation's banking system needed national regulation because that would interfere with private property. A strong defender of personal wealth and the right of private interests to avoid governmental control, he could attack railroads and other monopolies for ignoring the public's welfare. Newlands was a liberal in a conservative states rights

party—a politician far closer to the New Nationalism of Theodore
Roosevelt than to the New Freedom of Woodrow Wilson, except on
issues of foreign policy.

Newlands's life, which spans the turn of the century, affords an
unusual insight into the social and political context of the nation and
Nevada. To seek political preferment in Nevada at the close of the
nineteenth century Newlands rode the roller coaster of the free silver
movement while he tried to make Reno a modern city and encourage
the growth of a stable agricultural society. This was no simple task.
Nevada was an impoverished state with a declining population; its
competing economic interests had developed the art and science of
political corruption to a high level. To make matters even worse,
Newlands carried into the political arena the unsavory reputation of his
father-in-law, William Sharon, the notorious Comstock-lode millionaire, who had virtually bought himself one of Nevada's seats in the
United States Senate. The political hacks of Nevada expected the best
of times when Newlands took up residency.

Newlands had been forced to leave California to defend not only the
Sharon family's fortunes but also his own reputation because of the
senator's scandalous personal, business, and political behavior. It was
an onerous burden, even for a talented man, but proved especially
difficult for an individual who prided himself on his personal honesty
and integrity. Newlands was indeed a living embodiment of the Horatio
Alger myth. He was determined to make a useful life for himself, his
community, and his country. He did it during a period of great national
change. All of this and more is explained in William Rowley's graciously
written and meticulously researched biography. It is both a successful
evaluation of Newlands's life and a fine mirror of the age.

This book is one of a series dealing with the West in the twentieth
century. It is a splendid companion volume to three earlier works in the
series: Richard W. Lowitt's *The New Deal and the West*, William H.
Mullins's *The Depression and the Urban West Coast, 1929–1933*, and
Donald L. Parman's *Indians and the American West in the Twentieth
Century*. The series is intended to provide the general reading public
and the scholarly reader with a deeper understanding of important
individuals and aspects of the recent past of the American West.

MARTIN RIDGE
WALTER NUGENT

ACKNOWLEDGMENTS

Bringing the biography of Francis G. Newlands to publication has tapped the good will and cooperation of many people laboring in the vineyards of historical studies. Howard Lamar facilitated my research in the Newlands papers at Yale's Sterling Library and made my several visits there always a pleasant task. Martin Ridge, senior researcher at the Huntington Library, insisted over the years that I bring the project to a conclusion and provided essential editorial comments and deletions. Professor Donald Pisani of the University of Oklahoma generously shared his keen insights gained from many years of research in western water history. Likewise his colleague at Oklahoma, Richard Lowitt, offered encouragement in the early years of this study from his own challenges with political biography. Professor Richard Orsi of California State University at Hayward has made important suggestions, as has Judith Austin of the Idaho State Historical Society. In Reno, I have had invaluable help from the staff of the Nevada Historical Society: Director Peter Bandurraga, Librarian Lee Mortensen, Curators Phil Earl and Eric Moody. In the Special Collections Department of the University of Nevada Library, Kathryn Totton was always ready to help and Mary Ellen Glass, in her former capacity as head of the University of Nevada Oral History Program, opened many research doors. My colleagues at the University of Nevada have provided a rich academic environment. Special mention should be made of Jerome E. Edwards, chair, James Hulse, C. Elizabeth Raymond, Dean Ann Ronald, and emeriti professors Michael J. Brodhead and Russell R. Elliott. Graduate student and Ph.D. aspirant, Penelope Anne Carlson helped and, of course, Patricia Rowley did much. Thanks to all for this endeavor whose shortcomings whatsoever are my responsibility.

RECLAIMING THE ARID WEST

I

SENATOR NEWLANDS

FIRST AMONG THE
"IRRIGATION CRANKS"

United States Senator Francis G. Newlands was delighted. Three years to the day after President Theodore Roosevelt signed the National Reclamation Act on June 17, 1902, water flowed to the deserts of Nevada. Saturday, June 17, 1905, was a clear, warm day in the dusty sage desert twenty-four miles east of Reno on the banks of the Truckee River. During the previous two and a half years at this site federal reclamation engineers constructed foundations, poured tons of Portland cement, and dug canals, all in the task of building a diversion dam on the Truckee River for the irrigation of the desert.

Now, just before 10:00 A.M., a special train from Reno stopped. Dignitaries, almost 200 from all over the nation, filed from the passenger cars. They included members of the House and Senate Irrigation Committees, the governor of California, local citizens, and Nevada Senators Newlands and George S. Nixon, as well as the now retired and aging Senator William M. Stewart. Others among them were Senators Francis E. Warren of Wyoming, Henry C. Hansbrough of North Dakota, Fred DuBois of Idaho, Thomas Kearns of Utah, Charles H. Dietrich of Nebraska, and Charles W. Fulton of Oregon. The slate of names represented the champions of the western irrigation movement. As the crowd trooped from the train and began inspecting the dam, Newlands made preparations for his role as master of ceremonies to mark the completion of the first dam in the West authorized by the National Reclamation Act of 1902 and built by the newly created Reclamation Service.

Senator Newlands, with his tailcoat blowing in the wind and a broad white hat to shield his balding head from the sun, announced that this was an auspicious day for Nevada and the entire nation. Here in the deserts of Nevada, he said, the federal government had built a great work. Out of it will arise storage reservoirs and ditches to deliver water to freeholders upon the land whose acreage shall not exceed a limit of 160 acres. The future of the New West lay with these small farmers and not with the land monopolists who by law were excluded from the benefits of government reclamation. While this program was humanitarian, it was also a business proposition. Water rights were to be sold to small farmers interest-free in return for their repaying the government over a period of ten years for reclamation works necessary to bring water to the land. The water was not a gift but a sound business loan to open the deserts for the growth of new communities that would add to the common welfare.

While Newlands graciously received applause for his leadership in the Democratic party in the struggle for national reclamation, he briefly abandoned partisanship and praised the cooperation of Republican President Theodore Roosevelt in the cause. He saw it as a part of the president's program to restore the democracy and traditions of Abraham Lincoln and extend the prosperity and happiness of the entire people. Newlands was particularly pleased that the first project was inaugurated and completed in Nevada, a "state whose development has been retarded by so many untoward conditions." Newlands, like other progressive-minded citizens of the state, believed it was unfortunate that Nevada's youth "was spent not under the open skies . . . but in the deeps of the darksome mines." The future of Nevada, Newlands asserted, was upon the land in the open light of day in "harmonious development," with agriculture, commerce, and industry marching arm-in-arm as the vast powers of nature "hitherto unharnessed, [were] brought under man's control by this great national enterprise."[1] Newlands's vision not only saw the deserts watered but also foresaw the link between water storage and hydroelectric power for the state and the West.

After his speech, Newlands presented Congressman F. W. Mondell of Wyoming, who compared the present occasion to celebrate the diversion of water from the Truckee with a gathering on the banks of the Nile more than six thousand years ago for the dedication of similar works built under governmental auspices that made fertile a valley for a vast population through the ages. The completion of this diversion dam, said Mondell, represented the first fruits of western people to secure the aid of the general government in the construction of works so mighty in their character as to be beyond the possibility of private enterprise. It was appropriate that this first work occurred in Nevada, a state represented by Senator Newlands, "who has always been earnest, faithful, forceful and effective in bringing about the recognitions of the national character of this work and in securing the legislation which made this construction possible. Whatever other men have done," Mondell said, "no other man in the country did more than Senator Newlands to make possible these works you find here now."

In the next breath Republican Congressman Mondell complimented Democrat Newlands for appreciating President Roosevelt's work on behalf of national reclamation, and for noting that while the president was "no less a Republican now than he was in the past he is as Senator Newlands has well said the foremost exponent of that grand democracy to which all of us belong." And then as if in benediction Mondell wished the people of Nevada Godspeed and blessed "the waters that today shall be turned from their natural channels to take their course through the canals which have been constructed to fructify the desert, to bring life where death now dwells and to make possible the establishment of the highest and the best and the most perfect institutions of civilization in this splendid mountain land."

Following the congressman, Newlands introduced Governor George C. Pardee of California, the newly elected president of the National Irrigation Congress and the first governor of California to praise the benefits of irrigation to the California legislature. Pardee congratulated Nevada on this project, but also said that this enterprise means as much to the state of California as it does to Nevada. It means, he said, looking forward to the future nation-state greatness of California that the "waters now running to waste in the state of Nevada and in California, will be put upon the land to support a population which will only be equaled by some of the European nations."

Senator Newlands then spoke to the great work at hand: a dam built by the Reclamation Service, a branch of the Geological Survey of the Interior Department. He traced the evolution of the Service, starting with one or two men to make irrigation investigations and gradually enlarging into a regular force of five or six hundred engineers and their assistants. "This reclamation service has performed a work for the public," he said, "far beyond that simply involved in the construction of this enterprise or the completion of other irrigation projects in process of construction." They are teaching the greater lesson, continued Newlands, "convincing the people of the United States of the capacity of the nation to do things that have hitherto been regarded as belonging exclusively to the domain of private enterprise." One of the principals in this work was Frederick H. Newell, who came to Washington as a young man in the Geological Survey and who took up the subject of irrigation with enthusiasm. "I remember," said Newlands, "he approached me when I first entered congress in a deprecatory kind of way, as if the subject of irrigation required an apology for its introduction. That young man has gone on earnestly . . . until today he is at the head of that great service, in charge of all of this great irrigation work of the United States and he has impressed upon the entire service his character, his earnestness and his integrity."

At that he yielded the podium to Newell, Chief of the Reclamation Service. Newell expressed appreciation that so many statesmen and great men of the country were present to witness the completion of the project. He said he would let the works speak for the engineers. He asked Newlands to move toward the gates of the diversion canal and take one of the positions at the handles of the gates, and each one of the gentlemen who have by their interest in the subject earned the title of "irrigation cranks" to take their positions at the other handles. At a signal given by Newlands the works should be started in operation. At the same time the supervising engineer of the project, L. H. Taylor, directed Lieutenant Governor Lem Allen of Nevada and others to close the gates on the diversion dam across the Truckee.

The time was 11:23 A.M. as Senator Newlands signaled for his wife Edith McAllister Newlands to crash a bottle of White Seal champagne against a metal crank on the gates of the canal. The gates began to open while on the dam across the Truckee the other group turned cranks to block the normal course of the river. The Truckee rolled through the openings into the canal that carried water south toward the Lahontan Valley and brought national irrigation to the deserts of western Nevada. The crowd cheered, but in the river bed that took its course north to the ancient desert lake—named Pyramid by John C. Frémont—fish flopped about helplessly as the water drained away to the desert. With the effectiveness of the diversion dam demonstrated, Chief Engineer Taylor directed that the river resume its course. At a wave of his hand the river did so, and to the satisfaction of all the power to move rivers if not mountains seemed to be at the command of the Reclamation Service and its engineers.[2]

Among the crowd at the ceremonies was leading irrigation publicist William E. Smythe, author of *The Conquest of Arid America* (1900). As a frequent employee of Newlands and contributor to the magazine *Out West*, Smythe possessed all of the credentials as a journalistic "irrigation crank." In reporting this event he wrote that when the water turned from its ancient channel, where it had been wasted for ages, it rushed along the canal to enter upon its mission of making homes in the wilderness. He declared that on this day, "National irrigation was an accomplished fact!" It demonstrated that the nation could build irrigation much better and more quickly than private enterprise. As he stood in the crowd by the banks of the Truckee, his mind wandered back to the early days of the national irrigation movement, when he met many of its prominent pioneers. He remembered John Wesley Powell, scientific explorer of arid America and "the first to comprehend the meaning of its strange environment." Powell, he believed, would have "swelled with the pride and joy of achievement if he stood under that clear Nevada sky when the Great Dream came true!" Richard J. Hinton, too, would have cheered when the water turned sharply from its channel to pass through the hills to the waiting valley beyond. Then there was Judge James S. Emery of Kansas, friend of Abraham Lincoln, who had painted "the coming glories of Arid America." And finally, he recalled "that finest of Mormon diplomats, George Q. Cannon" who not only preached Mormonism, but also "the gospel of irrigation from a heart which always beat true to the interests of the American settler in the desert." Smythe wished he could have seen "his radiant smile when the headgates were lifted and the Truckee sped upon its mission to make homes and fill the silence with the laughter of children!" Surely these shadowy forms "stood on the banks of the Truckee at the memorable hour when national irrigation became a fact."[3]

After a quick trip by rail, following the new canal on a spur line to Hazen, Nevada, closer to the actual lands that were to come under the ditch, the train, provided by courtesy of the Southern Pacific, raced back to Reno for an evening banquet. The fifteen congressional wives with the party dined separately at the Riverside Hotel and following the meal presided at a reception to meet the women of Reno. At the men's banquet, long-time Renoite, irrigation advocate, and official of the Southern Pacific Land Company, Robert L. Fulton acted as toastmaster. Lieutenant Governor Allen, Governor Pardee, Surveyor General of Nevada E. D. Kelly, Senator Fred J. Dubois of Idaho, Congressman Mondell of Wyoming, Congressman James C. Needham of California, F. H. Newell, Congressmen Wesley L. Jones of Washington, William A. Reeder of Kansas, and Allen F. Cooper of Pennsylvania all spoke glowingly of the future of irrigation in arid America. Because of the large number of distinguished guests, Senator Newlands insisted that he not be called upon, but that the time be given to the visitors. It was 11 P.M. when the speeches came to a close at the announcement of train time, and the visitors departed for the station on their journey east. Newlands retired to his home in Reno after the most triumphal day of his political life.

Reno's press was ecstatic over the events. A typically partisan presidential race concluded in 1904, in which President Roosevelt trumpeted throughout the West his and the Republican party's initiative in passing the National Reclamation Act. In response, Newlands as a Democrat touted his party's role in achieving national reclamation and his own key efforts. These partisan themes lurked in the background during the celebrations on the Truckee. Characteristically, the Republican newspaper and anti-Newlands sheet in Reno, the *Evening Gazette*, regretted that President Roosevelt was not present, because after all it was the president who brought about the actual accomplishment of the work. It failed to mention Senator Newlands either in the news stories or the editorial that praised only Roosevelt for bringing about one of Nevada's greatest days. A new publication and "Nevada's only magazine," *Progressive West* also ignored Newlands when it praised Roosevelt in an article, "The Big Stick and the Big Ditch," which cheered the president's wide command over both domestic and foreign affairs.

On the other extreme, the Democratic paper, the *Nevada State Journal*, was almost worshipful of Newlands in bringing about National Reclamation: "Future generations will rise up and call him blessed." It referred to the National Reclamation Act as the Newlands Act and saw the "passing of the desert," because of Newlands's work. The national reclamation project came just at the moment that Nevada experienced a new gold and silver mining boom, yet this publication proclaimed that the precious metal discoveries at Tonopah and Goldfield that had given Nevada a long-needed mining boom faded in comparison to the opening of the gates that let water into the diversion canal yesterday. It painted a future of growth and prosperity for the desert state: "Lurking death will be banished from the alkali plains and the sand clouds of the arid wastes will give place to the wreathing smoke of civilization and new life."[4]

The partisanship of the press dogged Newlands's career in Nevada even as he tried to make a broad appeal for all Nevadans and westerners to rally behind the cause of irrigating and developing the natural resources of the region. As a twentieth-century western progressive politician, Newlands promised much. For him the National Reclamation Act of 1902 was merely one part of his general view that the power of the national government should be utilized to bring efficiency and greater opportunity to American life. Newlands also hazarded the opinion in 1906 that he had "long believed theoretically that the government could undertake many things which are now within the domain of private enterprise." In the past he hesitated to advocate such governmental operations "because of the complexity of our government and its weakness in points of administration." He wished to adapt to the American scene some of the more constructive aspects of state socialism, such as the nationalization of some industries.[5]

Despite his commitment to western development, Newlands always remained an outsider in Nevada. Nonetheless the fluid society of turn-of-the-century Nevada offered him a political life. His impressive wealth promoted his admission to the Nevada political fraternity. In the ensuing years he built a national reputation as congressman and senator—his prestige and aura of competency and legitimacy struck a chord of pride in the Nevada electorate. For decades Nevadans had heard complaints about their impoverished state: that it was marginally qualified to wield sovereignty and ridiculed as the West's most notorious "rotten borough." The figure of the impeccably dressed, well-spoken, urbane Newlands in the Senate belied these notions.

Newlands's career in Nevada and the nation resembles a Horatio Alger story written large. Like many who rise quickly into the privileged circles of wealth, he was admired, resented, and even dismissed as a dilettante whose residency in the state was, as one critic sarcastically remarked, "more constructive than real."[6] Yet only the most partisan of sources denied that he had earned the reputation as a foremost supporter of national reclamation. And it was as a noted "irrigation crank" that he turned the metal crank at the dam site on the Truckee in June 1905 to pour forth water to the lands of Nevada. Little wonder that on this day Francis G. Newlands was delighted.

II

TOWARD THE PROMISES
OF CALIFORNIA

In 1848 Francis Newlands was born to Jessie and James Newlands in the thriving river town of Natchez, Mississippi. The family had traveled a difficult road after emigrating from Scotland in the early 1840s. Newlands was the fourth of five children. He had two older brothers, John and James, an older sister, Annie, and a younger brother, William, born in 1850. His father, a physician, had received his training at Edinburgh and subsequently practiced in Scotland and India. Such credentials might suggest that the Newlands family could look forward to the future in their adopted country with every expectation of enjoying the prosperity of a growing nation. The move to America, however, began one of several relocations that Newlands's father undertook to escape a fatal alcoholic affliction.

New surroundings, far away from old associations in Edinburgh, offered opportunity for a new beginning. In Edinburgh James married Jessie Barland from nearby Perth, but his affliction persisted even after marriage and the arrival of children. Perhaps joining his brother Frank in America would lead to a better life. For a time James Newlands did overcome his Edinburgh debility in Troy, New York, but in 1845 he succumbed to it. Jessie, now with two children and pregnant with a third, sought a separation. His brothers, Frank in Troy and William in Scotland, were divided on whether to advise Jessie to leave her husband. Frank felt that "a separation might suck him headlong into destruction," but William felt that "duty to herself and children" justified her departure. It was the husband who left to seek the "water cure" in St. Louis.[1]

The separation lasted a year, then Jessie joined her husband in St. Louis. Afterwards the family sought a new start downriver in Natchez, where prospects appeared bright. Jessie's fourth child, Francis Griffith Newlands, was born August 28, 1848. But James once again took to the bottle. All the advantages he possessed in life were washed away by it. His brother wrote, "With great natural talents, a first rate education, gentlemanly manners, address and accomplishments he seemed formed for success. . . . I see him a dashing handsome man, full of life and good nature. . . ."

Again a move was necessary for a new start, where patients would not be driven away by the doctor's reputation for drunkenness. Moving to Quincy, Illinois, made a temporary improvement in his life. Jessie became pregnant with her last child, and the family started to blend and mix in the best circles of the town. But again the "unfortunate failing neutralized all his advantages." In this bout with the demon, his body failed as well as his will, and he died in 1851 at the age of forty-four.[2]

A forty-year-old widow with five young children, Jessie Barland Newlands faced several decisions about her life in America. She chose to remain in Quincy, borrowing from relatives and accepting the help of friends. The family found an easy acceptance in the growing society of this commercial river center. The spirit of growth, opportunity, and promise that engulfed much of the Illinois frontier must have played a role in Jessie's decision not to flee to distant relatives either in the United States or in Scotland. In 1853 she married a well-situated businessman, banker, and ex-mayor of the city, Ebeneezer Moore. Moore's comfortable income from his banking business gave Jessie the means to raise her family, provide them with a large home, tasteful surroundings, a piano, and schooling. Unfortunately, the general financial and banking crisis of 1857 destroyed many small businessmen, including Moore. After several difficult years in Quincy, Moore obtained a low-paying political position, which took the family to Chicago for two and a half years.[3]

The eventful decade of the 1860s began poorly for the family. The oldest son, John, enlisted with the Seventh Illinois for three years' service in the Civil War, while his mother worried incessantly as battle casualties mounted. Daughter Anne made an unfortunate marriage that ended in divorce, bringing Anne and her small daughter back to the struggling family. All of this occurred against the background of the dreary, poorer neighborhoods of Chicago and the family's incessant money troubles.[4]

Finally, in 1863 Orville Browning, a close friend of Moore's in Quincy and a political ally of Abraham Lincoln, used his influence to obtain for Moore a clerkship in the Treasury Department in Washington, D.C. Like other moves in her life, this one also prompted Jessie to new hopes and new plans for the future. Among them were plans for Frank Newlands to enter Yale College at the young age of fourteen, where he could acquire the credentials for success and social position that other men enjoyed. The advantages of education and well-placed friends did not escape the observant eyes of Jessie Moore, who lived on the fringes of society in Washington. But Jessie's plans for young Frank met obstacles. He did go to Yale, but he was forced to withdraw in March of 1866 because the family could no longer support his education, and he refused to borrow further from a classmate who had already extended loans to him. His "shortest, gladdest years" came quickly to an end.

Other reversals and tragedies struck the family. In 1864, John was gravely wounded, and Jessie brought him home to nurse instead of permitting him to die in an army hospital. Seven years later he succumbed to complications from his war wounds. In October 1866, Ebeneezer Moore died of a sudden attack of cholera. By the end of 1866 the household stood without a major income and faced the necessity of supporting an invalid brother and a divorced sister with a small child. The next three years saw Newlands and his brother James working hard as clerks in the postal department. To meet expenses Jessie took in "house guests." Still Newlands found time and ambition to undertake legal studies at Columbian University, later to be named George Washington University. For three years under these difficult personal and financial circumstances at home, he studied law. Newlands was admitted to the bar in the District of Columbia in 1869.[5]

Various tensions, centering mainly on finances, dominated Newlands's life in the years after he left Yale. In spite of the pressures, Newlands continued his studies by night and his postal job by day and even found time to make appearances at Washington social affairs as a protégé of the Secretary of the Interior, Orville H. Browning. Like so many in the federal city, Newlands stood outside the inner circles of society, but he was learning the social graces and proper conduct that would mark him as a person of breeding and education.

During these uncertain years in Washington after her second husband's death, Jessie managed to hold the family together on the meager salaries of Frank and James and the "letting of rooms." Still the family was able to do more than just get by. In the summer of 1868 Jessie and her daughter escaped the sweltering Washington summer heat for a holiday in Saratoga Springs, New York. Jessie Moore also made it a point to continue her friendship with Mr. and Mrs. Orville H. Browning.[6]

This friendship proved important from the standpoint of shaping the life and views of the young Newlands. Browning had become an influential figure in the post-Lincoln days in Washington, identifying closely with the Andrew Johnson administration. Like President Johnson, his origins were in a border state, Kentucky, close to Johnson's home state of Tennessee. Previously he had enjoyed close contact with President Lincoln, as a senator from Lincoln's home state when he served out Stephen Douglas's term after the "Little Giant's" death in June 1861. His appointed senatorship continued until January 1863. By that time he and Lincoln came to differ sharply on the issue of slave emancipation. Browning, a noted Illinois Democrat, objected to this emerging doctrine of the Republican party and to making it one of the principal goals of the war. He never accepted the Fifteenth Amendment and Newlands later called that amendment, which guaranteed political rights to all citizens regardless of race, a great mistake. In the remaining years of Lincoln's life, Browning always had access to his office, although the questions they now discussed avoided the course of national policies.

This former senator and friend of the fallen president gradually moved to a position of influence with soon-to-be President Johnson. Their backgrounds, moderate viewpoints, and anti-radical positions on Reconstruction and black suffrage brought them together. As late as 1869 Browning spoke in opposition to a clause in the new constitution of Illinois that granted black suffrage. In September 1866 he became secretary of the interior—a post he would hold for thirty-one months, until the end of the Johnson administration. During this time he moved in the highest circles of the beleaguered administration. In these months Newlands found time to accompany Browning on many of his official and social calls in the city. Newlands was received into circles friendly to the administration and also attended receptions given by the president. Jessie Moore had done well to keep up the acquaintance with the Browning's not only for the political appointments that had kept her husband employed during the last years of his life but also because Francis Newlands enjoyed the benefits of Washington society. Newlands must have caught the fascination of political and social life in post–Civil War Washington. He doubtless absorbed many of the political and party viewpoints of his sponsor. He knew full well that a career in law could eventually lead him to a political life, as it had for Browning, and also yield some of its considerable benefits.[7]

Several factors in 1869 forced Newlands to assess his career. He had successfully passed the examination for the bar. With the end of the

Johnson administration, Orville Browning left the city for Illinois. Washington had served Newlands well by introducing him to the ways and manners of government. In these circles, "he made a favorable impression despite his lack of dress clothing and generally meager wardrobe." All of these activities—law school, a lively social life under the tutelage of Browning, work at a daytime clerkship in the "distasteful" Postal Department—testify to his youthful energy. But without Browning's influence Newlands would be adrift in Washington. As a result Newlands turned his eyes and his hopes away from Washington, away from the Midwest and Illinois to the Pacific Coast and California. Mindful of his future, Newlands set out for San Francisco in 1870.[8]

Before departing, Newlands collected letters of introduction attesting to his good character, industry, and association with Yale. One such letter to the Chief Justice of California, Lorenzo Sawyer, stated, "His habits are remarkable, correct, and such as entitle him to the warmest recommendation. He neither drinks, chews, or gambles—qualities rare now-a-days in young men." Cautiously, Newlands took a salaried clerk's job in San Francisco with the law firm Parker and Holliday, providing him a small income and an opportunity to study California law. In six months he felt confident to strike out on his own for, as he recalled, "The time had come when he must make money instead of borrowing it."[9] A former Yale man, John B. Harmon, gave Newlands a place in an established practice.

It was an excellent opportunity, but the young Newlands attracted few clients and faced destitution. Pushed to desperation, he decided to immerse himself in the "basest legal transactions" in the city in order to learn the tricks of the trade. He offered free defense in the police courts of the city to the indigent, thereby making a name for himself through the conduct of successful defenses. Many young lawyers went through this apprenticeship to prove their worth and draw attention to their abilities. It was an exercise that most hoped to avoid. But at this point, Newlands had no other choice than to plunge into the effronteries of the police court, if it would lead him on to some successful prospects.

A judge in the police court soon took notice of Newlands—Newlands was too often defeating the cause of justice by defending the scoundrels brought into court. Judge Delos R. Lake recommended Newlands to a friend, Solomon Sharpe, who began to employ him in more complex civil cases. This not only saved Newlands from the "corrupting influences" of the criminal justice system but also, and more importantly, earned him an income of nearly $3,000 a year by the end of 1872. His civil practice and modest success demanded long workdays, but the long hours did not prevent Newlands from embarking on a lively and expensive social life in the city.[10]

Despite Newlands's busy schedule he attended to his family's problems in the East. By the summer of 1871, he encouraged his mother to move west and take rooms in Oakland, where he judged the climate more suitable for her health. Still he was unable to assume all the expenses of her trip. As Jessie put it in a letter to her sister, ". . . if it Be God's will that I should go he will open up a way." And the way was opened with the "painful and unexpected death" of John Newlands. John had belonged to the Masonic Relief Fund and upon his death it paid for his funeral and gave his mother "the means with what Frank has sent to get a pretty fair wardrobe and pay expenses out." As Jessie boarded the train in June of 1871, she left many burdens from previous years. She had lived "a most afflicted life," but now she looked forward to witnessing the successful advance of a promising son in San Francisco.[11]

Barely had the train descended from the Sierras into the foothills of California before Francis Newlands came aboard to meet his mother and ride with her to Oakland. Jessie described this joyful reunion: ". . . there jumped upon the cars a youth so bright and gay that I did not have to look twice to know that he was my Frankie." Although her emotions ran high Jessie Moore relates that ". . . we behaved with all the proprieties knowing that many eyes were upon us." For the summer Newlands had taken board for himself and his mother in Oakland because he believed it better to avoid the heavy fogs of San Francisco. His mother was delighted with the situation, "with acres laid in fruit, shrubbery, and flowers." Her room was, "the sweetest and coziest room in the world with Brussels carpet, and walnut furniture with marble tops." In addition the rooms had been filled with flowers and Newlands had provided "a decanter full of delicious port wine, and in the closet a gallon of the same." Jessie Moore was, as she wrote to the remaining family in Washington, D.C., ". . . deeply touched by Frank's thoughtfulness and delicate attention."[12]

Jessie was pleased with her new surroundings, and she was overjoyed that her son's ". . . associations are all among the elite of the place, people of wealth with much refinement and intelligence." Newlands had been in the city a little more than a year, and although he had no important success as yet in his law practice, he had established himself in the social life of the city. He possessed all of the attributes for acceptance. He was seen as a young lawyer from Yale and Washington,

D.C.; not from an obscure law school in the nation's capital. He was cultivated, well read, mannered, and attractive. San Francisco society at the time was well known for welcoming new arrivals, who brought any vestiges of culture, good upbringing, and refinement. Newlands, with his easy conversational manner, proper attire, and youthful energy possessed the prerequisites for admission to San Francisco's fluid society. Jessie rather incorrectly believed "the first circles of San Francisco society very difficult to enter," but not for one with Newlands's attributes. Apparently Newlands had chosen well the city for his future as it opened its arms to him socially—though not necessarily its purse.[13]

Newlands glided smoothly into the loftiest of San Francisco's economic and political circles. However harsh the estimates of San Francisco's early society—such as the generalization that "Fashionable society opens its arms to the man who has gold, be he knave or fool"— did not quite bear truth as far as Newlands was concerned. The budding "parvenuocracy" of San Francisco admitted the young lawyer from the East. But the city's social merry-go-round required a bottomless purse, for which Newlands was forced to labor at a quickening pace. Jessie noted that he had laid nothing away and barely met his own expenses. "I do not think he has to any extent the spirit of accumulation," she wrote shortly after her arrival. Of more concern to her over the next three years prior to his marriage was whether Newlands's not too robust health could keep up with the work and social demands of the city. Even after three years in San Francisco, Jessie Moore reported that "Frank is doing well, but cannot lay a penny away."[14]

Newlands's social and professional life demanded much of him. He lived in a respectable hotel, as was the standard for people of position in San Francisco's bustling social life. He was a member of the newly formed Bohemian Club and participated in its "high jinks" and regulated naughtiness that provided opportunities to depart from and make fun of conventional Victorian mores. He attended dinner parties at former Senator William Gwin's home, where the Gwin's attempted to be the city's representatives of southern society and where dinner was served by French waiters in black livery coats. He courted some of the prominent daughters of the city, including the daughter of Judge E. B. Crocker, brother of Charles Crocker, one of the "Big Four" responsible for the building of the Central Pacific Railroad. More exciting to the city's gossips was the continued display of mutual interest that Newlands and Clara Adelaide Sharon showed throughout the early months of 1873. Her father, William Sharon, a prominent investor in the Bank of California and the Comstock Lode in Virginia City, Nevada, was possibly the wealthiest man on the Pacific Coast.[15]

Yet courting the daughter of such a wealthy man put a further strain on Newlands's tenuous finances in the months prior to the engagement and during the long months before the wedding, when nothing could be done "shabily." His mother constantly worried over how Newlands was making ends meet, although he was clearing as much as five thousand dollars in 1873 and 1875. Moreover, his work load and social commitments drained his health. In the summer before his marriage Jessie relates that "I think we will have to leave our comfortable home in this Hotel to go to a miserable boarding house that everybody dreads." Everything depended on his health, which was showing itself to be fragile even at the age of twenty-six. She related in the spring of 1873, "Frank has not been well again. After pleading a case he suffers and feels prostrated. I feared it would be so." Perhaps she overemphasized their straitened financial condition in letters to her sister because her sister occasionally asked for money. In any event, in the spring before her son was to make one of the most talked about matches in San Francisco, Jessie Moore told her sister, and probably accurately so, that Newlands's financial outlook was bleak: "I am so saving now that I do not even send you a box, but Annie and I rip and wash breadth by breadth and make over everything. Frank has so many to care for now that I feel I cannot be economical enough." No doubt Newlands's obligations were heavy. He made monthly payments to his Yale school chum from whom he had borrowed during his last year at Yale. He supported both his mother and his sister and had been instrumental in obtaining an army doctor's appointment for his brother William and in moving his other brother James to the West Coast. Added to these personal expenses were the demands of keeping up with the everyday expectations of San Francisco's high society in whose circles he moved with confidence and increasing stature after his engagement to Clara Sharon in October of 1873.[16]

Newlands's engagement not only created talk and raised eyebrows but also excitement in his immediate family. In a letter his mother described her son's fiancée as ". . . the only girl he has ever loved" and also mentioned that "She is the daughter of Mr. Sharon, a man of great wealth." She said that Newlands paid attentions to her for more than a year. At one time he seemed discouraged in his courtship because of her great wealth, ". . . fearing he might be considered a fortune hunter and on several occasions ceased even to visit the family." But inevitably he would receive an invitation to a party or a dinner and "... as time wore on he came to the happy conviction that he was preferred beyond all others. . . ." With the full approval of Clara's parents, they were to be married in one year. But Jessie Moore did have "one objection to Frank's choice . . .": Clara and her mother were Roman Catholics, ". . . though by no means bigoted ones." Jessie was a devoted Episcopalian who found Catholicism disturbing, as well as Mr. Sharon who was ". . . like too many men of the present day, a free thinker." Sharon advised Newlands not to interfere in religious matters. Although Jessie regretted the Catholicism, she admitted that she would rather have him marry a good Roman Catholic than any of the numerous Unitarians that were to be found in San Francisco, "I believe half of San Francisco are Unitarians."[17]

The marriage of Newlands to Clara Sharon was extraordinary in several respects. Daughters of wealth in the United States and particularly in California were making a practice of marrying European titles rather than ambitious young lawyers from among their countrymen. One critic of California society suggested that millions had been drained from the state in this matrimonial manner. Sharon's youngest daughter, Flora, married Sir Thomas Hesketh in 1880 in an enormous wedding ceremony at Belmont, Sharon's summer home on the San Francisco peninsula. Sharon brought the entire Metropolitan Orchestra from New York for the affair. The bridegroom sailed his yacht *Lancashire Witch* through the Golden Gate, bound around the world from Liverpool. After the wedding Flora and Sir Thomas sailed away on their honeymoon back to England. On the male side, Sharon's son, Frederick, married and chose to spend his life in Europe pursuing art and leisure with little interest in business affairs. In effect this left no practical heir or caretaker of the accumulated fortune that Sharon's good luck and shrewdness had built by the mid-1870s.[18]

Astute observers saw in the Newlands-Sharon union practical advantages to the growing Sharon estate that a titled European could not offer. A well-trained, hardworking, and loyal son-in-law close to the family could provide Sharon's many enterprises with the legal defenses, leadership, and careful attention to detail that would be needed in the coming years as public sentiment cried out for the regulation of great wealth and its proprietors. From Sharon's point of view, Newlands's abilities brought strength to his operations. In the wake of Sharon the builder, risk taker, and flamboyant displayer of wealth, came Newlands, the skilled lawyer with an eye to fine legal points and methods more characteristic of an administrator than a daring capitalist.

Expectations ran high in San Francisco society over the grand scale in which William Sharon would entertain at his daughter's wedding. It was to be the social event of the autumn. By 1874 over a decade of development on the Comstock Lode in Nevada added millions of dollars to San Francisco. The Bank of California crowd, of which Sharon was the Nevada representative, prospered as it became the largest financial institution of the Coast. Sharon's mansion and grounds on Sutter Street was at least a $300,000 tribute to the prosperity that the Comstock brought the investors of San Francisco. Jessie believed that the wedding of her son to the daughter of the most prominent and powerful Comstock personality would be ". . . the grandest affair which has taken place in this already extravagant city for a long time." She correctly felt, "Everyone is on the tiptoe of expectation and I hope nothing will occur to change the program." As Newlands moved toward marrying into a family whose millions flowed from the Nevada mines, little did he realize that events in the Silver State would soon begin to shape his life.

Suddenly in September 1874, after almost a year's engagement, Sharon announced that the October 21 wedding date must be postponed until after the Nevada elections. After establishing the Bank of California as the chief economic power on the Comstock since his first appearance there in 1864, Sharon now sought the most prestigious political office available from the State of Nevada. It was no matter that he kept his residence in San Francisco. The San Francisco *Chronicle* quoted the Virginia City, Nevada, evening newspapers that Mr. Sharon had gone into the senatorial campaign with a determination to win, "regardless of the expense." It related that one saloon in Carson City had forwarded a bill to Mr. Sharon's cashier for $800, ". . . for drinks furnished to the boys." In a state where more truth is likely to be found in out-of-state papers instead of the local press, the *Chronicle* offered the following analysis of the Nevada senatorial election process. A Nevada senatorial election was an expensive process where, according to Senator John P. Jones, who had achieved election in 1872, "Millions may be expended and no one corrupted." Votes were not bought outright, but as the previous Jones campaign demonstrated the payrolls of the mines were increased with non-workers who promised to vote for legislators committed to the candidate, and the same was expected of other working employees. The open nature of the ballots permitted a check on the loyalty of the votes to the desired legislative ticket since the ballots were of different colors for each candidate.[19]

A United States senatorship would take Sharon to Washington and focus his financial interest on the East Coast as well as the West Coast. Why Sharon wished to delay the marriage until after the elections is not clear. Perhaps a flamboyant wedding display in San Francisco society would draw attention to Sharon's residency in San Francisco and not Nevada. Certainly it would mark him as a San Francisco Nevadan, or member of that circle of men who drew their living from the Comstock while living in the luxury of the city by the bay. Perhaps with the Nevada campaign in its final stages he did not have time for wedding festivities. Whatever the reasons, the decision disappointed Newlands and Clara and illustrated how Nevada affairs impinged on his life as he moved closer to the Sharon family. The Sharons would not only involve him with Nevada but also with Washington, D.C., when his father-in-law invested in suburban property during his senatorship.

Newlands and Clara were given the choice of making the wedding private or postponing it a month until after the Nevada elections. They were despondent at the news and believed it to be an ominous sign for their marriage. They agreed that the wedding should be kept public but postponed for the required month. November 19, 1874, was the new date for an affair that promised to be one of the most extravagant in the history of the city. After overcoming the initial disappointment, the couple became cheerful with the prospect of a month's delay to allow for more thorough preparations for the event of the season.[20]

The invitations to the wedding reception were simple and in good taste, according to the San Francisco *Chronicle* (which generally fawned over such affairs). The wedding was to take place at Sharon's spacious mansion on Sutter Street at 8 o'clock on the night of November 19, 1874. The reception that would host "the most honorable names in California" would be held from 9 until 12. In the newspaper's description of the wedding, William Sharon and his spacious mansion received as much attention as the bride and groom. Sharon was described as the republican who had become a king, "not by reason of primogeniture, nor because of divine right, but because he has conquered the right to rule by simply showing that he had the active brain and shrewdness of intellect that enable him to acquire money and to make it productive. The rich in a free country exemplify in a fashion, the theory of the survival of the fittest." Sharon was indeed the "Monarch of the Comstock Lode."[21]

Sharon's home was "magnificent in its proportions," even in a section of the city where imposing private homes were not exceptional. It was estimated that the estate, including the grounds, was worth over $300,000. This was an important testimony to Sharon's genius as the financial wizard. In only ten years since his arrival on the Comstock as a representative and employee of the Bank of California, he had made the bank the most powerful financial institution in Nevada and himself the most powerful person in Nevada. He had gained a partnership in the bank itself. His belief in the Comstock and financial development east of the Sierra had brought him wealth and unquestioned status in San Francisco—a city that was built on various mining discoveries in the West and which particularly benefited from the Comstock strike.[22]

The Sharon mansion contained some of the finest and most elaborate furniture ever brought to the Pacific Coast and was "unsurpassed in cost and richness by that of the most magnificent dwellings in the East." In the library the corner bookcases were ornamented with bronze figures of Schiller, Goethe, Pizarro, and Cortez. Such surroundings for the marriage ceremony must have signaled to Newlands that his days of genteel poverty were at an end. Four years before he had arrived in San Francisco with hardly $75, in possession of only a law degree, letters of introduction, a Yale association, and the good manners of genteel society. The intervening years had been filled with the struggle to survive in San Francisco and to maintain its expensive lifestyle. Not only had Newlands married into one of the wealthiest families in California, but his father-in-law had entered the uncertain waters of Nevada politics, seeking to be a United States Senator. Politics as well as the Sharon fortune loomed in Newlands's future.

The newspaper reported that as hard as it may have been to put the future aside on that night, it seemed that for a moment time had stopped in the large home on Sutter Street as Francis Newlands and his bride, Clara Sharon, pledged their devotion to each other. The bride was described as a beautiful, stylish demi-brunette, and as far as the press could learn, "Her marriage is according to her own wishes and of her own free choice. . . ." Jessie spoke of the marriage as "a love match on both sides." His brother William, however, recognized that Newlands would now have "new ties and new interests," but he felt confident that there was "no danger of his love ever being weaned from his family." The writer for the *Chronicle* concluded that as far he could sweep "the matrimonial horizon with his glass, it shows only azure weather and serene happiness."[23]

After the wedding "the blushing bride and the pale-faced groom" received congratulations from guests "beneath a gorgeous floral arch."

1. The young Newlands at the beginning of his career c. 1870s. Photograph courtesy of the Francis Griffith Newlands Papers, Manuscripts and Archives, Yale University Library. Used by permission.

The newspapers gave the standard description of the groom—a little above the medium height of five feet eight inches. At twenty-eight years of age, his features were regular and attractive "with a mouth indicating decision of character, and a forehead high and intellectual. His complexion was more fair than florid and the face exhibited neither beard, mustache nor whiskers." His hair was "reddish-blond with curling locks." He generally moved with a hurried step, "as though trying to crowd five minutes into one." The newspaper account of Newlands judiciously concluded, ". . . if there be great wealth on one side in this match, there is unquestionably no lack of genuine worth on the other." The writer for the *Chronicle* somewhat apologetically continued, "While it cannot be claimed for him that he is rich in worldly possessions, yet he is beyond measure wealthy in all the sterling traits of young American manhood." Above all he was not a titled European fortune hunter.[24]

With the marriage ceremony solemnized, the life of Newlands took new directions. His membership in the Sharon family made him part of a far-flung economic empire with interests in California, Nevada, and very soon in the suburban development of Washington, D.C. Shortly after the marriage, his mother discounted reports that Sharon had made her son a millionaire, because he was a man of too much sense to do that overnight. She wrote, "He [Sharon] had made himself and such men think that young men are only developed through struggling." It is true that years of hard work stood ahead of Newlands as he worked to show his "genuine worth" to the Sharon estate. The leadership that he exercised, however, was of a far different kind and style from the founder of the family fortune.[25]

III

IN DEFENSE OF PROPERTY

Newlands's world was the comfortable one of the Victorian rich. Unfortunately, the Comstock, upon which so much of the prosperity of the "San Francisco–Nevadans" depended edged toward depression by 1877. The era of vast fortunes accumulated in quick succession in Nevada and in California ended. Now began a long period in which the rich attempted to consolidate their positions and advance themselves in less spectacular enterprises. Newlands, one of the captains charged with guiding the Sharon estate in this less-adventuresome period, sought avenues for the protection of wealth against radical assaults.

The first of the older generation to tumble from the dizzying heights of wealth and power was William C. Ralston, president of the great Bank of California. Less than a year after Newlands became part of the Sharon family, Ralston, the builder of San Francisco and financier of the Comstock, fell. On August 27, 1875, he lost his life in the waters of San Francisco Bay either by his own decision to take a swim of no return or because of circumstances of stress and fatigue. He was the most spectacular of "San Francisco's magnificent Medici." Ralston's death and the collapse of the Coast's most powerful financial institution previewed the inability of the Comstock to rescue the bank with new bonanzas.[1]

The bank's failure seriously affected Sharon's financial empire and the course of his son-in-law's career. Sharon, as a partner in the bank, faced the task of regrouping its finances and claiming many of Ralston's assets, such as his home and the nearly completed and spectacular Palace Hotel. In less than two months the reorganized bank opened its doors. Sharon emerged the kingpin of San Francisco's financial world, and as an additional tribute the Nevada legislature gave him a United States senatorship.[2]

If Sharon's star shined brightly, it burned with a tarnished light. His financial empire needed fortification against the economic and political storms of California society. After the death of his wife in 1875, he became involved with Sarah Althea Hill, who eventually sued him for divorce on the grounds that they had a common-law marriage. His political career was short-lived—one unillustrious term—because of his complete lack of interest in the Senate. Local tax assessments and rate regulations on public services authorized by the new California Constitution of 1879 plagued him. Sharon lived another decade, but Newlands assumed a larger role in defending him and the vast interests of the estate.

Newlands's marriage to Clara Sharon provided neither immediate wealth nor instant leisure. He found himself cast into the institutional structure of great wealth and he took to its cause as an avid defender and promoter of corporate interests. Over the next decade Newlands devoted his energies first to helping Sharon reopen the Bank of California, supervising the management of the Palace Hotel, defending the water monopoly that Sharon's Spring Valley Water Company held over the delivery of water to San Francisco, and protecting the estate against the divorce claims of Sarah Hill.

Amid the Kearneyite agitation, the rise of the Workingmen's party, and the adoption of a new California constitution in 1879, Newlands helped steer a safe course for the Sharon fortune. His strategic role in the reorganization of the Bank of California was not publicized and only revealed some years later during a court case in which one of the creditors of the bank brought suit against Sharon for the settlement offered during the reorganization. Ralston's debts totaled over four million dollars, but Sharon would not commit the bank to their liquidation. Newlands bought Ralston's debts for half their value, fifty cents on the dollar. The bank claimed that Ralston was worth only two million dollars and that this was all that was available to pay creditors. The action protected Sharon and eliminated the necessity of his paying off Ralston's debts in the total of four million dollars. Sharon restructured the bank in one of the most artful financial maneuvers in the history of American business. For this he drew severe criticism from creditors who were paid only fifty cents on the dollar. Sharon also gained control of many of Ralston's properties, most notably the Palace Hotel, Ralston's home at Belmont, and the Spring Valley Water Company.[3]

Sharon's acquisition of so much local property within a year after Newlands's marriage forced the mobilization of all the legal talent that Sharon commanded. These windfalls came to him as California entered a period of difficult economic times. The difference between the haves and have-nots was great and obvious. Agitation against conglomerations of wealth produced an array of protests, a Workingmen's party, single-tax advocates, and anti-Chinese riots. All decried the excesses of property and those who controlled it amid the spread of poverty in the Golden State. Dislike of the nouveau riche heightened because of their blatant disregard for public interest and their ostentatious display of wealth before those who had nothing.[4]

In these strife-filled years Newlands provided Sharon with legal expertise and talent. The Spring Valley Water Company became a chief target of reform groups in the city and Sharon's spectacular divorce suit brought his life to an untidy end in 1885. Moreover, the next ten years also brought Newlands personal tragedy and loneliness. His wife of six years died in 1881, leaving him a widower with three small children. His mother had died two years earlier. Personal losses and the burden of work produced in Newlands a nervous exhaustion from which he would suffer periodically during stressful periods the rest of his life.

Symbolic of Newlands's new life was his residency at the Palace Hotel. Although it was consistent with his social level, it offered the opportunity to keep a close managerial eye on the workings of this opulent hotel. His central focus, however, was his law practice, which now concentrated on his father-in-law's problems in San Francisco. Sharon was never as popular in the city as Ralston had been. His reputation was that of a man of sharp financial practices whose only concern was the building of his own fortune and prestige. Sharon's interest in San Francisco embraced large real-estate holdings, especially the Spring Valley company. Its monopoly over the city's water supply made Sharon the target of reform groups who demanded that the city either purchase the company or set water rates.

The company raised the banner of the sanctity of private property to protect itself from government interference. On one side stood the interests of a large corporation bent on monopolizing water delivery; on the other a local government that resented the arrogance of wealth and determined to chastise it. The contest simplified itself into a struggle between the privileged corporation and the people of San Francisco. The "water struggle" was an offshoot of the tumultuous events in the San Francisco of 1877. An elected Democratic administration, which usually campaigned against the company prior to election and then befriended it afterwards, announced its intention to obtain free water for all uses of city government. This was proposed in 1874, but the California Supreme Court sustained the company's objections. As Newlands filed suit against the city in early 1877 for its appropriation of water, he expected another favorable decision in support of private property, but he was mistaken. The court accepted the argument that private public service corporations must perform public services. Newlands denounced the decision as a naked, undisguised attack upon private property— the court sanctioned "systems of legalized plunder."[5]

Newlands marched to only one drum: the protection of property from the designs of government. His petition for a rehearing revealed him as an economic and political conservative with an underlying suspicion of majoritarian rule. Reformers saw Newlands in 1877 as the spokesman and hireling of Sharon, the city's foremost and most disliked capitalist. Newlands uncompromisingly denied the right of government to interfere in any manner with the free operation of private enterprise.

It was 1877—a year that brought a national railway strike, the rise of the Kearneyite agitation in the city, and the formation of the Workingmen's party in San Francisco. If nothing else, Newlands found that his views offered no basis upon which to build a future political career. But Newlands in the mid-1870s had no need for popularity. He resided within the sheltered circle of wealth as an employee and family intimate. If he had any political ambitions, his minority viewpoint must have been increasingly distressing. Forthcoming court decisions accepted the traditional powers of government over property and demonstrated the hopelessness of a position that denounced the destructive growth of governmental power over enterprise in the nation.

Newlands's problems paled when viewed in the light of events in San Francisco in the summer of 1877. A general mining depression caused by the failing Comstock mines in Nevada began to affect the city, drought in California drove many from the farms to the city to seek employment, and sympathy rallies for striking railway workers in the East produced dangerous tensions. Gatherings on the sandlots in front of city hall drew large crowds of the unemployed, who heard speakers like Denis Kearney denounce capital, which oppressed workers and their unions, and attack the Chinese as another cause of unemployment in the city. The harangues against the Chinese resulted in the burning of Chinese properties and a general threat to the safety of the city. On July 23, 1877, Chinese laundries were set ablaze throughout the city. In reaction, San Francisco's elite resorted to past methods. William T. Coleman was called to form a protective committee as he had done in San Francisco's Vigilance Committee of 1856. A public meeting of vigilance-minded citizens met on the afternoon of July 24 to organize a force of volunteers, a "Committee of Public Safety," to which local, state, and the national government pledged aid. Even this show of force did not prevent riots and burnings on the night of July 25.[6]

In Nevada, where dividends from the Consolidated Virginia mine had stopped in early 1877, the general manager of the Virginia and Truckee Railroad (a Sharon enterprise) Henry M. Yerington agreed with Sharon that the mobs in the city were "ugly beasts." He placed his faith "in a strong vigilant Committee powerful enough to take the scalp of every evil doer in the town." The mob he declared was "ruinous to every business interest on the Coast. We certainly shall have no trouble on the V&T," he reported, "and can see no reason why there should be any among the miners in Gold Hill and Virginia." But he did say that "the Gold Hill *News* has had some villainous, Communist editorials on the great strike," and that he was trying to get hold of the editor, Alf Doten, "to see if he won't put a stop to it—for that is just the kind of work to start a row in our midst." Nevadans feared anything resembling the turmoil in San Francisco. Failure of the Comstock in the late 1870s threatened the economic stability of the entire Coast, but migration out of the state appeared to be labor's answer to depression in Nevada.[7]

For Newlands, too, the disruptions and displacements of the late 1870s prompted a departure. In the fall of 1877 his health failed and by June 1878, he could remain in his office only a few hours each day due to nervous exhaustion. During this summer he decided to travel to Europe with his physician brother, William. All the family agreed that he should seek rest and relief from the nervous tension he had developed in fighting unpopular causes for the Sharon interests.

He visited relatives in Scotland, delved into the family genealogy, and observed the comfortable position they enjoyed in Edinburgh. Travel afforded him the opportunity to view some of the major cultural and architectural sites of the continent as well as to buy fine presents and furniture to send home. His visits to the elite tourist resorts in Switzerland placed him among a class where he felt at ease, given his wealth and social achievements. In November 1878, he delayed returning home for a month "on account of having overfatigued himself on the mountains of Switzerland." This sojourn gave Newlands time out from the fast pace of events over the previous seven years to discover, perhaps, himself and the larger world beyond San Francisco.[8]

Newlands returned in January 1879 to seek opportunities and confront new obstacles. But Newlands was a different person, and possessed new physical and mental energy. And well that he did because the California Constitution of 1879 offered little to those who espoused

2. Newlands with friends and in-laws at Yosemite in the late 1880s. Photograph courtesy of the Francis Griffith Newlands Papers, Manuscripts and Archives, Yale University Library. Used by permission.

the sanctity of private property and the limited role of the state in imposing regulation upon it. It asserted that "the exercise of the police power of the State shall never be so abridged or construed as to permit corporations to conduct their business in such a manner as to infringe the rights of individuals or the general well-being of the State." And in relation to water usage it stated: "In cities and towns it is compulsory on the Board of Supervisors, or other governing bodies, to fix annually the price for which water shall be sold to the cities or towns and the inhabitants thereof, and enforce such regulations by suitable penalties."[9] This clause was designed, stated the San Francisco *Chronicle*, to "cinch" the Spring Valley company.

If Newlands was to assume a commanding role in his father-in-law's affairs, now was the moment to demonstrate talent and energy. His careful cultivation of diplomatic skills in his social and professional life prepared him for a new role. Now he spoke of the higher ideals in society, the partnership between private enterprise and government, of fairness on the part of government in dealing with private property. At the same time he supported the duty of property to the community and, of course, the obligations of the community to property and the services it was hired to provide. Diplomacy was essential if property interests such as Spring Valley were to survive in post-1879 California. Newlands, who had moved from being an impoverished lawyer into one of the richest families on the Pacific Coast, was equal to the task. Legislative lobbying and the bribing of elected officials—Sharon tactics, the crass practices of an earlier era—must give way to sound argument, evaluation of a company's assets, and explanations of essential profit margins for a company to continue its services. This presented opportunity for a skilled lawyer and one attentive to the details of profits, losses, and the need for future investments and also one in tune with the sensitivities of elected officials in the city government. Newlands proved he was up to the task.[10]

Not only would he be called upon to guide Sharon's interests through the thickets of governmental supervision, but he was also confronted with family problems in 1879. The first was to extricate his brother, James, from a scandal involving the Justice Mining Company, a Comstock property. Newlands's influence secured James the job of treasurer of the company, but it was evident that the president and secretary were swindling Sharon and other stockholders. Although James was not involved, it was apparent that he was ignorant of many of his tasks as treasurer. Newlands, determined to save as much of the situation as he could, argued the stockholders' case in court. It was an embarrassment to him and one that the newspapers cited as additional evidence of why the Comstock mines were failing. Toward the end of summer 1879 his mother died, and for months he could not write because "my pen is arrested by the flood of sad memories." Only after the death of his mother did Newlands become a man of great wealth. As a representative of wealth with middle class origins, ideas, and education, Newlands had a clearer vision of how to impose some order and rationality on the chaotic California events in which he found himself.[11]

There was no need for him to view himself as a hireling of wealth or a cog in Sharon's economic machine—he possessed his own identity. He could see more clearly the hopelessness of the legal struggles he had undertaken in San Francisco as he attempted to defend the interests of property against the demands of an ever-changing political universe rooted in popular democracy. He could not wed himself irretrievably to arguments irrelevant to the social context if he ever hoped to pursue a career beyond the vineyards of the Sharon family.

Newlands moved to more creative approaches in his perception of

the rights of society and the rights of property. His conduct of the Spring
Valley Water Company's defense against the rate-fixing powers of the
San Francisco Board of Supervisors reflect a man accommodating himself to the new political realities of California. Great wealth could not
continue to demand laissez-faire from the state under the banner of the
sanctity of private property. Clearly the state was determined to control
public service corporations, but in return the corporations wished
assurances against confiscatory actions on the part of publicly elected
rate-fixing bodies. What possible recourse could there be for private
property, if rates were too low? No institutionalized system existed for
the purposes of rational, objective negotiation.

Newlands moved to meet the requirements of the new California
constitution. He negotiated with San Francisco's supervisors, showing
them the cost to Spring Valley of delivering water to the city and
convincing them that the company needed a 9 percent return on its
investment. Facts, figures, and reasonable argument carried the day
with Republican officials of San Francisco's municipal government in
1879. Peace between the city and the corporation prevailed, since the
supervisors accepted the argument that in setting rates it was performing a judicial rather than a political function. The board also accepted
the idea that the company should have a role in rate-making.

Newlands was the voice of reason, fair play, and moderation in
making the case that fair profit on investment was a reasonable expectation. These were not the heavy-handed lobbying techniques that
Sharon had used with the legislature. This was a new and sophisticated
approach by business to governmental regulatory powers. It presented
a workable method by which government could be dealt with on a
sound and predictable basis.

Such stability, however, was not to last. The "water war" revived in
the spring of 1882 as San Francisco newspapers noted that water rates,
despite a reduction, allowed more than a 9 percent return because of the
city's increased population. The *Call* and the *Bulletin* renewed their
attacks. They took aim not at the company but at the supervisors, who
were, of course, responsible for the reduced, yet favorable rates for the
company. Political attacks relieved the company of criticism that was
now aimed at elected officials.[12]

Newlands's arguments before the California Supreme Court during
the previous year, however, still had the ring of the mid-seventies. He
continued to praise Judge Stephen Field's dissent in the *Munn* v. *Illinois*
decision of 1876 and contended that the police powers of the state were

limited by the original federal Constitution. He reiterated an argument, increasingly attractive to corporation lawyers, that rate-fixing by elected bodies violated the "due process" clause of the Fourteenth Amendment. Beyond constitutional arguments, he spoke in terms of the classical liberal position of the nineteenth century when he said that "self-interest is the foundation of society . . ." and that "this instinct, properly protected and guarded, could be made a factor in the advancement of civilization and progress, and the promotion of art and science."[13]

But in 1882 Newlands struck a new course. Based on his experience in negotiating water rates and upon his need to depart from the traditional Sharon motifs of dealing with government, he saw a world far different from the one Sharon had operated in during the formative years of California's "winner-take-all" mining society. In a surprising turnabout he emphasized, in argument before the state high court, that ". . . the power of society over the individual is absolute. It is called the power of government, or the police power." This was a radical shift from his earlier praise of Judge Field's dissent in *Munn*. But make no mistake, Newlands's shifting ideology was designed to protect the interests of Spring Valley. One point of contention arose over whether the company's franchise to deliver water to and within the city was a taxable privilege subject to assessment and a fixed valuation. He unsuccessfully argued all "rights" or "privileges" enjoyed by individuals or corporations were in a sense a grant from the government. Included were such rights as suffrage, trial by jury, freedom of speech, and freedom of the press, which could all be termed "franchises" but certainly not subject to normal taxation process. The court quickly brushed aside his argument.[14]

The important point to acknowledge in analyzing Newlands's litigation is not his acceptance of the all encompassing power of government as expressed in *Munn*, but his turning away from the doctrine of laissez-faire that had characterized the Sharon organization. His now greater reliance on the historical and traditional development of American law as seen in his more traditional legal education asserted itself. Of course, this served the interests of Spring Valley. In the following year he continued to pursue this new line of argument and to refine it to an even greater degree, but still to serve not only the interests of property but also of society, which he believed to be one and the same.

In 1883 there was a hotly contested election for the Board of Supervisors. Newspapers attacked the old board for pandering to Spring Valley and new candidates pledged to reduce water rates by 33 percent.

The three-year honeymoon between the company and supervisors ended. Newlands went into the federal courts to argue not the sanctity of property and self-interest but a line that he had pursued two years earlier, that elected representative bodies should not perform the judicial function of determining fair utility rates. The case came before the U.S. Supreme Court in November 1883. Newlands argued more pointedly that elected representative bodies cannot fix rates for services that they and the people who elected them receive because this made them arbiters or judges of their own cases. But Newlands did not deny the right of government to regulate the financial behavior of property; rather he argued only against this manner of direct regulation by elected officials.[15]

Both Newlands and Vermont senior senator George F. Edmunds presented arguments on behalf of Spring Valley. As expected of a skillful corporation lawyer, Edmunds seized upon the due process clause of the Fourteenth Amendment to argue against rate-fixing by elected bodies. It represented a taking of the company's property without due process. The due process argument was also implicit in Newlands's argument, which he had presented to the California Supreme Court in 1881 when he called for "some fair and impartial tribunal." There was no question about the right of government to regulate, but regulation must be "just" and "reasonable." A long-term appointed expert commission would avoid the spectacle of "public mass meeting . . . aroused to fury by the appeals of incendiaries and demagogues." An appointed commission, acting only "after notice and upon inquiry," would be "a much more rational system." Clearly the 1879 state constitution delivered private property performing a public service into the hands of the voters and the politicians, many of whom were ignorant and foreigners, "easily controlled by the prevailing interest of passion or prejudice."[16]

Newlands, like others of his training, spoke for an emerging middle class that sought a rational society. Newlands was not committed to laissez-faire or dedicated to Spencerian Darwinism—both of which, James Bryce observed in the 1880s, the middle class had rejected. Advocating such doctrines would only serve to foster more turbulence, discontent, and vicious resentment on the part of the masses.[17]

Government's power and regulatory procedure, according to Newlands, should take on new forms with the establishment of tribunals or commissions. These bodies should ensure that both the great corporations and the public behaved in a civilized manner toward one another.

Such development would assure society that "the science of government . . . like all other sciences, is progressive; there is evolution in government as there is in physical and vegetable life." No one, Newlands said, should deny that the role of government changes and as it changes it evolves to a higher and more rational state. To deny this would be as irrational to assert, "that the man of today, endowed with a soul, possessed of rational faculties, hope, sympathies, and aspirations, is identical with his progenitor, Darwin's prehistoric man." The courts must promote this progressive change and the positive use of government power in society. Newlands's arguments might be good progressive philosophy on the proper function of government and quite within the paternalistic tradition of the mid-nineteenth century, but it was asking the Court to move beyond the immediate questions of the case and endorse the concept of impartial tribunals. Edmunds presented the more direct, less complicated argument to the Court with respect to the violation of the due process clause of the Fourteenth Amendment. The Court rejected both arguments.[18]

The 1883 decision fell within the *Munn* doctrine: "That it is within the power of the government to regulate the prices at which water shall be sold by one who enjoys a virtual monopoly of the sale, we do not doubt." The Court dismissed Edmunds's arguments by saying, "Regulations do not deprive a person of his property without due process of law." In response to Newlands's argument that elected officials were prone to act irresponsibly under the pressure of uninformed public prejudices, the Court simply said such questions were not pertinent to the issues under discussion: "What may be done if the municipal authorities do not exercise an honest judgment, or if they fix upon a price which is manifestly unreasonable, need not now be considered, for that proposition is not presented by this record." Newlands believed he had won a concession in this statement for his argument in favor of a judicial review or process in the procedure of rate-fixing beyond the legislative bodies. This did imply that the courts would be open to such questions if and when they were brought to court. Newlands counted this as a modification of the strict *Munn* doctrine and a step toward his view of a "fair and impartial tribunal." The Court answered Edmunds's argument more directly in admitting to possible judicial review or at least that a commission should be established, as in the mid-seventies, with representatives from the company. It said: "It will be time enough to consider consequences of the omission of the company when a case involving such questions shall be presented."[19]

With hindsight and the subsequent development of court decisions, Newlands wrote in 1891 to a biographer employed by the Bancroft Company that the case had succeeded in modifying "the extreme doctrine laid down in the case of Munn v. Illinois . . . that the power of regulation was a legislative power and that the judiciary could not interfere with it." From his vantage point in the early 1890s, he saw it as "the commencement of a series of decisions" that afforded greater security to property performing a public service. The search for an accommodation between the power of government and private property's demand for security formed the basis of Newlands's developing political views. But other events intervened to slow the emergence of Newlands's public career.[20]

IV

THE "WRETCHED CASE"

In September of 1883, just as Newlands was refining arguments for the courts, Sarah Althea Hill accused William Sharon of adultery and sued for divorce, alleging a common-law marriage. The tragic-comic course of this trial consumed Newlands for the next three years. The suit infuriated "steely eyed" Sharon, who vowed that Sarah would never receive a cent from him or his estate. She pursued a community property settlement through the Superior Court, the State Supreme Court, and the Federal District Court. Not only were the legal talents of the Sharon estate called upon for protection against the encroachments of government, they were now mobilized to guard against the consequences of the indiscreet amours of its founder. Hill, a formidable opponent commanding impressive legal talents, saw the possibility of a lucrative victory.

The story was sordid. Sarah became Sharon's hostess at Belmont in 1880. From 1880 to 1883 she frequented his residence at the Palace. The public nature of their relationship was not in dispute, but rather whether Sharon entered into a written contract with her. During the trial she dramatically produced a piece of paper with such an agreement. On this evidence she claimed a handsome settlement. Sharon's vulgar defense: Hill had been only one of several mistresses entertained by Sharon and the document was a forgery.

Two court cases resulted from the dispute. In *Sharon* v. *Sharon* Sarah sued for divorce on grounds of adultery. The second case, *Sharon* v. *Hill*, filed in Federal District Court by the Sharon estate, claimed she was a paid mistress; therefore, her claim was out of the question. The latter case was filed because Sharon claimed he was a resident of Nevada and also because he believed a more favorable judgment could be received from the federal court. The trial in state courts received nationwide newspaper attention—Sarah bedecking herself in fashionable clothes each day of the trial. A sympathetic Sharon-hating press portrayed her as an innocent woman betrayed at the hands of a lord of property who had used and deceived her in the same ill-mannered way he had acquired his fortune.

Newlands's defense was wearisome and exasperating. The press had a field day. The *Call*, the *Bulletin*, the *Chronicle*, and even Ambrose Bierce's trenchant little literary page *The Wasp* sensationalized the trial, beginning in January 1884. Public opinion cheered on Sarah as she pushed her claims against the millionaire mogul. *The Wasp* had no sympathy with Sharon and ran an elaborately colored cartoon depicting the trial episodes over the caption, "The Social Cancer." The cancer was a shapeless and growing form at the bottom of San Francisco Bay on which Sharon, in the body of a crab, was feeding. Above on the docks, a frightfully evil fisherman named "Scandal" had set his line into it. Both sides resorted to bribery to obtain evidence and witnesses to the point that the antics of the trial became almost as interesting as the subject, not only to the local and national press, but also to European newspapers.[1]

After doing battle in the courts, Sharon hurried away to attend the Republican National Convention where he openly boasted of his role in the sordid spectacle. The Chicago *Herald* for June 4, 1884, reported that he spoke of the trial "with the frankness of his kind and the training of a Pacific Coaster." Talking to a group of cronies, among them Senator John P. Jones of Nevada, Sharon declared, "I'll admit it; I've been indecent. But I'd like to know what any of you fellows would have done under the same circumstances." He said, "Yes, it was pretty tough to go on the stand and admit that I had been such a fool; but what are you going to do—be blackmailed?"[2] A roughneck to the end, Sharon exuded a certain gusto for the battle and enjoyed the notoriety.

Initially, Newlands was not involved in the trial. But events in the summer of 1884 brought him to the center. When Sharon filed a countersuit in Federal District Court against Sarah Hill, it was not without the knowledge that Judge Stephen Field sat on that court. Field, already a friend and frequent visitor to San Francisco, where he resided without charge at the Palace Hotel, had also received a $25,000 loan from Sharon that he never repaid. Victory could hinge upon the good favor of Judge Field. His presidential ambitions and his desire for support from the California Democrats were well known. At this point Newlands strengthened the good relations between the judge and the Sharon interests, but ultimately hurt his own political calling in the state.[3]

At the June 1884 state Democratic convention in Stockton, Field hoped to gain support for his presidential bid, but the temper of the convention was against him. He had been on the wrong side of two important issues. He had favored the Chinese and the railroads, which meant he was an unabashed servant of corporate wealth on the Coast. The convention openly entertained a resolution announcing its opposition to Judge Field's presidential aspirations. When a motion was made to drop the anti-Field resolution from the platform, only Newlands rose to speak in its favor. For almost an hour amid ". . . outcries of rage and execration from an insensate and ruffianly mob," Newlands delivered what he termed his "Strike and Repent" speech. His defense of Field may have seemed foolhardy if he had any future political ambitions with California Democrats, but it was much appreciated by Field. This was more important from Sharon-Newlands point of view. Newlands's first loyalty was the defense of the Sharon estate.[4]

After this the color lithographs of *The Wasp* included Newlands in its caricatures of the trial. In "Re-opening the Ball," the trial was depicted as a grand formal ball with the defendants and their entourage of lawyers. Newlands was sketched as a fawn in an evening dress being escorted into the ball.[5]

Newlands was caught in the web of this "wretched case." It frustrated his plan to seek the U.S. senatorship that would be appointed by a California Democratic-controlled legislature. Newlands had been outside party politics and the forces that directed its anti-monopoly and anti-Chinese stands. His support of Judge Field probably assured his defeat. His hopes demanded vigorous effort to give himself a new image, particularly if George Hearst's quest for the senatorship was to be thwarted. The most immediate problem was the divorce suit. Another was Sharon's unexpected death in 1885. Mourned by few, he did not escape a damning obituary by Ambrose Bierce:

> You'll lie among the dead you helped to kill
> And be in good society at last,
> Your purse unsilvered and your face unbrassed.[6]

With robber-baron Sharon gone, an era passed, but the legacy persisted. By terms of his will, the heirs were obligated to continue the fight against Sarah, not only to protect their inheritance but also to carry out Sharon's wish that she not obtain one cent.

For Newlands, the lonely years between his wife's death in 1882 and his father-in-law's demise were a time of growth. He refined his views on the relationship of the state and public utilities and turned away from Sharon's crass tactics, toward an accommodation with the demands of government. He realized a political future was impossible if he continued the bullying and bribing course of the old Sharon machine. The divorce case interrupted his plans, casting him back into the role as Sharon's mouthpiece. The "wretched case" (his words) undoubtedly damaged his public image. Not only were these years unpleasantly busy, they were sad as well. He confessed to his mother's sister in 1885, "As for myself life is dragging very wearily with me." He spoke of the afflictions of the past few years that "have contracted the area of my affections and made my path hard and strong." His three daughters were his only personal comforts, in addition to "absorption which hard work temporarily brings."[7]

Increasingly, the hard tasks of directing the Sharon estate fell upon his shoulders. The co-executors of the estate were Newlands and Sharon's son, Frederick, but in 1886 Fred Sharon resigned. He "preferred the quiet and repose of private life, and the pleasures of literature, art, architecture, music, travel, out-door sports, and the society of congenial friends." Sharon's estate was divided among Sharon's son Frederick, daughter Flora, and Newlands's three daughters, Clara, born 1875, Janet, born 1876, and Frances, born 1878. As both a trustee for his minor daughters and an executor, Newlands conducted investments and defended its income during the divorce suit. Sharon's will demanded the heirs fight Sarah to the bitter end. The task fell to Newlands because Flora and Frederick lived abroad.[8]

For a time it even appeared that Sarah Hill and her lawyers would be triumphant in their claims for millions of dollars from the estate. By early 1888 Newlands was "tired beyond expression." The Supreme Court of California affirmed the right of the Superior Court to try the divorce case and to issue a decision against Sharon. Other appeals, however, were readied that might make it necessary for both Newlands and Frederick Sharon to take up residence in states other than California to ensure that a federal court would ultimately rule in the matter. Newlands received legal advice to this affect. He told Sharon, who was in France, that he might have to return to New York and take up residence there. "In any event," he said, "I shall move either to Nevada or New York."[9]

Another pressing concern for Newlands was his political career. After his disastrous appearance before the 1884 Stockton convention, he sought to build a political base in the Democratic party. The Democrats regained control of the legislature in 1886, placing them in the position to select a senator in 1887. Prior to the Democratic victory, Newlands shrewdly organized the California Democratic League. This occurred one year after the party had been defeated. Newlands could point out that the people had rejected the candidates of the Stockton convention. He was the principal force behind the new Democratic League that he hoped would eventually lead to a California senate seat. Newlands, in his "call" for members, said that the regular party, because of the reckless policies opposing legitimate business interests in their state, had brought the party to defeat.[10] He sought to restore "harmony" and called upon Democrats to repudiate the old leadership and its harsh attacks on private property. The league promised to restore the party's lost strength at the polls.

Others saw the league for what it was: a power play, offering not "harmony" but "insurgency." Still the appeal of the league forced the leadership to absorb it rather than fight. League men were well represented on committees in the 1886 convention and there were no anti-railroad planks in the platform. The league's success within the party placed Newlands in a strong position. If the Democrats won the 1886 legislative elections, he would be an important prospect for the Senate. He knew this well and took pains to assure the party that the Sharon estate would discharge the over 500 Chinese it employed and replace them with white labor. But Newlands carried with him all of the liabilities of the Sharon heritage—the infamous divorce trial, unchecked corporate wealth, and Sharon's misspent senatorial career. To overcome some of these criticisms, especially a much-repeated observation that Sharon had left nothing in his will to charity, Newlands raised an earlier grant for a children's facility at Golden Gate Park from $55,000 to $100,000 in late November 1886.[11]

The Democrats won the fall election, and although Hearst was still the most likely to succeed with the legislature, Newlands had enough votes to challenge him. After several days of determined struggle the Newlands men capitulated to Hearst. Still Newlands's enthusiasm for California politics and a Senate seat were not dampened. After all, Leland Stanford's seat might be a possibility in 1891, and he was not yet forty years old, with a vast fortune behind him. In March 1887, he issued a general call for civic improvements in San Francisco. He wished to keep in the public eye and to be known as a builder of San Francisco in the tradition of Ralston and an economic developer such as Sharon on the Comstock.[12]

San Francisco was at the center of California's politics. It was the staging ground for a new career. Newlands's goal was clear when he asked San Franciscans to join him in a campaign to make the city "the

Paris of America" and the center of "intellectual, musical, artistic and social life." New streets and sewers must be built to ensure the city's growth. Schools, especially kindergartens, should be supported because Newlands believed that the "hoodlum" developed from idleness even before he entered grade school. The provisions for the grand boulevards and parks exemplified the refined values Newlands admired, as well as his desire for social order through a widening of the educational system.

Moreover, Newlands did not believe that all of these things could come about through the good intentions of like-minded citizens. Funding was needed, but if his "plans for improvement were typical of a man of his breeding, the methods he proposed were not." Out of the chaotic growth of late nineteenth-century America, Newlands proposed city planning, and he urged the city to float a bond issue for four million dollars and engage in deficit financing. Clearly the young lawyer with good manners planned a national political career based on his talents, his programs, and his access to the Sharon estate.[13]

But events blunted his immediate plans. While in Washington visiting Judge Field and surveying the Sharon real estate properties in suburban Washington, he received news that his middle daughter, Janet, was seriously ill in Europe. She was with the Fred Sharons for the winter in Paris and in Ragatz. Fearful that the illness might be a fatal one, Newlands rushed to Europe in late April to be with her. He carried with him a letter from Judge Field to the American ambassador in London describing him as a "warm personal friend" and a conservative Democrat who supported everything that is good in government and everything that tends to advance the interests of society or the individual. The hurried European trip hurt him in California. Janet recovered by the time of his arrival, and he missed rallies at home in San Francisco on behalf of his civic improvement schemes.[14]

Although Newlands's absence from the civic improvement rallies was "an ill omen" for his political plans, it was not decisive in bringing about an end to his efforts. By fall Newlands returned to the state to discover that all was not well. After the unfavorable court actions in 1888, Newlands retreated to Virginia City ". . . to get rid of the worry caused by the Sharon decision." This was the same path followed earlier by Sharon himself when suit was brought in federal court against Sarah Hill to stop her allegations of marriage. The suit was brought by Sharon on the basis of his claim to be a Nevadan and, therefore, his diversity of citizenship.[15]

Newlands was obligated to take these extreme measures, although he did not believe that the divorce represented a major threat to the estate. He told Fred Sharon the common property "will not amount to much." Newlands probably preferred to seek a settlement and be rid of the entire matter as quickly as possible. Certainly an early end of the divorce uproar would have helped his political strategy in California. As it stood, he felt compelled to leave the state not only because of the pressing matter of divorce but also because his groundwork for a political career had not succeeded. As Ambrose Bierce predicted, Sharon and his heirs would be shackled with it as long as they had a dollar to fight it with and "as long as greed shall stimulate aggression and perversity encourage defense." Legal advice urged a change of residency. By the end of 1887 both political disappointment and the divorce question turned Newlands's interests away from the state that had given him so much opportunity. Even prior to the court decision, he wrote of his disappointments in San Francisco and indicated that his career there was at an end.[16]

From late in 1887, Nevada Senator William M. Stewart, counsel to Newlands on the divorce case, tried to interest him in the emerging silver crusade in Nevada and the nation. Newly elected after a fifteen-year absence from the state, Senator Stewart saw a future role in Nevada affairs for the wealthy San Franciscan and virtual heir to the Sharon estate. Key to this role was the passage of national silver legislation. The prospect was a sharp rise in the price of silver, with benefits to Nevada mining, to the estate holdings on the Comstock, and to Stewart's own mining investments. With these goals in mind Stewart asked Newlands to contribute $2,000 to publicize the silver cause. In making the request, Stewart did not want to be considered a "beggar in this matter, on the contrary, I am willing to do my part, but if we expect to be successful there must be cooperation." By 1888 the silver issue faded in comparison to what Stewart considered the more pressing divorce crisis for Newlands and the estate. Newlands and Sharon should move their residency from California because, "Everything depends upon an impartial tribunal to determine the question." He warned that, "Delays in this matter are dangerous."[17]

Newlands's choice of New York rather than Nevada was made possibly because it was so far removed from the recent debacles in California and also no doubt because he could not see himself easily adjusting to life on the eastern side of the Sierra. At the same time, Fred Sharon prepared to return from Europe to New York, where he would purchase a fine home on Fifth Avenue some distance from Newlands's fashionable new address in Gramercy Park. This enabled estate lawyers to file suits in Federal Circuit Court against the decisions of the state court and to reaffirm the decision of the federal court in 1885 that state courts had no jurisdiction because of the dual citizenship of the parties involved. Yet New York held little promise for a political career. No sooner had Newlands moved to New York when the advantages of Nevada suggested themselves. After all, Nevada had been his father-in-law's choice earlier because of his large properties there and his brief, if inglorious political career.

Moreover, Senator Stewart was still interested in Newlands's removal to Nevada. Stewart saw him playing an important role in the new silver movement that could possibly help fuel Newlands's ambitions for a political career, as well as Stewart's ambitions for silver. Stewart reported to the manager of the Southern Pacific Railroad in California that he had a long conversation with Newlands on the subject of coming to Nevada instead of staying in New York. Afterward Stewart could write with some confidence, "I think he will make the change as soon as he is satisfied it will not prejudice litigation."[18]

A new avenue appeared to be opening for Newlands as he prepared for a summer visit to the Hesketh estate in England, where his sister-in-law, Flora, lived with her husband, Lord Hesketh. He departed for England with the strong possibility of returning to a vigorous career in the rough-and-tumble arena of western politics in the least populated and most prostrate of all of the so-called western "rotten boroughs." When he returned it would not be to a refined life of wealth and polite New York society, which the fashionable Gramercy Park address suggested. He could have chosen this life, "the life characteristic of many other heirs to large fortunes, full of ease and beautiful things but devoid of significance." Frederick Sharon had already pursued this course. Rather, Stewart and others opened the doors for Newlands to re-enter politics from the venue of another western state on the high tide of what Stewart saw as the national silver movement.[19]

Vacationing at the Hesketh estate, Newlands joined another young San Francisco visitor and friend of Lady Hesketh's. Edith McAllister was the daughter of a leading member of the San Francisco Bar, Hall McAllister, and niece of one of the leading figures in New York society, Ward McAllister. She was twenty-eight years old. Newlands was a forty-year-old widower of important wealth and future political prospects. Edith had been away from San Francisco for several years studying languages and music in Europe. Their reacquaintance and courtship during the summer provided Newlands with the opportunity to escape the dismal state of his personal life. They were married at the Hesketh estate on September 4, 1888. West Coast and Nevada newspapers, unaware of his course in politics, merely reported the circumstances of the wedding and noted that after a short stay in Paris the couple intended to return to the United States and reside in New York.[20]

The second Mrs. Newlands represented refinement, taste, and the highest virtues of feminine society in the late nineteenth century. Newlands had married "upward," but this time into the ranks of society, not wealth. Ward McAllister, arbiter of New York and Newport society, was known to have once remarked that "good society numbered no more than 400 in the United States." The McAllisters were social leaders, but certainly not as rich as the Sharons. Newlands's new father-in-law, one of the founders of the San Francisco Bar, had come to California from Georgia in 1849 with the first wave of the gold rush. Like the Sharons the McAllisters were the victims of Ambrose Bierce's pointed pen. Of Hall McAllister, Bierce wrote in 1892:

> No doubt, McAllister, you can explain
> How honorable 'tis to lie for gain,
> Provided only that the jury's made
> To understand that lying is your trade[21]

But Newlands's life was suddenly quite removed from the circles of Bierce's San Francisco. His new marriage rescued him from a desperate loneliness and encouragements from Nevada opened new political doors. Finally the estate began winning divorce case decisions. In England he received the news that Judge Field ruled in favor of the Sharon estate in Federal Circuit Court. The ruling against Sarah, who had married her lawyer, David Terry, said that the earlier court ruling that the Superior Court had no jurisdiction must stand and required that she hand over to the court the alleged marriage contract. It was the end of an effective litigation against the estate on the part of Sarah Terry. In the courtroom during the reading of the verdict, she interrupted Judge Field in an outburst asking him how much Newlands had paid him for the decision. Field ordered her removed and when her husband forcibly attempted to prevent this, he was himself subdued and dragged from the courtroom. Contempt charges followed that created a lasting enmity between the Terrys and Judge Field. In 1889 David Terry was killed by Field's bodyguard during what the guard said was an attempt on Field's life.[22]

In addition to this victory, the California Supreme Court unexpectedly ruled in favor of the estate. Both court actions could have opened the way for Newlands to return to California politics, but they did not. While the court rulings helped clear the clouds from Newlands's public life, he coupled his taste for a new political career with intentions to explore new economic adventures with the wealth of the vast estate over which he now presided. These months presented themselves as a threshold for new directions, new creative energies that began in this fifth decade of life. By early December 1888, Newlands and Fred Sharon visited the offices of Senator Stewart in Washington. Less than a month later Newlands told Fred, who was planing to resume his leisurely life in Europe, "I have concluded to make my legal residence in Nevada." He would, however, "spend a good deal of time in the East." In further talks with another chief legal adviser, William Herrin, Newlands was also urged to identify himself with Nevada to "strengthen myself politically as a means of influence and power in matters and litigation relating to the Estate." Convinced of the soundness of this advice, Newlands wrote Fred of his decision to take up residency in Nevada and his decision to pursue a political career in the state—not only for his own personal reasons but also for the interest of the estate, as Herrin had put it. "I must be on the Coast a good deal," he wrote, "I might as well pursue my career." And he added, "I have no idea at present of contesting Jones' seat." Newlands declined any challenge: "I simply intend to hold myself in line and wait. . . ." He did not wish to be the target of criticism as a carpetbagger, like so many other Nevada political figures, now including Jones, and certainly including Sharon. He said emphatically, "I don't wish to imperil the good faith of my residence here by a mere Sharon sojourn."[23]

Both Nevada and San Francisco newspapers announced Newlands's imminent move to Nevada and speculated about the new life his presence would bring to Nevada politics. On Christmas Day, the *Morning Appeal* in Carson City authoritatively reported, "Frank Newlands will occupy Senator Stewart's home during the winter." The San Francisco *Examiner* observed that, "if Senator Jones intends to hold on to what he has politics will be lively in the state . . . and stand in marked contrast to the last two senatorial campaigns that have afforded not very much fun and very little picking." The *Nevada State Journal* innocently rejected political motives or any threat to Jones on the part of Newlands and suggested Newlands came to Nevada merely, "because he has large interests in some mills along the Carson River and also in the Challenge, Confidence, and Yellow Jacket mines." As political forecasters, the San Francisco papers spoke the truth.[24]

V

NEWLANDS AS A NEVADAN

In late December 1888, Newlands crossed the mountains. Nevada was poor in natural and human resources, but rich in the history of a departed Comstock mining era. The gold and silver strikes on the Comstock from 1859 to 1880 transformed the western counties of Utah Territory into a new state with a bustling urban and transportation frontier centered in Virginia City. But the failure of the mines in the late seventies threw the state back upon agriculture, livestock, and transportation. Depression and an exodus of population followed so rapidly that many suggested Nevada statehood be relinquished. It was an empty shell of a state with an electorate of under 20,000, far less than San Francisco. In this setting Newlands chose to seek prestige, power, and even national influence.

Newlands became Senator Stewart's political protégé. Newlands even asked to rent Stewart's Carson City residence. Although surprised, Stewart believed it was an important first step in identifying as a resident and "not merely a transient." He requested no payment, but he would accept a nominal sum if Newlands thought it necessary. He instructed his renter to take care of his library and refrain from lending his valuable books. Stewart, of course, saw Newlands as a wealthy ally in state and national politics.[1]

Newlands was well aware of Nevada's unsavory reputation: it was a pocket borough of California and considered by the national press a "rotten borough" where political offices were sold to the highest bidder. With the advantages of wealth, many assumed that Newlands would plunge boldly into the traditional game of Nevada politics. Newlands surprised many by refusing to play the brazen role of a carpetbag politico. He hoped to avoid the crassness of William Sharon's previous "political sojourn." He faced the task of gaining entrée to state politics on some other basis than wealth, and he sought a way to overcome the tarnished image of his ex-father-in-law.

In Nevada, Newlands carried the liabilities of the Sharon heritage. But the Sharon name also brought back memories of money and the good days of the Comstock Lode. Everyone knew that most of Nevada's wealth had escaped to California. Newlands's presence suggested that some of it had returned at a time of great need. This was exactly the redeemer image Newlands wished to portray as he became a public figure. In California, Newlands spoke of progressive community development and of San Francisco's future as the Paris of America, echoing the early San Francisco booster William Ralston.[2] In Nevada Newlands proclaimed a great future for Reno, with its beautiful Truckee River, surrounding mountains, and briskly mild climate. Moreover, Reno and Nevada in general offered growth to agriculture, manufacture, and commerce as a redistribution point to a vast area for trade goods.

By early February 1889, Newlands was comfortably settled in Carson City. Rumors abounded about his intentions. Stewart wrote reassuringly that despite all of the political suggestions, "people have generally come to the conclusion that your business interests called you there," and, "That is the best view of the question at present." Stewart went on to advise him to build a home in Nevada: "It will look more like improving the country." And he was certain Newlands would find Nevada a very healthy place for his family. If he decided to build in Reno the educational facilities would be excellent, "if the legislature takes care of the university."[3]

Newlands beckoned others to join him in building for the future of the state in a public statement that set forth the opportunities he hoped to realize in his newly selected home. His remarks, reported by the Reno *Evening Gazette*, revealed a man who intended to play a personal role in the state. In May 1889, the newspaper announced that Newlands had purchased property overlooking the Truckee River in Reno, employed a New York landscape gardener, and hired an architect to design a house for his family. Asked if he intended to enter the senatorial fight in 1892, Newlands replied, "I have come here to stay and not for a political purpose . . . there is no politics in it. Nevada is very ably represented in Senators Stewart and Jones and I have no ax to grind." As Senator Stewart had indicated earlier, the best view was to give the impression of "improving the country."[4]

Less than a month after his arrival in Reno Newlands talked to the local press about Nevada's resources. He urged Nevadans to turn away from the region's mining heritage toward the "unlimited possibilities" of irrigated agriculture. Obvious resources of sun and soil existed in the state; now man should intervene to apply water to the land. Abundant snow in the high mountains produced runoff that only irrigated adjoining lands served by diversion ditches. Much of this water, he acknowledged, was in dispute in suits over priority rights, but Newlands believed such contests could be avoided if the supply of water were made more plentiful and constant.

The beginning of a lengthy interview in the Reno *Evening Gazette* of February 25, 1889, sounded like the plan Newlands had urged for San Francisco. Whether Newlands realized it or not he spoke to the central questions of Nevada's future—how to justify the state's existence beyond mining and how to free it from the rotten-borough image by providing it with a viable economic and population base. Unfortunately, Nevada's boundaries existed without reference to water resources. This crucial question opened a new chapter in Nevada's quest for economic growth and stability.

Newlands thought federal land cessions to the state could underwrite development. But he believed state irrigation acts, like the Wright bill in California, represented "unwise legislation," because he thought irrigation districts with their power to issue bonds would promote "extravagance." He opposed government ownership: "I believe it much better to limit such enterprise to private capital." Property rights, he told the *Gazette*, transcended state lines. The people of Nevada could acquire water storage sites in the mountains of California. He asserted, "An imaginary line should not stand in the way of private negotiations and enterprise."

Newlands did not rule out legislation to lay the foundations of a new Nevada. At this date, 1889, he announced, "I believe in national legislation on this subject." The government had already spent large amounts on investigations of the irrigation question, but the results gave only a preliminary report to the public; it would be years before the national government acted. Meanwhile, individuals and communities should not sit idly waiting for legislative aid, but along with private enterprise should consider action. He admitted that there were problems, such as sectional rivalries within Nevada. The financing of projects by state government presented difficulties because of the state's constitutional debt limit of $300,000. Both made the state an uncertain vehicle for development schemes. To resolve rivalries, Newlands suggested a program of state aid to local community projects as the beginning of a general program intended to embrace all of Nevada. To deal with deficit financing, he believed the state constitution should be amended to allow increased indebtedness for the financing of irrigation works. In Nevada he invoked the same method of deficit finance he had proposed for beautifying and improving the public services of San Francisco.

Newlands further argued that in western Nevada there were multiple uses for water that need not compete destructively with one another. Agricultural and industrial sectors, especially ore processing mills, could cooperate. Actually, he noted, they complemented one another, as industry and agriculture should. For example, the mining population of Virginia City depended on the operation of ore crushing mills along the Carson River, while at the same time Virginia City provided a market for the agricultural goods of the Carson Valley. Disagreements over the use of Carson River water were not a conflict among private interests. A larger issue was at stake. "It involves the public good and prosperity," he insisted. "Why," Newlands asked, "should not these two interests come together and unite in this enterprise for the common good." These remarks revealed his sensitivity to the dispute between the mill owners on the lower Carson and the upstream ranchers in Carson Valley because of the Sharon estate's interests in the Union Mill and Mining Company.[5]

In discussing Truckee River water, Newlands emphasized that he had familiarized himself only with the western part of the state. Three weeks earlier he had visited the upper waters of the Truckee with a delegation from Washoe County. The excursion involved talks with people in the community of Truckee and at the source of the river in Lake Tahoe. He found water flowing freely from the lake even though it was not needed for agricultural purposes. He believed the gates of the dam should be closed to store the water for future use. This simple action would be an example of solving problems ". . . by energy, determination, and cooperative enterprise on the part of individuals." Newlands's interview underlined his interest in the state. Nevadans should not be content with the present system of water diversion ditches for sawmills, flour mills, reduction works, and limited irrigation. "It is to the interest of all that water should be kept running in the river as long as possible and that none of it should be wasted."

More reliable studies were essential, Newlands continued, because no one in Nevada had a definite knowledge of how much water could be stored. Efficiency minded, Newlands called for studies by experts on the costs of irrigation enterprises, the quantity of water available for storage, and land that could thus be irrigated. He introduced the name of former California State Engineer William Hammond Hall, under whose direction information-gathering on stream flows and land subject to irrigation was going forth in California. Nevada, he declared, needed to undertake a similar survey, "but in addition to this there should be some legislation with reference to the storage of water and priority of rights."

With this interview Newlands marked the beginning of his campaign to advertise the benefits of irrigation and the modern scientific approach needed to bring water to the underdeveloped lands of Nevada. "Its essence," as a leading conservation historian wrote, "was rational planning to promote efficient development and use of all natural resources." On the water issue Newlands early became identified with a national conservation movement that saw the proper utilization of resources as the highest form of conservation and progress. Not so coincidentally, the 1889 Nevada legislature took a first step toward rational water planning. It sought to determine the priority of all water rights in the state.[6]

At the invitation of Senator Stewart, he joined the Senate Committee on Irrigation and Reclamation in a tour of western states. Stewart also assured Newlands, "This will give you an opportunity to meet prominent men at these points and become acquainted, and make such arrangements as you may desire for some active work in the campaign." Stewart's invitation included copies of his recent speeches and concluded: "I hope you will not fail to accompany me on this trip." After a hesitant reply by Newlands, Stewart urged him to go along at least part way: "If it is impossible for you to accompany me through Washington and Montana on my way to St. Paul to meet the Committee on Irrigation . . . , you can meet the committee when it reaches Montana and go west with us through Washington and back through Idaho." The senator also congratulated Newlands on the recent favorable decision of the Supreme Court in the Sharon divorce litigation. The tour of irrigation sites reinforced Newlands's belief that irrigation was the key political issue in the arid West. The development of the region, including Nevada, depended on the stable economic base that irrigated agriculture could provide.[7]

Newlands also turned his attention to other issues. In a speech before the State Agricultural Society he noted the decline in population and demands that Nevada be returned to territorial status. Without referring to the "Crime of '73," he paid homage to the emerging silver crusade when he spoke of the "clandestine and dishonest legislation" that destroyed silver currency and charged that Nevada suffered from it more than any other state. This was his first public statement on what became the strident issue in Nevada during the 1890s and showed he was learning the rhetoric of silver as well as irrigation.[8]

Little did he suspect that the silver issue would eclipse irrigation and monopolize the state's politics for over a decade. Newlands made the point that eventually became strict doctrine among the silverites when he said, "owing to the demonetization of silver the prosecution of mining enterprises is almost at a standstill." This provided him with what he believed the perfect opportunity to introduce the issue of irrigated agriculture as the new hope for a state whose economy stood ruined by national legislation. The crimes against Nevada's mineral industries were great, but the shambles could be transformed into opportunity and eventual prosperity. The salvation of the state lay not in the doctrine of silver or even bimetalism. Rather, he announced his faith in what he believed was a far more concrete plan of action than the magic words "Free Coinage of Silver." He merely said, "This was an age of material progress," and agricultural development of Nevada represented a doorway to a new age. There was no need to wait for government action because the community could act to purchase properties and secure for all time water for the great enterprises of Nevada. "When this is accomplished can you form any conception of the great wealth that can be produced by the proper utilization of water?" he asked.[9]

Besides capturing headlines, Newlands became directly involved in the ownership of water supplies. He might proclaim that the mining era had passed, but with some embarrassment he joined the side of mining interests in a dispute over the use of Carson River waters. The issue pitted upstream ranchers against the processing mills operated by the Union Mine and Milling Company on the lower Carson. He claimed that the mills had a vested right to the water. Moreover, "Union Mine and Milling Company had no intention of compromising its property right to the water." The demands of ranchers denied water to the downstream mill works, violating Newlands's concept of justly sharing available resources.[10]

The Carson River dispute illustrates the complexities of Nevada water politics. For many years ranchers on the upper Carson forks confronted the owners of the downstream mills. Important court cases, rendered as early as 1872, attempted to divide the water between agricultural and mining-milling interests. The Carson River forks rise in the central Sierra and flow from the California mountains in a northeasterly direction. In Nevada the river flows below Virginia City's Comstock mines, beyond which it eventually disappears in the Carson sink. The Carson's proximity to the Comstock made it an ideal source of water power for the stamp mills processing the ore as it came from the Comstock, and for working tailings that continued after the exhaustion of the mines. Because it owned the principal mills on the lower Carson, the Sharon estate was the ranchers' chief antagonist both in the Comstock period as well as in the very moment when Newlands entered Nevada politics.[11]

Water storage, use, and distribution were not new questions to Nevadans, who had long struggled over definitions of beneficial use of the state's limited water. State-sponsored irrigation proposals appeared in the 1883 legislature. Newlands's leadership put a new twist on an old question. Could Newlands act as a catalyst for innovative irrigation actions from both communities and private enterprise? Ranchers, who recently benefited from the sale of selected school lands, saw a threat to their appropriated water in state reclamation systems and in a revamping of state water law. Moreover, people from eastern Nevada feared that funds for projects would aid only ranching interests in Washoe County. Mining and transportation interests wished not to disturb their present access to water or increase the light state tax burden. Therefore suggestions of state-sponsored reclamation roused a wide range of opponents.[12]

Drought forced the Nevada legislature to review water matters from 1887 to 1889. The 1889 legislature passed laws that anticipated many of Newlands's early remarks. The new laws also represented concessions on the part of the mining, ranching, and transportation interests for distribution and storage of water resources. Newlands started his campaign for irrigated agriculture at an opportune moment in the state's history.

The new legislation, however, proved ill-fated. The act to build storage systems with an appropriation of $100,000 from the state school fund met immediate protests. Administration of the statute provided for a four-member Reclamation Commission appointed with the power to mark out irrigation districts in the state. They could employ an engineer to select reclamation sites and begin storage works. The comprehensive Water Law of 1889 was modeled on a Colorado statute. Seven irrigation districts were created with the power to determine water rights in each district. All rights had to be filed with county recorders by September 1, 1889. An important provision made unappropriated water the property of the state. No addition to present water claims would be allowed without the consent of the water commissioners. Calling it a raid on school monies for the purpose of building reservoirs on the upper Carson, critics damned it as a benefit to the mill owners.[13]

The Water Law of 1889 spurred interminable controversy. To Newlands's chagrin as a major stockholder, the Union Mill and Mining sued ranchers on the upper Carson. The case came when he tried to portray himself as a disinterested party presenting programs for the benefit of all citizens of the state. Again Newlands's business interests ran contrary to his public ambitions, as they so often did in California. He regretted the suit, but the company pressed for it. Newlands's solution was a comprehensive storage system on the Carson to guarantee water both to ranchers and mill men. But the ranchers, particularly Carson Valley land baron Frederick Dangberg, eager to bring thousands of additional "sagebrush lands" under cultivation, could not admit to compromise. Agriculture now challenged the preeminence of industry in the state and would eventually win the suit in 1897. Newlands could not concede to agricultural interests all the water of a river whose power for years had turned mills that ground out the riches of the Comstock.

He insisted that he did not stand against the agricultural interests, but rather against the "large landed proprietors" who constantly expanded their acreage. Cattle ranching did not represent the type of agricultural development he envisioned. Newlands unhappily observed that the matter now would go into court and the money that could have been used to build reservoirs would be spent on litigation. He noted that in the previous two years before the filing (1887–1888) ranchers had appropriated all the Carson River waters from July 4 to January, forcing the mills to close. Small farmers downstream, who had prior rights to water, were also adversely affected by the upstream ranchers, he asserted. Thus Newlands cast himself in the role of champion of the small farmer, not simply as a defender of the milling monopoly. Farmers represented a forward looking group for Nevada, while ranching interests seemed wedded to Nevada's frontier past.[14]

For Newlands the Nevada situation rendered neither easy solutions nor immediate acceptance of the broad plans he outlined. Years prior to his arrival, comprehensive water planning, storage, and irrigation were topics of public concern. The present laws were products of previous years, but almost immediately water users in the eastern part of the state challenged the new state water law in District Court in Winne-mucca. By June 1890, the court declared the law unconstitutional. The statute threatened vested rights in water and delegated too much law-making power to the governor. The decision returned Nevada water law to a legal wilderness. It has been described as a "set-back" for Newlands who "forced" it through the legislature. It is clear that water questions were already under debate and certainly California's Wright Act was well known in the state. Newlands quickly boarded a band-wagon that was already under way when he addressed the Nevada irrigation issue. The new measure fit his plans to establish water allotments along all of Nevada's rivers. But the law, which sought to clarify water demands on the various rivers, resulted only in exagger-ated claims like those on the Carson. It did offer order and consistency to the state water picture.[15]

After the legislature passed what must have seemed to Newlands encouraging water and irrigation legislation, he moved ahead with his own plans to promote irrigation and storage facilities along the Truckee River. The Reno *Evening Gazette* for October 17, 1889, described "What F. G. Newlands is Doing to Develop Our State" in glowing terms. The first grand scheme was to lay claim through Newlands's private land purchases to the waters from Tahoe, Donner, Independence, and Webber Lakes with a view to bringing the water to the Truckee meadows for irrigation. Newlands agreed to act as a private agent, advancing money for land purchases and even for the construction of some storage facilities. He hoped that the community might ultimately reimburse him, with 6 percent interest. Newlands explained his ven-ture in terms of sound business practice and said that even Mr. Sharon, if he had lived, would no doubt have invested largely in Nevada, "where the foundation for this vast estate was laid." As doubtful as this was, by referring to Sharon he convincingly insisted that his actions should not be mistaken for altruism. The *Gazette* concluded that, "Mr. Newlands is showing his faith in the state's future . . . in an honest endeavor to solve the perplexing irrigation problem."[16]

A week later at the Washoe County Court House following a meeting of the Washoe Improvement Association, "prominent gentlemen," according to the newspaper, addressed the irrigation question in a public forum. Among them were Newlands, Robert Fulton of the Southern Pacific Land Company, Robert Foley, representing the State Irrigation Commission, and F. W. Sharon. The *Gazette* featured New-lands's remarks, but it also focused on the critical remarks of former

Nevada Congressman Thomas Fitch, long-time Republican carpetbag politician. Truckee meadow irrigators, Fitch argued, should incorporate independent of Newlands or the state. Successful irrigation works, he charged, could be carried on outside of Newlands's financial empire.

Others disagreed. Robert Fulton, whom Newlands later employed to advise him on land and water investments, emphasized that "if the General Government held the water we might have all sorts of restrictions and red tape placed upon its use." In addition he saw many problems associated with state ownership, but, "If farmers could not act, let the country, if the country could not act, let the state." He and others agreed with Newlands that farmers, ditch owners, and other water users should form a corporation to build and manage water storage facilities. Newlands assured the gathering that he would move ahead with the purchase of dam and reservoir sites on the upper Truckee and even at its source where it flowed from Lake Tahoe. A businessman could make such decisions quickly, and without the delay that community action encountered. He hoped that the community would follow his lead. In referring to $100,000 appropriated by the state legislature in its irrigation law of 1889, he said that there were too many restrictions to expect it could be used in this project. "In reaching out for a great enterprise," he said, "my disposition is to fix my eye on the goal and to jump all the intermediate fences." Already negotiations had been initiated with Southern Pacific's Leland Stanford and former governor of California on an agreement to permit the waters of Lake Tahoe to be stored for eventual release to Nevada. Senator Stewart also was active in efforts to devise a plan for this with the governor and meet his demand for any scheme that would "advance the general good."[17]

Immediately after Newlands made this proposal to tap the waters of Lake Tahoe, Alexander von Schmidt, civil engineer and surveyor of the line separating California and Nevada, wrote a letter to the *Gazette* charging that Newlands's plan to use the water of Lake Tahoe was part of a scheme to keep San Francisco's water supply under the monopolistic control of the Sharon estate's Spring Valley Water Company. "Don't you know," he wrote, "that his kindness is prompted by his Spring Valley Water Company of this city. He represents the interest of the late William Sharon, which was the controlling interest." Von Schmidt said that his dam, owned by the San Francisco Water Works, controlled the waters emanating from Lake Tahoe, and, "Whatever Mr. Newlands may do cannot take away the rights of the Lake Tahoe and San Francisco works." The *Gazette* replied that von Schmidt's rights had

expired because he proposed to divert waters from Tahoe to San
Francisco fifteen years before and, "Any right he may have had has
lapsed when he failed to appropriate water at the time he built the
dam." The editor indignantly objected that no sooner did Newlands
make a constructive proposal than von Schmidt came forth with "Its
mine."[18]

Newlands replied that von Schmidt was in error on two counts: the
Spring Valley Water Company had no interest in the waters of Lake
Tahoe, and the Sharon estate now owned no controlling interest in the
company. Moreover, state partisanship should not be an issue. Nature
had already decided that the waters of the Truckee, the Carson, the
Walker, and the Owens Rivers were for use by people living on the
eastern slope of the Sierra. "Tahoe's water will never go to San Francisco. It is not needed there. It is needed here," he asserted. Newlands
also dismissed von Schmidt's claims to the waters of Tahoe by virtue of
his dam on the headwaters of the Truckee. A dam owned by the Donner
Boom Company was farther upstream than von Schmidt's and controlled the waters of the Truckee at their source. Senator Stewart
endorsed Newlands's rebuff of von Schmidt: "The von Schmidt
scheme is a fraud. Nobody here takes any interest in it," said Stewart
and referred to von Schmidt as a man who "talks wildly and fanatically
in regard to his scheme."[19]

Still, in this late fall and winter of 1889, despite the in-state and out-
of-state complications, Newlands remained optimistic about Nevada's
water and land development. Nevada could overcome "the apparent
hardness of life, the lack of comfort, the lack of beauty," that drew the
attention of any stranger arriving in the state from a settled community.
No doubt this remark reflected his own impression of Nevada as he
settled into his new home.

Although he occasionally employed the silverite rhetoric when he
attacked the legislation that destroyed the mining industry, Newlands
generally deplored mining society. He asserted that Nevada's lack of
refinement "largely arises from the mining character of the country, and
from the general belief that life here is temporary and conditional."
Newlands stressed that Nevada was emerging from "a mere mining
community" to one where agriculture and industry would flourish.
Nevadans should turn their thoughts to "more comfort and happiness in
life, pleasing the eye and the ear and senses." Reno, he asserted, could
be "one of the prettiest towns on the Coast." He noted that the Truckee
River presented the perfect setting for a promenade where people

could gather and walk with their families in the heart of the city, just as Europeans did in their cities.

Still Newlands preferred practicality to aesthetic beauties and qualities. The leisurely pursuit of art and literature was not to Newlands's taste as it was for his brother-in-law, Frederick Sharon. He was far more imbued with the desire to organize great schemes to utilize the resources at his command. Still he enjoyed the refinement of the children of great wealth and mixed easily with them. To Nevadans, he emphasized that material progress opened new vistas in practical education and training. Education must not concentrate entirely upon the intellect or "the head" as he put it to his audiences. Gymnastics should be stressed: "Physical sports should be more general and embrace both men and women." Something more was needed than merely baseball, "a spectator sport like spectator sports of ancient Rome," he said.

Establishing cooking schools for women was an area where practical education could better serve the community. The neglect of the stomach he found ". . . particularly noticeable in frontier life." The word "frontier" summarized Newlands's view of Nevada society. Certainly the "frontier" atmosphere played a role in all that he thought, talked, and wrote about Nevada. The symbol represented waste, squandered resources, and backwardness. The proper preparation of food was an example of this general condition of "frontier" life. Incredulous, he said, "In a country abounding in cattle of every kind fresh meat is but little eaten, and the great reliance is ham and bacon swimming in fat and destructive of digestion." To one of Newlands's fragile constitution, diet, health, and physical education were matters of great importance. So intent was his interest that he could not resist relating dietary habits to an entire social attitude that prevailed on the frontier.[20]

For many Nevadans, Newlands's views represented cultural arrogance rather than a vision of progress, but he appealed to those seeking a more modern state. For his friends, Newlands's presence in Nevada was a modernizing force in a neglected land in the intermountain West. To others he was a "city slicker" whose big ideas and big money served only the cause of his own ambitions. Regardless, Newlands meant to reform Nevada's society and government. Mining and open-range ranching symbolized Nevada's frontier past. He sought to channel the robust, wasteful energies of that era into an orderly and planned society of small homes, busy cities, and industry. In the post-frontier era, the jack-of-all-trades gave way to the expert. His opponents feared such a post-frontier society as too disciplined, orderly, bureaucratic, and accountable.[21]

Newlands, however, managed quickly to "get right with the silver question." Stewart urged him to attend the 1889 Free Coinage convention in St. Louis. "Now is the time to act. The recent elections showed great discontent on the part of the people," Stewart wrote, "and whatever others may say there is no doubt in my mind that want of money is the cause of all the trouble." No one could foresee that silver would overshadow every other political issue. Newlands, however, paid only passing lip service to remonetization when he referred to the "clandestine and dishonest legislation" that had destroyed Nevada's silver industry.[22]

Nevada Senator John P. Jones saw silver as a political issue in the late 1870s and gave appropriate mention to it throughout his career. By 1882 a "silver" plank appeared in the platforms of both Nevada state political parties. Senator Stewart took time to impress upon Newlands silver's crucial bearing upon Nevada politics. Yet Newlands was unaware of the stormy and disruptive impact the silver question would have upon state politics.[23]

Acting on Stewart's advice, Newlands not only attended the St. Louis convention but also praised Nevada's leadership on the silver issue. In reply to the toast "Nevada, may she live and prosper," he denied the allegation that Nevada was a "rotten borough," noting that the distinguished senators John P. Jones and William M. Stewart represented the political system of Nevada. Jones in his great "silver speech" a decade earlier "gave utterance to all the ideas upon the question silver which have constituted the text of the literature upon the subject since. . . ." Newlands called Senator Stewart "the peer of any man in the senate" and the ". . . restless propagandist for silver." The crusade for silver, he asserted, was not only in the interest of his own state but for the debtors as well—the farmer and the planter ". . . whose best interests have been mercilessly trampled underfoot."

Newlands won excellent coverage in the Nevada press. As an aspiring Silver State politician, he spoke the language of his new state, of a new decade, and of a new phase in his career. In the past he had defended property rights. Now he talked of injustices.[24]

While Newlands spoke grandly of Nevada's future, he could not foresee the severe national depression that struck in 1893. The economic crisis forced Newlands to curtail investments in Nevada. Moreover, neither the state's new irrigation law nor its water law of 1889 proved workable. As one correspondent told Newlands, "the Nevada connection" has not been entirely satisfactory. Meanwhile his political

career was held in abeyance. Neither a congressional seat nor a senatorship stood immediately available.[25]

Newlands spent Christmas 1889 in Nevada as work began on his
home overlooking the Truckee River in Reno. After the holidays he and
his family planned to leave Carson City to spend the winter in the East.
The newcomer's initial journey to Nevada accomplished numerous
objectives. Newlands became a resident of the state, and his political
and economic moves provoked much discussion. He identified himself
with the sensitive Nevada issues of irrigation and silver through speech-
making and personal contacts with key individuals. Now he could
temporarily leave the state with a feeling of some satisfaction, until the
time for political activities arrived the following summer. The office to
which he would aspire in Nevada would certainly be a national one, and
a senatorship most desirable.[26]

The politics of Nevada could be put aside for the winter. His good
political tutor in Nevada politics, Senator Stewart, had opened his home
to him in Carson City and advised him on important issues. Stewart
encouraged land acquisitions, the building of a home in the state, and
most important, support of the silver issue. Newlands himself cast his
considerable influence over the Reno *Evening Gazette*; he formed a
coterie of influential men who were drawn to his ambitious visions for
Nevada. Newlands's influence prompted the 1889 legislature to create
a Board of Trade designed to stimulate agriculture and encourage
farmer immigration into the state. To command some of his plan for
irrigation-farmer development, Newlands turned to a long-time employee of the Central Pacific Railroad, Land Agent Robert L. Fulton
of Reno.

Fulton had long been a booster of Nevada. Years before, as the
Central Pacific field agent, he saw the benefits of careful range management for a larger ranching economy. Now he also foresaw the rise of a
small-farmer population in the state based on irrigated agriculture. As
early as 1884 he wrote that the railroad lands from Wells in eastern
Nevada to the Utah line could provide range for a quarter of a million
cattle with proper winter feeding arrangements. Six years later he wrote
of a more diversified crop agriculture in this country. Fulton was excited
about Nevada's growth, foreseeing colonies of people coming into the
state to dig canals, construct irrigation works, and plant crops. Fulton
emerged as an important advisor to Newlands as manager of the Nevada
State Board of Trade, with responsibility for many of Newlands's views
on the challenges of water storage and reclamation. In January of 1890

Newlands issued a widely distributed pamphlet entitled "Storage and Reclamation" in which he detailed the promises of irrigated agriculture for Nevada.[27]

Prior to Christmas 1889 Newlands sought ways to enlarge Fulton's "sphere of usefulness in Nevada" and, as he put it, "increase your income." He proposed that Fulton should consider managing a company that would oversee all the properties acquired along the Truckee for irrigation, power, the ice business, and water storage. Further, he hoped Fulton could head up the new Board of Trade. As a man with fifteen years of training and experience. ". . . obviously you are the man for the place," said Newlands in one of his extensive letters to Fulton. He continued he would also like Fulton to manage the development he contemplated on the Carson River. This would involve a series of three reservoirs: one near the head of the Carson in Long Valley, another about five miles from Carson City, and the last below Dayton for the irrigation of about 7,000 acres to be selected from state lands. Newlands anticipated that these reservoirs on the Carson River would irrigate thousands of acres and also provide the necessary water for the operation of three quartz mills on the Carson.

These plans reinforced Newlands's views that ranchers and mill interests could live in harmony with the river if adequate reservoirs existed. Ranchers on the upper Carson did not share his views of concord and community interests. Newlands correctly identified Frederick Dangberg as the chief instigator of a suit against the estate's Union Mill and Mining Company for the waters of the river. He declared to Fulton, "As I am satisfied that Dangberg is an obstructionist and is impeding the prosperity of that entire country and is contemplating the absorption of all the water, I am making movements to surround him in every way. . . ." Newlands instructed another agent, Herman Springmeyer, to purchase a Long Valley reservoir site and 4,000 adjoining acres. Newlands's also toyed with the idea of buying the "Twelve Mile Ranch" which owned half of the oldest and highest ditch leading from the Carson River. Dangberg owned the other half, and through it expected to irrigate his own 8,000 acres. Newlands's plan to own one half of the ditch would place him in a position to block Dangberg's movements and "compel him to come to some agreement with reference to his 8,000 acres." Instead of Dangberg monopolizing the land, irrigation facilities could be constructed and the thousands of acres turned over to immigrants in small lots at reasonable prices. Newlands believed if he could buy up enough land he could control the river's water and settle any disputes to the advantage of both agricultural and milling interests.[28]

Unfortunately Newlands's great pronouncements about the future of Nevada deserts were not self-fulfilling prophecy. As with all prophecy, and especially desert prophecy, the events of the real world intervened. The real world of Nevada in the 1890s meant idle mines, declining silver prices, squabbles over limited water, and unproductive sagebrush lands. With the remnants of a mining population hanging on in the state, the vision of a mining revival was more meaningful to Nevadans than talk about a new Nevada based upon farms and commerce. Higher prices for the white metal offered more immediate rewards than dams, reservoirs, and irrigation ditches. In a mining state the issues of irrigation politics paled before the energetic and colorful cries for Free Silver and protests against the goldbugs of Wall Street. A revival of silver, the politicians averred, would instantly return prosperity to the state while irrigation prophets could talk only of distant futures. Not only were silver politics more appealing and exciting, but growing demands for sweeping economic and political reform became allied with an upstart third party political movement in the agricultural states of the Midwest and South—Populism. Populists called for, among other measures, government ownership of railroads and communications, greater regulation of business, and more democracy in the political process. As it would happen, the silver cause became attached to the Populist party as a part of its attempt to increase the money supply, reduce interest, and increase the prices of farm goods.[29]

Depression in the 1890s spurred interest in third-party political radicalism. In the mining states of the West, Silver party politics overshadowed Populists, especially in Nevada. The politics of silver and populist reform imposed political adjustments on Newlands, forcing him to embrace silver ardently and to speak less often about irrigation. Newlands could not conscientiously subscribe to the more radical reforms of Populism. His political draughts were more moderate; he had no intention of becoming a passionate populist or for that matter a straight-out free silverite. Nonetheless, "to get on" in Nevada politics, he realized that devotion to silver was essential. He wished to avoid silver's populist campaigns and moderately offered support to the cause. In his visions of a new Nevada, Newlands did not bargain for the uproar of silver politics. The issue of remonetization imposed personal and public adjustments upon his aspirations in the state. But bargain he must, if he was to win (or buy) political office in Nevada. Even a well-financed campaign would not win if it did not pay tribute to the silver cause. As the new decade began, silver politics demanded its place as the paramount issue in any vision of Nevada's future. Silver could be neither subordinated nor tamed without severe risk of rejection.

VI

MORE THAN NOBLE WORDS

As Newlands left Nevada for Washington, D.C. in January 1890, the uncertainties of Nevada politics went with him. Meanwhile, in California the Oakland *Tribune* maintained that Newlands did not go to Nevada for political reasons nor did he become a Republican because he discovered it was the dominant party in the state. He abandoned the Democratic party because of its free trade doctrine. Henry M. Yerington, General Manager of the Virginia and Truckee Railroad, befriended Newlands early as a welcome addition to the ranks of Nevada Republicans. The Sharon estate was also a principal stockholder in the railroad. On the Comstock, Yerington controlled the *Territorial Enterprise*, and he immediately sent the Oakland *Tribune* article to Virginia City with "instructions to publish same." The *Gazette* also republished the piece. But other editors charged the Reno paper with booming Newlands for the Senate and waiting for a sack of money. Many, of course, hoped to profit from an "old time" political fight with ample spoils of battle for everyone. In March 1890, Yerington remarked: "The boys are talking politics a little, just sharpening their tools for the lively rattle that we are to have this fall." Meanwhile, the Jones people, it was reported, were trying to get Newlands to run for governor "... to get him off the track."[1]

Nevada politics appeared to be a struggle among men who could afford to play expensive games. There could be few serious contenders outside this circle who played high stakes for the state's top offices. Newspapers, controlled by the various political factions, told the public only what the political moguls wished to publicize. Occasionally a reckless editor attacked the powers within the state, but at the risk of missing handsome payments for the publication of political tracts. Newlands did not wish to create a spectacle, arbitarily forcing himself into office through the influence of property and wealth. Such a move would further proclaim Nevada a "rotten borough" and brand Newlands a beneficiary of sordid politics.

Although away in Washington attending to estate business, he kept in touch with Nevada events. He feared that heavy winter snows and rains might lull the community into forgetting the necessity for water storage in the mountains. And he kept alive his pro-silver credentials. By May the *Gazette* carried articles relating an extensive interview by Newlands in the Washington *Post* showing him to be, in the words of the *Gazette*, ". . . eminently sound on the silver question." The Reno paper also published a letter from Newlands to Secretary of the Treasury William Windom attacking the Republican administration of President Benjamin Harrison for failing to carry out platform promises to re-monetize silver.[2]

Still Republicanism seemed the best route for Newlands's goals, with Senator Stewart his chief mentor. A congressional seat offered Newlands a respectable entree to Nevada politics without threatening the Jones faction of the party or creating the resentment that a Senate battle promised. From the House of Representatives he could attend to estate business, such as developing valuable Chevy Chase real estate in the suburbs of Washington. The governorship was unacceptable because it would confine him to Nevada when business interests demanded his presence elsewhere. But there was a problem: what to do with Congressman Horace F. Bartine? Some arrangements needed to be made to enable Bartine to retire gracefully and without resentment from the congressional race.

By mid-June those who made decisions in Nevada politics were seeking to ease Congressman Bartine into a federal judgeship, in order to clear the way for Newlands's nomination for congress on the Republican ticket. But the president had refused to appoint Bartine to a judgeship because he did not wish to take a Republican out of Congress and reduce the party majority. Stewart promised another Republican to replace him almost immediately. More to the point, Stewart told Newlands that he awaited some expression of opinion from Nevada, "to avoid the appearance of making a candidate in Washington." Stewart's delay reflected advice to assess the local situation before pushing hard for the Bartine appointment. His support for Newlands did not extend to the point of risking his own security among factions in the state.[3]

On August 15, 1890, nineteen prominent citizens of Nevada addressed an open letter to Newlands asking him to be a candidate either for governor or Congress. Newlands replied the following day. He ruled out the gubernatorial nomination because as trustee of the Sharon estate he must be in Washington several months of each year. He could accept the congressional nomination without endangering "the interest in my charge." Newlands noted his own limited residence in the state and his short affiliation with the Republican party. All of these, he said frankly, "present considerations of delicacy and embarrassment which precluded a personal canvass for the nomination. . . ." Newlands understood that his drive for the congressional seat conveyed the image of a carpetbagger trying to seize political office. However, he wished all to know that he also stood for a program of state development. He would yield to a demand for his services from the upcoming Republican state convention in Virginia City, which under the circumstances, he said, "I could hardly expect." But expect he did.[4]

Constant appeals to ideals and programs rather than to party maddened Newlands's opponents. His attempts to place ideology and programs above party identified him with a style employed by politicians in the Progressive Era. Woodrow Wilson, Robert LaFollette, and George Norris successfully adopted the political tactics of the new age that coupled ideals and ambition but de-emphasized party.

Despite his words, Newlands pursued the congressional nomination at the Republican convention. His backers, Yerington, Will Sharon (nephew of his late father-in-law), and Newlands, met at Sharon's home in Virginia City where they determined that Bartine would eventually receive a judgeship. Promising a judgeship to Bartine would leave "the door open for Mr. Newlands to run for Congress in a decent way and to which I have no doubt he can be elected," wrote Yerington.[5] Newlands also gained press support. The *Gazette* said that Newlands came into the state with "a sack full of Nevada money," but of all the men with similar means he was "the first to show any interest in developing Nevada's agricultural possibilities." The Winnemucca *Silver State* spoke of a "New Development promoted by Newlands." But, the editor asked, what would become of the two old parties? This was an ominous question coming from an editor, George Nixon, poised to organize the Silver party that would sweep all before it in Nevada politics by 1894.[6]

These private meetings and press reports preceded the Republican state convention in Virginia City on September 5, 1890. With Bartine still in the race, the Jones faction worked successfully for the incumbent's renomination. When it became clear in the convention that the motion to renominate Bartine would be accepted, Newlands rose to second the nomination. His speech, however, betrayed resentment. He was confident of victory had he received the nomination, but the opposition to his candidacy, he said, came "from a source and was urged by a power from which I had a right to expect better faith." He could not entirely conceal his bitterness when he said, "Before the campaign closes there may be a contest within the party in which I may partici-pate, but there will be none against it." The statement was widely quoted as a possible challenge to Jones in the Senate race. The *Gazette* charged that a combination of the Jones forces and the railroad, led by chief lobbyist "Black" Wallace, had defeated Newlands.[7]

When news of Newlands's treatment at the Republican convention reached Stewart, he expressed surprise at the events. He could not understand why the Jones people opposed Newlands. But if Stewart had followed the pages of the *Gazette*, there was little doubt why Jones felt threatened by Newlands. Stewart insisted that Jones would benefit more from cooperation with Newlands and himself: "Nor do I see why they should be unfriendly to me. I have never injured them and it seems to me that it is for their interest to be friendly to both you and me." Stewart also referred to consulting with California railroad magnate Collis P. Huntington for direction on Nevada matters.[8]

Stewart cautioned Newlands against a vengeful contest with Jones. Personally Jones disavowed any control over the convention and hoped Newlands would not hold him responsible. With this explanation Stewart expected to maneuver Newlands away from a confrontation with Jones. "The question now is," he said, "what is best for you and me and the party." Stewart declared, "if you do nothing which will enable the politicians to disparage you, you will be invincible in Nevada." He praised Newlands's action at the convention and predicted that he had made many good friends who would be useful in the future. "Every day will strengthen you," he said, "No combination can be formed against you, unless you give the enemy foundation for opposition." Stewart assured Newlands: "Your energy, enterprise, and ability, if you pursue the course you have hitherto pursued, will secure for you anything that Nevada has to give without combination with or dependence upon any other human being." Stewart urged that Newlands take a leading part in campaigning for the Republican ticket and, "Above all, do not let the people think that you are lukewarm in the cause for the reason that you were not properly treated in the convention."[9]

By mid-September Newlands decided to follow the advice of his moderate friends, Yerington and Stewart. Perhaps at this point he regretted some of his earlier statements not to engage in deal making and bribery to win what he wanted. He was convinced Jones was "very unpopular in the state, and it would not be difficult to contest the senatorship with him, if I were disposed to go in for blood." Instead, he chose to stump, and in the words of Senator Stewart, "Keep Nevada in line for the future."[10] Newlands's decision meant that there would be no lavish outlay of funds in an extravagant campaign. He would deliver only good words for the Republicans, not "the sack" to newspaper editors and legislators.

His decision "not to go in for blood" in 1890 was based on self-interest and idealism. He refused to enter a spite contest against Jones that would require huge outlays of money reminiscent of the old Sharon ways in Nevada politics. He would remain the good citizen and build a list of credentials to make himself an even more attractive candidate at the next election. The decision reflected Newlands's determination to resist the temptations of riding roughshod over the opposition. Jones represented an earlier era of rotten-borough politics and was an example of what Newlands deplored in the state's history. Chairman Robert Fulton of the Nevada Board of Trade said Jones had not even bothered to attend any of its meetings that fall and after the election hurried off, "to go below to the bay . . . and this state will see him no more forever except when he comes to treat the boys who vote for him."[11]

Meanwhile the Board of Trade issued Newlands's pamphlet entitled "Storage and Reclamation." The Carson City *Morning Appeal* editor said it was ten times more comprehensive and exhaustive than "the useless and wholly impractical work of Major Powell, who spent $55,000 of Government money, accomplishing nothing." This publication and Newlands's various appearances before Republican clubs prompted Fulton to state, "No man did more for the ticket than Mr. Newlands. He made hosts of friends for it and for himself."[12]

Newlands left Nevada in the winter of 1890–91 with little more than applause, but he remained politically active. In Washington he took up the silver issue by testifying before the Senate Committee on Coinage, Weights, and Measures. The Washington *Post* gave extensive coverage to his views and the *Gazette* in Reno loyally reprinted them under the headlines, "Although Newlands in Washington, He is doing much for Nevada."[13]

By 1891 Newlands supported Nevada's enactment of an irrigation law similar to California's Wright Act. Previously he had rejected the plan because he believed irrigation districts, with their power to issue bonds, promoted extravagance. From Reno, Fulton advised that the legislature would do nothing unless Newlands pressed matters. An inquiry with legislative leaders about, "What pressing would be necessary?" produced the answer of $10,000. "Black" Wallace, professional lobbyist on railroad affairs, could not be moved without $2,500. Fulton protested that Newlands would not use money, but in apparent reconsideration let it be known that Newlands could probably "afford to do some work for such a cause." Newlands could not have been shocked; he had worked the California legislature in affairs relating to Sharon's Spring Valley Water Company. Now, however, Newlands justified his efforts as being on behalf of the public interest.[14]

Newlands was also interested in tax reform. The issue at stake was the establishment of a State Board of Tax Equalization. Newlands supported the concept. In a letter to the *Gazette* he said: "As it is now, the counties of the state are engaged in a disgraceful race to escape their proper proportion of the state tax by diminishing the local assessments." Newlands's early support of tax reform places him squarely in the ranks of reformers who came to regard it as an essential element in reform platforms. The measure was not entirely popular with "the people," who saw the measure removing their assessments from the elected assessors and placing this power in the hands of a remote state board.

On this issue Newlands displayed an exasperation with popular politics that surfaced from time to time in his public career. He could not understand opposition to the Board of Equalization among the people. Some were opposed to a state Board of Equalization because the railroad companies were for it. "I hardly know how to meet this kind of reasoning," Newlands complained. By the end of the legislative session of 1891, both an irrigation bill and a Board of Equalization measure passed. Most likely money changed hands to achieve these legislative successes. Certainly the lobbying efforts of H. M. Yerington and Robert Fulton played an important role in pushing them through the legislature.[15]

Newlands's intervention in legislative affairs in the 1891 session marks the beginning of his attempts to direct the course of state legislation toward such goals as the Australian ballot law. Some believed that it would upgrade the state's electorate by excluding from the franchise those who could not read English. The Eureka *Sentinel* asserted: "The disfranchisement of the class who are not able to read is the key note to the measure." The voter from now on could not simply cast a paper ballot of a particular color in the election and fulfill his obligation to vote for a certain party. With the secret ballot Nevada took a long stride toward home rule. Not unsurprisingly, railroad lobbyist "Black" Wallace opposed the secret ballot system and denounced it as unfair. The direct purchase of votes would be more difficult if they could not be checked by color ballot as voters went to the polls. The relationship between the advent of the Australian ballot law and the rise of single-issue parties, such as the Silver party, did not escape Newlands's notice and others already established in Nevada politics.[16]

Development was the key word in the Newlands vocabulary. He was delighted with an article in the New York *Tribune* by his Nevada associate Robert Fulton describing the resources and possibilities of Nevada. As he returned to Nevada in the spring of 1891, Newlands saw ranges covered with grass, which for the first time in years had the chance to go to seed and sprout in the spring. He realized the advantages of the bitter "White Winter" of 1890 that virtually destroyed the open-range stock industry in eastern Nevada. He was confident the ranges could be restocked using "more rational methods" of raising cattle at less expense. Newlands also envisioned the work of irrigation districts, "which would doubtless soon be formed," as coordinated under the direction of a state Irrigation Bureau with ties to the land-grant state university and its new Experiment Station supported by Federal Funds from the Hatch Act of 1887. All of this looked to rational methods of production, the establishment of government coordinating bureaus, and partnerships with the university. With these varied institutional supports Nevada could be transformed from a defunct mining and livestock economy into the stable society of agriculture, commerce, and industry.[17]

Newlands's penchant for development even became an object of domestic humor. His wife, Edith, declared, "When he dies and enters the door of Saint Peter's famous health resort, he will immediately discover many ways of improving it, and will at once suggest to the management a general re-organization of the whole place." Edith told the story during an interview on the landscape improvements at the Newlands home in Reno.[18]

As early as March 1892, Newlands announced for Congress. A great deal of "laying pipe to that end" had to take place, according to Yerington, if the Republican nomination was to be acquired. In terms of traditional Republican politics, Yerington believed it absolutely necessary to take Republican stalwart and lobbyist Abner C. Cleveland, a man he called ". . . the cleverest political manager of Nevada," into camp to handle the fight. Yerington said to hire Cleveland although

3. Newlands with two of his daughters at their home in Reno.
Photograph courtesy of the Francis Griffith Newlands Papers,
Manuscripts and Archives, Yale University Library. Used by
permission.

"He is somewhat expensive." But all of this was changed by the death
of the Newlands's two-year-old infant son. Newlands spoke of aban-
doning all idea of public life. Grief brought illness both to himself and
Edith. To recover, they decided to leave the country for the Hesketh
estates in England and abandon personal involvement in the congressional race. If the nomination were to be achieved, Newlands's friends
would have to carry on the battle. He indicated that this should be the
answer to any inquiries about his political plans, but "The rest I must
leave to my friends." In December 1893 Edith lost another baby in
childbirth.[19]

Newlands's political fortunes rested with state senator Will Sharon.
From his home in Virginia City, Sharon (or "Willy" as he was known in
local politics) early on assumed the role of Newlands's political manager. Despite all of Newlands's expansive ideas, his friend Fulton
believed only money would give him the Republican congressional
nomination in Nevada. In a letter to Sharon, Fulton concluded that if

Newlands intended to count the cost of the election, he might as well stay in England and withdraw from the contest. "It is very distasteful to me," he said, "to write you recommending the use of such means here but I see no other way." He said, "You must make your points [about irrigation and silver] in the minds of men and appeal to other considerations that have controlled elections heretofore." Fulton saw Newlands's interest in silver politically appropriate. While Newlands preached about matters of irrigation and water storage, Fulton kept emphasizing that "the masses are not guided by such considerations and one good drink has more effect than a sermon on the mount would have." Clearly Newlands needed more than issues to win. But how could cash be effectively used in Nevada campaigns governed by the new Australian ballot law? As Fulton said, the distribution of good cheer in the form of drinks always helped candidates in Nevada. Buying influence with key newspaper editors also was an effective use of money, in addition to liberal contributions to the campaigns of other party members running on the same ticket. All of it amounted to a traditional use of "the sack" in the election process.[20]

Newlands returned to Nevada to find politics astir over the silver question. The Republican party nominated incumbent President Benjamin Harrison on a gold standard, or hard-money platform. Nevada Silver League Republicans swore not to support the ticket. The Nevada Silver League was formed in June 1892, and there was a strong indication a new party was in the making. The politics appeared confused and volatile, but Senator Stewart told Newlands: "Do not be discouraged about the situation in Nevada. I am confident that the forces can be harmonized." But in this campaign Newlands did not rely solely on grand pronouncements. As one editor said, "Newlands returned to Reno and he will soon open his barrel to capture the congressional nomination." The *Gazette*, championing Newlands's integrity, denied the charge. But Newlands spent handsomely to obtain his congressional seat. Two years later he remarked that he had spent $50,000—at least twice his personal yearly income from the estate—on the campaign of 1892.[21]

Did Newlands represent a new trend, or did he perpetuate California's established ownership of Nevada? Newlands had spent almost three years trying to overcome this impression. Further, he catered to the sentiments of home pride and localism that the silver movement embodied. But it was somewhat out of character for Newlands to champion the cause of the poor silver miner against the outside forces of corporations and industrialists. The interests of the mine owners, such as Newlands, and the mine workers, however, were exactly the same on the silver issue. Whatever the shortcomings of the silverite solutions to Nevada's troubles, the movement offered a crusading spirit to Nevada's politics and community life.

While Newlands made important efforts to establish his legitimacy in Nevada, money appeared more critical to his election. In this respect his foray into politics was little different than his California predecessors. Yet his style reflected his earlier experiences in California when he coupled his entrance into politics to improvement and development. At the end of August, by whatever means, Newlands received the congressional nomination from a badly split Republican convention. He accepted the nomination from the anti-Harrison or silverite element in the party. He rejected the handful of regular Republicans who supported the Harrison gold ticket. They also offered the nomination to him, but he quietly refused it. In his acceptance speech he pledged: "I shall be mindful always that I am not a Republican of Massachusetts or a Republican of New York, but a Republican of the State of Nevada." He professed loyalty to Nevada, to the Republican party, but most of all to the silver cause. Nevada and silver had become inseparable.[22]

Without the mark of silver, no candidate or party could win in Nevada. Both Newlands and Stewart sought and accepted the endorsement of the Nevada silverites who met in Winnemucca on September 15. Stewart said that when he returned to the Senate it would be as a representative of the Nevada Silver party. Newlands, already a member of the National Executive Silver Committee, the National Convention, the American Bimetallic League, had been elected president of the National Mining Congress in Helena, Montana, in July. His silver credentials were impeccable, although some people criticized him for devoting too much attention to irrigation as a palliative to Nevada's ills. In late October the *Gazette* repudiated charges that Newlands was a rich man, asserting that he was the only man of wealth who brought capital into the state instead of taking it out.[23]

With the backing of the Silver party, a well-financed campaign, and even the support of traditional Republicans, Newlands won the congressional seat from Nevada with a handy 4,876 majority over his nearest opponent. Of the 9,878 votes cast, Newlands received 7,171.[24] This was the smallest electorate in the nation to send a congressman to Washington. It was also a polity dazzled by the appeals of Free Silver and a new Silver party. Newlands would never again identify himself with the Republican party. His issues were the redemption of the state through irrigation and the remonetization of silver, but underlying these pronouncements lay the distribution of hard cash both to the press and "the boys." The realities of rotten-borough politics continued to demand these concessions, which Newlands disdained but nevertheless employed through various political agents.

Years later a critic claimed that Newlands spent $150,000 for both his election and Senator Stewart's reelection. He portrayed "Black" Wallace managing the money and forcing Newlands to finance the entire campaign for railroad candidates in return for the Silver party's nomination. With Newlands's arrival an entire slate of candidates were run on the beneficence of his purse in return for the congressional nomination. In this light Newlands appears as gullible, milked by the clever managers of Nevada's elections. If true, Newlands probably considered the price satisfactory, if he could remain aloof from crudely buying votes. While the figure of $150,000 appears exaggerated, by his own admission the "rotten borough" still responded to the power of money at election time. Newlands seemed to accept this as a hazard of any enterprise he undertook either in public or private endeavors.[25]

Newlands had forced the incumbent Bartine to withdraw in the face of determination and resources. Stewart's strong identification with the Silver party and nominal departure from the GOP left Republicans little choice but to ask someone else to stand for the Senate. Bartine accepted. More important, the shape of Nevada politics now included Newlands and would do so until his death in 1917. By the close of 1892, Yerington wrote with satisfaction that the politics of the state were secure from the viewpoint of the railroads. "Stewart and Newlands are our friends in Congress," he told D. O. Mills, and within the state, "local matters have all gone our way most beautifully and we are on top as usual which delights me exceedingly."[26]

In December, Newlands picked up his political winnings and departed for Washington. The electorate, largely bought and paid for, stood informed on the issues. He advocated the remonetization of silver, irrigation development, and protectionism. Over the next two years the silver issue intensified, forcing almost every elective officer in Nevada into the Silver party. Newlands stayed faithful to the cause: he stood for remonetization, not unlimited coinage. In the campaign this fine difference went unnoticed. In 1893 he fell ill from the strains of the fall campaign, the national depression, and the state of his investments. He was not too ill, however, to authorize Fulton to deny in the *Gazette*, "unequivocally that my views on the Silver question have changed at all. They remain the same as I particularly expressed them, in public in Nevada and elsewhere." He realized that a clear public record in favor of silver was as necessary as the private capital to finance a Nevada campaign.[27]

As the newly elected representative from Nevada, Newlands became both a man of public affairs and a figure in the well-to-do circles of Washington society. He bought the Woodley mansion on one of the highest points in the city. Built in 1803, it had sometimes been used as a presidential summer home. He and Edith entertained important figures of Washington society, and Newlands gave "political breakfasts" in which he presented legislative proposals to Washington notables. Back in Nevada, Yerington believed Newlands's position within the state impregnable, ". . . and will surely be so for years to come. . . ."[28]

Every sign indicated that Newlands sank deep roots in Nevada as well as Washington, D.C. His new home on the Truckee stood like a monument to progress amid the sagebrush. By spring orchards, shrubs, and shade trees grew around it "making it look like an old, established home," according to a Reno reporter. Newlands suggested that the Truckee be cleaned up and Reno's sewers diverted away from it. Reno like other cities should face the sanitary question and provide for the proper disposal of sewage rather than letting it flow into public waters. Unfortunately most of Newlands's plans for civic improvement called for public funding. His projects made little headway in a decade of retrenchment and depression. These were frustrating years that would only be reversed by events after the turn of the century.[29]

During the summer of 1893 President Grover Cleveland called for the repeal of the Sherman Silver Purchase Act, which was passed in 1890 to appease western demands to raise the price of silver. The move was necessary, the president contended, to restore confidence in the dollar and ultimately end the depression. Like every depression president, Cleveland sought to blame the economic chaos on events far removed from his administration. Silver served this purpose and received the president's unrelenting condemnation. Nevadans poured abuse upon the president for his stand. Attacking the president, Newlands said repeal spelled further economic disaster and greater dependence on England. Yerington wrote that "People all over the coast are delighted over your magnificent effort in the House the other day on behalf of Silver." Senators Stewart and Jones also opposed the repeal bill. Stewart spoke for three days against it and Jones for seven. Their efforts helped in a futile six-week filibuster by senators from the West and the South against the administration's repeal bill.[30]

As Senate voices fell silent, protests mounted in the western silver states. In Nevada the single-issue Silver party grew stronger. Senators Stewart and Jones openly severed relations with the gold Republicans in Congress. Inexperienced, Newlands miscalculated. He declared the issue dormant. The only possible course was to wait four years for the rehabilitation of silver under a more favorable administration. "In the meantime," he said, "we must direct our attention to agriculture." To a people agitated by the silver defeat, he naively declared, "The attention of the entire country is being called to the benefits of irrigation where the ground is watered by science, not by chance." The *Gazette* welcomed this departure from the thorny silver question and hoped for a return to normal politics. Still, Newlands failed to grasp the excitement of silver and that irrigation paled beside silver's allure. Silver became the foremost issue in Nevada in the election of 1894.[31]

Accordingly, Newlands changed course. He described the state as the most persecuted member of the Union in a speech on the floor of the House. Among the wrongs committed against Nevada were the repeal of the Silver Purchase Act, the lack of national reclamation legislation, and insignificant tariff protection for wool and borax. In debate over a Utah statehood bill, Newlands criticized speakers who said they might favor the bill if there was some way of turning out Nevada.

More to the point, Newlands complained, "It is taunted with being a 'rotten borough' and the home of millionaires; the place from which millionaires are returned to Congress." Sensitive, he defended himself and his millionaire colleagues by asking, "Point me a millionaire who has ever represented that State who has not had brains." He praised Nevada because, "In that State the mere possession of wealth is not a disqualification for office." And he contended that Nevada fortunes were won by "men of robust qualities of mind and body." They did not acquire their resources by money-lending or in the devious ways of Wall Street. They wrestled with nature in her very strongholds and the voters approved of this and sent them to Washington. At the moment Newlands wished to portray himself as just such an enlightened representative.[32]

The poor economic picture ruled out lavish spending on the campaign. No funds would be forthcoming from the estate, and he felt so uncertain that he expressed doubt about running because it involved "vexation" and considerable expense. His political position possessed advantages for the estate, however, and it was not unjustified to spend estate monies to retain political office. Newlands believed his congressional seat made him more effective in matters relating to estate enterprises. The post served him well in the successful negotiations for a loan to develop the interurban railway to the Chevy Chase properties. He believed his position grew stronger every day through experience and acquaintance. Newlands saw the advantages of his congressional seat, but detested the struggle to retain it. Without a well-financed campaign, he sadly concluded, "I daresay I shall make a cheap fight and get licked."[33]

Newlands easily regained the Silver party's nomination for Congress, but declined to endorse a part of the platform that called for government ownership of railroads. His forthrightness was unwise in the view of the old Nevada political hand, C. C. "Black" Wallace. Newlands recognized that he must retreat and agreed to support the platform. When Wallace and Senator Stewart, both servants of the railroad, embraced the railroad ownership plank, they had no intention whatsoever of working for such legislation, but they knew good politics. Wallace believed Newlands needed more political guile if he intended to stay in Nevada politics—his money alone might not be able to save him.[34]

Wallace was almost correct. The national railway strike during the summer turned voters against any candidate who might symbolize wealth and power. The summer months of 1894 brought federal troops to the major towns along the overland route in Nevada. Resentment against military intervention spread as troops took up positions ostensibly to protect the free passage of the mails, but in reality guarding railroad property. The Populist candidate for Congress, J. C. Doughty, a railroad striker himself, asked voters to defeat Newlands because of his doubtful support of government ownership of railroads and because he was a man of great wealth.[35]

The campaign was not all issues. The Dangberg crowd in Douglas County demanded direct money payments or they would vote against Congressman Newlands. "That means he must buy his pretended friends—a pretty state of things truly," said Yerington, who felt most Silver party members looked only for a handout in return for their support.[36] In this election, however, Newlands edged away from buying votes outright. Circumstances forced him to rely on more modern approaches. The Comstock Glee Club sang at his political rallies—to the tune of "Marching Through Georgia":

Our Congressman is Newlands, who loves Nevada true
He says our lonely deserts yet shall bloom as roses do, He'll irrigate our
valleys, and get free coinage through, So come along to victory

Come all Nevada silver men, we'll have a glorious song, The tune will
be free coinage, sung every voter strong, And 'though we're weak in
number, we'll win the fight ere long. Fore we're marching to victory.[37]

Newlands retained his congressional seat, but by a far smaller margin
than in 1892. The Populists and the Republicans took their toll on
Newlands's majority, reducing it to 1,807 votes, a figure far under his
4,876 majority in 1892. In the northeastern counties he ran behind both
the Populist and the Republican candidates, but won in the far-flung
mining communities. The campaign cost Newlands at least $7,000. His
failure to distribute enough money in the populated western counties,
plus the broader Populist appeal to small farmers and railroad workers,
drew votes away from him in Douglas and Washoe counties, while the
traditional Republican vote for Bartine remained strong.[38]

Business relations became a source of friction between Newlands
and Stewart by 1895. The hard times of the decade depressed real
estate values. As a minor stockholder in the Chevy Chase Land Company, Stewart complained of being treated as an outsider and of having
his stock in the company reduced. He believed the steps Newlands
took regarding this prejudiced Stewart's ability to pay his debt to Collis
Huntington, who had loaned him $150,000, taking stock for security. In
addition, Stewart asserted that the previous agreement to pay him a
salary as a co-manager of the company was not honored. He realized that
Newlands must settle the distribution of the estate among the three
principal heirs, as called for in Sharon's will ten years after his death.
Stewart did not wish to impair the progress of this settlement, but at the
same time he did not want any change in the arrangements that
damaged both his share and Huntington's loan.[39]

The growing crisis in his own financial empire influenced Newlands's
politics. Early in 1895 he denounced Cleveland's continuing efforts to
maintain gold payments by the government through a complicated
scheme borrowing on Wall Street. The congressman's rhetoric became
radicalized enough to demand "the unlimited use of silver" instead of
his previous more moderate demands of "restoration." The difference
was subtle, but sharp. Unlimited coinage of silver meant a virtual
conversion of the monetary system to a silver standard, while restoration only suggested a regulated use of silver in the nation's monetary

system. Newlands became a true professing silverite as the course of national political and economic events pushed him into the free coinage camp. By 1895 silver sentiment was so widespread, but at the same time totally anathema to the leadership of both the Democratic and Republican parties, that the issue became a force of its own. The silver movement and its Populist party allies in other states began to assume national dimensions.[40]

President Cleveland's adamant stand on the money issue assured the future of free coinage as the paramount political issue in the West and South. Newlands became convinced that as both parties stayed fixed to the gold standard, there would be a spontaneous national outcry for another party to sponsor free coinage. On March 6, 1895, the American Bimetallic League, with Newlands as a member of its Executive Committee, formed the "National Bimetallic Party" to campaign for free coinage of silver. This was the Silver party that Newlands hoped to nurture into the make-weight of American politics. Stewart for many years talked of this goal, but Newlands never believed it, for he saw only hopeful rhetoric in such talk. Now, with the deepening depression and the obstinacy of the administration on the monetary issue, he perceived a unity among silver men that could provide the foundation for a viable and influential third force in American politics.[41]

Nevadans detected in Newlands a not totally admirable trait. When he embraced a cause it was not enough that it pertain only to Nevada. He usually attached larger significance to irrigation as a plan for western American development or silver as the salvation of the American economic system. He strove to develop a style that came of age in the Progressive Era. He became comfortable in this new era where every political move and governmental program glowed with the light of idealism. The parallels with Wilsonianism seem remarkable. But unpleasant political tasks, quite divorced from idealism, haunted Newlands in Nevada.

VII

CHALLENGING THE
OLD GUARD

Newlands instinctively regarded his congressional seat as little more than a stepping-stone to a senatorship. But ascent to higher office depended on steering a careful course and convincing either Jones or Stewart to step aside for him. Persuading either to relinquish their membership in the most exclusive men's club in America became almost impossible. As his relations with the old guard deteriorated, Newlands moved closer to longtime silver advocate, George S. Nixon of Winnemucca. They came to believe that they represented the new political generation in Nevada and tailored their ambitions appropriately, setting their eyes on the two occupied Senate seats.

Newlands found Nevada politics tough going. He did not move with ease in the state's frontier saloon society, nor did he relish it. Sagebrush made him sneeze and opponents charged that he much preferred his Chevy Chase properties or English vacations. Newlands could claim little in common with his Nevada constituency. He had never worked in a mine, on the railroad, or on a farm. He far preferred the role of statesman to that of politician. Newlands detested the bombast of American political campaigning, especially in the limited environs of Nevada's sagebrush and mountain valleys. But participate he must.

The Venezuelan Crisis with England in 1895 gave Newlands an opportunity to mix foreign affairs and the silver issue.[1] When Great Britain threatened Venezuela in a contested area of British Guinea, Secretary of State Richard Olney asserted that Britain had violated the Monroe Doctrine. His saber-rattling demanded British withdrawal. In a speech to a Reno gathering Newlands declared war with England would guarantee the silver standard for America and break the bonds of gold by which England held America. His speech reaffirmed his support of silver; it played both to the anti-British bent of many Irish miners and to a jingoism that fired American's when given the chance to twist the British lion's tail. His words seemed to disprove charges that he was more at ease with his English relatives than among Nevadans.[2]

The local press cheered Newlands's war talk, but others reacted with scorn and disbelief. One local judge said that these remarks could be expected from an ignorant backwoodsman, but "Newlands, if he has his senses, certainly knows better. . . ." California journalist and poet Ambrose Bierce scorned this latest utterance by a Nevada officeholder. The famous newsman quoted Newlands as declaring that, "War is a public blessing for it means free coinage of silver." Bierce suggested Newlands should be in the front ranks of the charging warriors and, "When he shall fall let us give him a hero's burial in congenial [Nevada] alkali."[3]

As the days moved rapidly toward the national party conventions in the summer of 1896, Newlands's rhetoric emphasized that silver was the elixir to solve most of the domestic and foreign problems of the United States in this troubled decade. In Nevada, and with silverites throughout the West, this placed him on the popular side of all issues. There was only one issue—Free Silver. He gave little time to irrigation. It was not as spectacular a question as war with England, the silver cause, or the anti-Chinese question. Even the protective tariff, which Newlands supported, surpassed the appeal of irrigation. Increasingly, Newlands sounded more like a politician gearing up for a major election than a statesman.

By the mid-1890s the disastrous depression deepened. Meanwhile the administration committed itself to gold and special deals with New York financiers, the courts convicted Eugene Debs's Railway Union for its actions in the Pullman strike, and struck down income tax legislation. Both decisions favored corporations and wealth. Nowhere in the political system, it seemed, were the needs of ordinary people served. Populism, according to Newlands, advocated too many reforms in government and society for conservative men. The free coinage of silver presented a safe and conservative rallying point that offered cheaper money to the agrarians in the Midwest and to the debtors of the South. It promised a rejuvenated silver-mining industry in the West.[4]

Westerners, including Newlands, believed the Silver party offered avenues to national political influence. Although the party could not hope to win a presidential election, it might gather enough votes, as Senator Stewart long contended, to block either of the two older parties from a majority in the electoral college. From this position the new party might be able to name the next president—most likely their favorite, Senator Henry M. Teller of Colorado. In this spirit Newlands became a principal participant in a bizarre scheme to nominate Republican silverite Teller at the Democratic convention in the months before the summer convention in 1896. Newlands, who was comfortable with the southern Democracy, gave political dinners for many at his Woodley mansion. He felt southern pro-silver Democrats would support Teller, but he paid no attention to western Democrats. He underestimated the appeal and oratory of Nebraska's William Jennings Bryan at the Chicago Democratic Convention in July, when Bryan pronounced in his famous Cross of Gold Speech that, "Thou shalt not crucify mankind upon a Cross of Gold." All of the well-laid plans of the western silverites evaporated when the Democrats, intoxicated by the boy orator of the Platte, nominated one of their own.[5]

The silverites, meeting in convention at St. Louis eleven days after Bryan's nomination, had little choice but to fuse with the Populists and support the Bryan candidacy. They did refuse to endorse the Democratic vice-presidential nominee, Maine banker Arthur Sewall. But this was a poor substitute for the dreams Newlands entertained only a month before. National politics, like Nevada politics, disappointed him.

In the public eye, however, he maintained good spirits. Before the national Silver party convention Newlands praised Bryan as a man close to the people, but not demagogic; he was a reformer, but had never given a single "incendiary speech"; Bryan was a man of ability and integrity. Newlands also explained that Free Silver was a non-radical and totally safe economic reform. It was not an inflationary giveaway to debtors, as the eastern goldbugs declared, but merely an attempt to adjust the money supply to a growing population. Despite the endorsements, Newlands remained unconvinced that Bryan could win the fall election. Accordingly, he quietly withdrew from the national campaign. Nor did he waste any efforts in effecting a fusion with the Populists. In contrast, Senator Stewart spent considerable energy in the fusion project and gave active support to the Bryan ticket.[6]

In Nevada the Silver party endorsed the Bryan ticket and nominated Newlands for Congress by acclamation. Stewart promised to "stump Nevada for Bryan," but Newlands made no similar commitment. He did not move beyond the Reno–Carson City communities for his own candidacy and failed to visit the areas of eastern Nevada that gave him majorities in previous elections. With the handful of Populists divided and Republicans in disfavor Newlands could be assured of easy reelection.[7]

The Nevada Silver party was made up of diverse factions—silver Republicans, Bryan Democrats, and Populists. In Nevada silver won every county except Douglas. In the nation the Free Silver standard and Bryan failed. Newlands sensed defeat. Although listed on the speaker circuit for the Midwest and the South, he delivered only one speech for Bryan, in San Francisco, and engaged noted Yale professor William Graham Sumner in a friendly debate on the merits of Free Silver while in New Haven on a business trip. The Nevada situation was intriguing. Strains within the Silver party reflected suspicions among the older ruling cliques. Senators Stewart and Jones stood unmovable in their possession of the two prize offices of Nevada politics. They strategically shifted with the tides to retain their positions.

But the ambitions of others were strong. George Nixon aspired to high political office. His only reward had been a brief term in the legislature and now an alliance with Newlands. He clearly desired more for his efforts on behalf of silver. Newlands too wanted more from Nevada than the congressional seat and onerous reelection campaigns every two years. Yerington advised Newlands that he could effectively challenge Jones. The congressman instead hesitated. After the fall elections, however, Nixon startled the Nevada political community with his announcement in Winnemucca that he would move against Jones in the legislature when it met in January 1897. The matter of even greater comment was the general suspicion that Newlands supported the Nixon effort. In letters to prominent men in the state, including Yerington, Newlands confirmed his support of Nixon.[8]

Yerington was dismayed: "To my mind this Nixon proposition is an awful tough one and likely to lead to very bitter feeling in the near future," he warned Newlands. Recalling his advice to the congressman prior to the November election that Newlands could take the Jones Senate seat, he complained, "You took no stock in what I said." Indeed Newlands seemed distracted from both state and national politics in the weeks before the election. Yerington painfully pointed out that before the election Newlands had appeared with Jones at political meetings in Reno, Carson City, and Virginia City supporting his reelection. He could not understand how Newlands could now consistently favor Nixon and cautioned that Newlands endangered his own position and popularity for a contest two years away. As rough and crude as Nevada politics sometimes appeared, Yerington insisted that Nevadans liked fair play.[9]

Privately, Jones branded Newlands a double-crosser. With "blood in his eye," Jones told Yerington that, "he knew you were behind Nixon in this affair." Jones appeared sensitive to the challenge because he was not as strong in Nevada as his years in office and impressive demeanor might suggest. His principal worry regarding reelection was that the Senate would refuse to seat him because of his questionable residence in the state from which he was elected. For this reason he wanted an overwhelming or unanimous vote in the legislature. His resentment grew as he realized the damage Nixon's candidacy could do to him. Newspapers favorable to the Newlands faction began emphasizing the issue of home rule—an issue that Newlands had taken great pains to avoid when he came into the state in 1888 and 1889. In many ways Stewart was also vulnerable on the home rule charges because of his absences from the state and his close connections to the Southern Pacific interests in California. The Newlands-Nixon assault upset the status quo and even Stewart recognized a threat to himself.[10]

Nixon, a short, balding man, invited ridicule from Nevadans who were accustomed to the tall, impressive Stewart with his flowing beard and the figure of the large, portly, dignified Jones. Even Newlands suffered attacks because of his middling height and taste for English-tailored checkered suits. He and Nixon seemed out of place in nineteenth-century Nevada politics. Newlands wished to recast the state's society and basic economy while many Nevadans were not convinced that they wished to have their society and economy remade. Nixon was a successful businessman, banker, developer, and investor with interests in nearly every financial enterprise in Nevada, but he brought no Comstock mining background to the political scene like Stewart and Jones.

Nixon proclaimed that the issue was "Nevada for Nevadans," and pointed to Jones's brief stopover in the state during the campaign before he hurried on to his family in Santa Monica. Perceiving a threat to themselves, Stewart and Wallace vigorously backed Jones, as did Yerington. According to Yerington, Nixon never had a chance. Yerington saw him as "a knuckle-headed Silver party man." As a good Republican he even begrudged Jones's desertion of the Republican party for silver, but he was much more acceptable than Nixon. Even Newlands's political manager in the state, Will Sharon, declined to back Nixon's cause. Yerington concluded that "less said on that subject the better for your personal interests."[11]

The first assault on the Nevada senatorial offices only embarrassed Newlands, but he was not deterred. Newlands now looked at the

Stewart seat as possible prey in the elections of 1898 and the legislative session of 1899. In the meantime he drifted away from the eroding battlements of silver. Bimetallism through international agreement seemed more appropriate. When the money question failed to elect a president, the tariff issue grew in importance with Newlands. He supported a protective tariff, if it shielded western products like wool and borax. Newlands also began to modify the antimonopoly rhetoric that had been part of the silver movement.

He spoke of "innocent combinations." He also talked in terms of good and bad trusts in a fashion that Theodore Roosevelt was later to popularize. "Whilst some trusts are oppressive," he said, "nine-tenths of the trusts which have been organized during the past few years are the result of an effort to stop the destructive effect of falling prices." Newlands cautioned that legislation against trusts should be very carefully considered. The labor union itself was one form of trust, as the courts had declared in the recent Debs case—a combination in restraint of trade and therefore subject to prosecution under the Sherman Anti-Trust Act of 1890. Moreover, the proposed southern program to limit the area of cotton planting in order to prevent over-production was a trust organization response to low prices.[12]

Throughout the spring and summer Newlands drew back from his support of Free Silver. He contended that the fall in silver prices would convince people that a constant value between silver and gold could never be achieved. Free coinage of silver would indeed mean destructive inflation and the driving out of gold from circulation. Even Senator Stewart admitted this, but he still spoke enthusiastically of the "war on gold bugs." But whatever unity Stewart and Newlands felt, the silver issue which once united them rapidly faded after Nixon's bid for the Senate in 1897. By the end of the year Stewart correctly believed Newlands had designs on his own senatorial office. In a letter to William F. Herrin of the Southern Pacific Railway, Stewart referred to Newlands as "our friend, the enemy," and, "what mean advantage he proposes to take." Stewart's letter, however, was more in the tone of a request for support against Newlands. He could only say, "I trust to your level head, in conjunction with Wallace, to checkmate the contemptible plan suggested by the gentleman while in San Francisco and Nevada. . . ." Stewart could be fairly confident of continued railroad support.

Even Yerington saw Newlands's course as too independent for the interests of the railroad. He wrote to D. O. Mills that Newlands saw the question of railroad taxation more from a political point of view than from that of the good interests of the railroads. This "political point of view" damaged Newlands's credibility with the railroad interests to the extent that they hesitated to give their welfare over to his care. Stewart remained the loyal servant. Still this not-so-invisible hand in Nevada politics must have realized that the power brokers faced a choice ultimately between the old-line politicians and the growing strength of a rival who was not completely dependent upon their resources. They would either have to fight Newlands openly or acquiesce in his drive for the Senate. The question uppermost in Stewart's mind was: Would 1899 be the year that the railroad chieftains would abandon him?[13]

Newlands accurately described his political course in early 1898 as one of drift. He believed it served both statesmanship and politics, but his friends thought otherwise. By June Will Sharon, Newlands's political manager, began pressing for a decision on some course of action.[14] On June 26, almost three weeks after Sharon's inquiry, Newlands admitted he had been "drifting along without any definite political plans or purpose. . . ." His outlook on the future was now more akin to what he believed was a policy of statesmanship rather than the dreary affairs of politics. He enjoyed questions bearing on whether the United States should become an imperial power after the war or resist that temptation and concentrate on internal development. Other questions relating to economic organization and the control of corporations intrigued him. "I much prefer," he said, "this way of securing public recognition to the chicanery and intrigue which have formed so large a part of Nevada's politics." Moreover, so long as the money question was the only theme and fusion and harmony of the silver forces essential to its success, he did not wish to inject controversy over personal ambitions for the Senate at home. In such a case he thought, "I might be chargeable with sacrificing the great issue to personal ambition. . . ." Now the war with Spain changed everything. "The public man," said Newlands, "who sticks to one idea is likely to be trodden under foot in the movement."

The man in Nevada least equipped to engage new subjects was the aging Senator Stewart. "I think Stewart's usefulness is at an end," he declared. Although Newlands appreciated Stewart's key role in the national silver fight, he believed the tide of events had moved beyond this all-embracing topic. Principal men both in the House and in the Senate, Newlands contended, felt that Stewart "has talked himself to death, and that his intolerance and abuse of people who differ from him have intensified enmities and alienated friendships."

Still, he frankly admitted that without this popular support he feared losing in a three-way contest against Stewart that would divide the opposition to the senator. To win, he admitted it would require that, "I should resort to the methods which have so disgraced the many senatorial contests in Nevada and have robbed the office itself of its honor." He wanted time to return to Nevada and travel through the state before making a decision on his candidacy.

To Sharon, Newlands's political strategy must have proved maddening. First he concluded that Stewart was obsolete as an effective member of the Senate, second, that he was weak in Nevada, but still no decision came forth. Finally Newlands did not know when Congress would adjourn because opposition to his resolution to annex Hawaii persisted. All in all Newlands seemed a difficult and fickle candidate for his manager. On top of all of this Newlands resisted the temptation of entering the contest along "old Nevada lines," but as Yerington noted, "it's wicked but I fear to the majority of our people it's mighty nice."[15]

Senator Stewart also pondered Newlands's intentions. Newlands predicted Stewart's reelection strategy. He sought the nominations of both the Silver and Democratic parties that comprised what was called the "Fusion" forces. Stewart noted unrest among strikers on the Comstock who hoped his reelection would be contested in order to make a few dollars from vote buying during the campaign. But he did not believe Newlands or anyone else would undertake such an unpromising task. Still, the Comstock was in a desperate condition, with people in need of money to buy bread, according to Stewart.[16]

The question persisted into early August: Where did Newlands stand? Newlands probably did not know himself. Newlands and Stewart met in Yerington's Carson City office in mid-August. Newlands agreed to stand for Congress and Stewart for the Senate. Yerington reported, "all is harmony between them—no war as was hoped for by their devoted constituents." Clearly Newlands did not wish to be drawn into an expensive contest against the stubborn and tough campaign tactics of the Stewart-Wallace machine. There was a truce but not peace.[17]

In the election campaign that followed, Stewart-Wallace and Newlands-Sharon forces clashed over accusations that Newlands and Sharon were secretly working for Republican and anti-Stewart legislators. In the Republican convention, Yerington blocked attempts by Wallace to promote a Republican nominee for Congress. The move also brought a threat from Newlands to campaign openly against Stewart, and Wallace withdrew. The compromise or stalemate called for Newlands to support the Silver party ticket, including Stewart, in the election and after, if the Stewart legislative ticket won. But if the Silver party did not sweep the legislative elections, the Newlands forces could claim a defeat for Stewart.[18]

The election of 1898 represents a nadir in the legislative process of electing Nevada's U.S. Senators. Unfortunately for Stewart, he failed to win a majority in both the assembly and the senate. Newlands and Sharon failed to fuse the Democrats and the silverites as in 1896, but they did obtain separate endorsements. Stewart appeared to be in a desperate struggle for survival and raged against his detractors, such as the *Territorial Enterprise*, which he accused of being under Yerington's control. In retaliation he promised to work for state regulation of V&T rates. Yerington, irritated, could only believe that these were idle threats coming from the state's most railroad-controlled politician.[19]

The Southern Pacific and Collis P. Huntington himself supported Stewart's election. Both Herrin and Huntington asked Yerington to support Stewart, but Yerington chose to remain neutral in the campaign. Stewart interpreted this as tacit support of a possible last-minute candidacy on the part of Newlands. The weeks after the November election were tense as eyes turned to signals from the Newlands camp. By the first week of December they were revealed. In Winnemucca Newlands made the announcement to challenge Stewart after conferring with Nixon, who immediately splashed the news in his paper, the *Silver State*.[20]

Stewart complained bitterly against Newlands in letters to newspapers and to Newlands personally. The break brought the two leaders of the Nevada Silver party into open combat. In December and in January of the new year (1899) the Silver party split irrevocably over the two candidates. Stewart arrived in Carson City for the opening of the legislature bitter, hostile over what he regarded as Newlands's treachery.

Newlands viewed Stewart as representing only special interests, such as the railroad or the sugar trust. From Newlands's position of wealth and independence, Stewart cut a somewhat contemptuous figure as a hireling. He was a lawyer vying to advocate the cause of the highest bidder. Stewart prided himself on the ability to serve these interests and still keep abreast of the political trends affecting the electorate. Stewart's rhetoric in the next two months expressed a sense of frustration and helplessness against a man who seemed to have things too easy in his pursuit of a political career. Newlands needed to serve only himself, his ideology, and his pet programs. In some circles this was called statesmanship, in others opportunism.

The old "pros" of Nevada politics felt that Newlands, for all his money, was inept or worse. Wallace told Stewart after the failure of Nixon's Senate bid: "I think as you that Newlands is an ass pure and simple[;] divest him of his money and he wouldn't rank above a dry goods clerk." Stewart thought Newlands a simpleton in state politics, but he always feared his command of riches. The only force that could counter him in state politics was unlimited corporate support. Stewart could confidently expect this from the railroad, and from sugar companies because of his promised support of a high tariff on sugar, and even from the giant Miller and Lux land and cattle company that had holdings in Nevada. Newlands had little need to cultivate these interests and as a consequence was an uncertain entity for corporate interests. Since he had no need of their aid, corporation's could not be fully certain of his loyalty to their interests.[21]

In the opening days of the legislative session a bitter duel seemed imminent. Through letters signed by Thomas Wren, defeated Populist candidate for Congress, Stewart accused Newlands of dishonestly and secretly opposing him in the legislative campaigns, although claiming to support him on the Silver party and Democratic platforms. Appearing in the Carson City *Morning Appeal*, one letter in particular abused Newlands for spreading the story that Stewart was defeated in the legislative elections. As a disinterested and concerned citizen the author wished to call attention to Newlands's "utter unfitness for any place of trust or honor in the gift of the people of Nevada." In personal correspondence, Stewart wrote that Newlands was little better than the outlaw, Three-fingered Jack.[22]

Stewart proved to be an irascible political opponent. He commissioned a series of cartoons of Newlands for the Carson City *Morning Appeal*. One showed Yerington, Cleveland, Coffin, Dennis, and Chartz, gathered around Newlands saying, "Continue to abuse Stewart. Anything to beat Stewart, but keep me in the background." Another cartoon depicted Sharon, Yerington, and Newlands at a table with some money sacks on it. In another Newlands is pictured dressed in a checkered coat and trousers seated in an English go-cart behind four bobtailed horses driven by a top-hatted English driver. Newlands says, "I will sweep the state with this rig." All the cartoons showed Newlands as effete, inattentive, deceptive of the public, and a traitor to a longtime friend.[23]

Few delicacies were spared in this struggle. Stewart took up headquarters in the Ormsby House and surrounded himself with a controversial group of lobbyists, employees of the Southern Pacific, and even

a) STEWART: -"What kind of a germ is this "Anything?"

b) M. Newlands in his study.

c) NEWLANDS — (In 1892) "I will sweep the State with this rig."

4. A series of political cartoons was commissioned by Senator William M. Stewart to parody Newlands and his political ambitions in the state. Stewart claimed that Newlands would do "anything" for high political office and become "anything": Republican, Democrat, or Silverite. Courtesy of the *Carson City Morning Appeal.*

the gunfighter Dave Neagle, already famous for killing David Terry in the defense of Federal Judge Field. The pro-Newlands San Francisco *Examiner* printed a cartoon of Stewart commanding the Nevada legislature with his gun-toting, knife-wielding bodyguards. The pro-Stewart Carson City *Morning Appeal* tried to pawn Neagle off on the Newlands forces by suggesting that Neagle's earlier shooting of Terry destroyed the efforts of Mrs. Terry, formerly Sarah Hill, to obtain part of the Sharon fortune. The headway Stewart had made with public opinion by emphasizing Newlands's shabby treatment of an old friend was undercut by his display of strong-arm tactics at the legislature.[24]

Stewart backers moved to eject Newlands from the Silver party because of his challenge to Stewart. Stewart and Wallace obtained proxies from members throughout the state. At the first assembly they did not succeed, but at a convocation in January 1899, the Central Committee dismissed both Newlands and Sharon from the Silver party. Sharon declared that the railroad had used the Silver party through Stewart and Wallace, who betrayed the party and its purpose. The power of the railroad over the Silver party through these men, Sharon said, brought shame and disrepute to Nevada's political process.[25]

Two days prior to the Central Committee meeting, Newlands openly attacked the Wallace-Stewart combine. With bonfires in the street and a brass band Newlands appeared before a large gathering in the Carson City Opera House. In one of his best political speeches Newlands sketched the history of the anti-Stewart movement. He assailed Stewart's undisguised service to the Southern Pacific Company and explained that Stewart's assaults on the V&T did not mask his solicitude for any legislation that might aid railroads and protect them from serious regulation by the Interstate Commerce Commission. To the approving crowd Newlands claimed the railroad knew that it had nothing to gain from his candidacy. It had everything to gain from William M. Stewart, its tried and faithful servant. He charged that Stewart had committed treason against the Silver party. Senator Stewart claimed to support the Silver party, but what did he do? asked Newlands. "He secured a position on the committee for the settlement of the Pacific Railroad debt and there faithfully, persistently, constantly and nefariously aided Mr. Huntington. . . ." This was true treason to the Silver party.

Furthermore, he explained, the Southern Pacific planned to make the trackage across Nevada a "dead line." The Central Pacific was regarded as "simply a bridge across a vast and expensive desert."

Newlands said this was "a business proposition—a policy for the interest of their own pockets." But what was the interest of the people of Nevada? he asked. "To have it vitalized; to have cars run over the country; to build up various enterprises along the road, in order to give the road its business and stimulate trade throughout the State." He did not presume to criticize the men of the Southern Pacific for pursuing what they regarded as their business interests but, he said, "What I do propose to question is the action of the representative of the State of Nevada, who assisted them in thus distracting and devitalizing this road, which is the great artery of the commonwealth." Thus, Senator Stewart committed treason against the State of Nevada as well as against the Silver party.

Stewart represented the corruption of past senatorial politics. The anti-Stewart forces, of which Newlands was now the leader, represented a popular indignation at the interest-group politics that Stewart symbolized. Stewart's politics, Newlands charged, did not care for the broader interests of the people, but served his master the Southern Pacific Company from first to last.[26]

Could Newlands hope to win in the legislature? It was doubtful. Some said he stood willing to spend as much as $150,000 if he could win. Stewart reportedly had over $40,000 in railroad money to distribute. Such charges are difficult to prove, but Newlands did not allow his name to be submitted to the legislature after his defeat in the Central Committee of the Silver party. He could only assume that Stewart had already "fixed things" in the legislature. The vote in the state senate confirmed this, but in the assembly Stewart lacked one vote of the majority. One legislator, W. A. Gillespie, from Storey County, failed to appear. Stewart's name was placed in nomination with twenty-nine of the assemblymen present to vote. He received fifteen, a majority of those present with the other fourteen votes scattered to various names, the most prominent of which was A. C. Cleveland, the Republican who actively campaigned against Stewart in the fall elections. Many said he was another "stalking horse" for Newlands. The absence of Assemblyman Gillespie was no accident since his vote against Stewart could have tied the assembly. He was spirited away either voluntarily or involuntarily to a home in Carson Valley for two days. Many speculated on how much he received for his absence, but within two months he held an office job with the railroad in Oakland.[27]

After Stewart's victory, Newlands addressed a somber group of supporters in Carson City. This was his second speech acknowledging defeat at the hands of Nevada politicos. "The issue," he said, "in the legislative contest during the last campaign was clearly Stewart and anti-Stewart." The results spoke of a rejection of Stewart and his coddling of the Southern Pacific railroad and Mr. Huntington. The anti-Stewart forces, according to Newlands, were composed of a broad section of the Nevada electorate—Independents, Silver men, Democrats, and Republicans. To unify these forces Newlands had offered himself as a candidate, "but always stated that I would withdraw in favor of any capable bimetalist upon whom the anti-Stewart forces could easily combine." "My name," said Newlands to the quiet audience, "therefore was not presented to the legislature." Although Newlands believed Stewart "entirely square on the Silver issue," he accused him of having sacrificed the interests of the party for his own continued ambition when he unfairly blocked Newlands in the legislature and refused to step down in the face of his own election defeat. As Yerington earlier predicted, Stewart would cling to his office, for he had nowhere to go except to die with the leaves of autumn.

With some bitterness, Newlands concluded with promises to press on in the future: "The victory by the people at the polls has been reversed in the Legislature, and the Southern Pacific is victorious. The question for the future is whether the administration of government in Nevada shall be controlled by the people or by the Southern Pacific Company." This rhetoric could be heard in other states by a new political generation plotting its way into high office. Soon it would be called "progressivism," or the struggle to place government in the hands of the people instead of the interests.[28]

Stewart, the stalwart, oldguard, nineteenth-century politician was overjoyed with his victory. The resolutions expelling Newlands from the state Silver party were telegraphed around the country and Stewart declared, "If ever a politician received a drubbing at the hands of the people he betrayed, 'Anything' Newlands received it. With all of his money he failed to receive one vote in the legislature. This speaks very highly for the honesty of Nevada Legislatures." Of course, Newlands's name was never presented to the legislature.[29]

Behind all of the rhetoric about honesty and the "will of the people," the question persists: how much money was used in the legislature and was Newlands on the verge of using extensive funds if he believed they would be effective? Newlands was always sensitive on such matters as illegitimate political channels. Legitimate political expenditures included contributions to party campaign funds, but even here he showed a reluctance to be saddled entirely with the burden of a campaign. For Nevadans, he was not as free with his money as they had hoped. Still, Newlands was probably not above spending money, if he thought the prize was within his grasp. When he realized he had been outmaneuvered he withdrew, making speeches about the will of the people versus the power of the interests. This is not to detract from his commitment to reform Nevada, but rather it suggests his realistic assessment of politics.

He admitted privately, "My Senatorial campaign turned out disastrously," but concluded, "we made it very interesting for Stewart and the railroad people." The contest clearly showed that Newlands lacked a personal appeal among the legislators. Even Will Sharon was of little value when it came to standing against the pressures of Wallace, Stewart, and the railroad money.[30]

What did the future hold for these two strong factions in Nevada politics? By mid-March Nixon reported Wallace wanted "to patch up a truce." Sharon brought news that the railroad did not want to engage Newlands in a continuing fight in Nevada. The price for such an agreement, Nixon suggested, should be the elimination of Wallace from Nevada politics; otherwise, open warfare should be pursued with railroad interests. Stewart and Jones, the politicians of the old order, which Newlands and Nixon sought to replace, found Newlands a curious political animal. The one drive that seemed to dominate him was personal. More puzzling, he represented no vested property interests except, perhaps, his own varied and far-flung real estate holdings. As a consequence, when he talked about appealing to the rule of the people and spoke of the higher ideals of social achievement many detected a discomforting strain of sincerity in his words.

But where were his loyalties? Probably unto himself and to the type of future he saw for Nevada, the West, and the nation. Here was the emergence of a non-interest group politician. Foremost, Newlands wanted high office to pursue programs of development in concert with government. His ideal involved change and reform not only in the conduct of government vis-à-vis private enterprise but also in the process of how government elected its personnel, enacted legislation, and administered it.

Nixon said that the key to Newlands's ambitions in the state was his position on the railroad question. "You strike the key note," wrote Nixon, "when you say, I shall be just but never subservient. Mere office holding means nothing to me, unless I can hold the office with honor and with a proper regard for the rights of my constituents." Nixon applauded these words and said, "That is just what the people of this state want." But he emphasized that although Newlands was "now in the right channel, the only thing necessary to capture the people is to make them believe you."[31]

A politician of Newlands's convictions and independent wealth did not stand in awe of corporations. He did not even stand for the exclusive interests of the Mine and Mill Company of which he was a large stockholder against the ranchers on the upper Carson River. From his detachment he could argue that there could be water for all if an adequate reservoir system was initiated on the river. Such a person in high political office in the state could be dangerous. In the view of the railroad, there was no need to make Newlands into an enemy: he showed no evidence of retreating and surely he would one day succeed. He was an unlikely heir to Sharon's old crowd that at one time ruled Nevada politics. He was also an enigma to Nevadans whose political outlook was jaded by the role of "the sack."

Newlands recognized that he failed because he lacked a political organization. The task for Newlands was to build such a group within one of the major parties, namely, the Democratic party. This meant Newlands had to establish a party system built on issues and programs. Thus, Newlands began to usher Nevada into a modern political era, replacing the temporary alliances assembled during the past. One reason that the Silver party had swept everything before it so quickly was that the older parties possessed little permanent organization. Also, it should be noted that the railroad itself supported the Silver party through the activities of "Black" Wallace. The silver movement conveniently offered the opportunity to destroy the state Democratic party as it started to take an interest in removing the Southern Pacific from state politics. But when the Bryanites in the national Democratic party adopted silver, this unexpectedly added strength to the reconstruction of the Democratic party at the state level as the need for an independent Silver party disappeared.[32] All of this strengthened Newlands's hand as an emerging Democratic politician in the state.

VIII

WITH WATER ON HIS WHEEL

The political plums of Nevada were never Newlands's for the picking. This became painfully clear in his struggle for reelection to Congress in 1900. Stewart and Wallace determined to block him, possibly aided by Jones and especially the power of the giant Southern Pacific Railroad. George Nixon believed that if Newlands could obtain the endorsement of both the Democrats and the silver men he would win handily over the Republicans, but if not, "the outcome would be problematical." Although Wallace claimed he was not seeking revenge for the events of 1899, nothing could have been further from the truth.[1]

If Wallace could prevent the fusion of Silverites and Democrats he could defeat Newlands and virtually deliver the state back to the gold Republicans, so he believed. But the persistent attraction of silver and its increasing identification with the Democrats and Bryan were powerful influences to promote fusion as was the diligent work of Newlands and his political manager, Will Sharon. Clarence D. Van Duzer, Newlands's ex-secretary who was now trying his hand at county and state politics in Winnemucca, warned that Edward S. Farrington, a railroad lawyer from Elko, was being groomed by Wallace to run as a Republican candidate for Congress against Newlands in the general election. Van Duzer urged Newlands to pay less attention to foreign affairs and corporation regulation and give more to local matters relating to irrigation, reservoir storage systems, and federal buildings in Nevada, for "it would rebound to your benefit." In eastern Nevada he reported that, "Either national legislation or private capital investment would mean a great deal for Nevada and the Humboldt field."[2]

By the end of February, Will Sharon planned the course that must be followed for Newlands's success. Both the Silver party and Democratic party must work for "fusion and harmony," and hold conventions at the same time and place and agree on nominations. "If this cannot be accomplished," Sharon declared, "they will both go down." By late March, Sharon worried "there is no disposition to harmonize." The date and place for the Silver party Central Committee meeting was April 12 in Reno. The Democratic Central Committee called their meeting for two days later at the same place. Sharon was convinced that Wallace and his friends would control the Silver meeting so he would "not kick up a row in the committee." His strategy: prepare for control of the state-wide convention later in the year.[3]

When Wallace arrived in Reno a few days before the Silver party Central Committee meeting, he made no secret about his opposition to fusion. He declared Newlands a "dead duck" for Congress or any other office. Sharon urged Newlands to contact Comstock "Bonanza King" John Mackay in New York to instruct leading Democrat Joe Ryan on the Comstock to support Newlands in the Democratic party. "Ryan will be governed and controlled largely by Mackay," wrote Sharon. Apparently the request was sent, because later in the campaign Stewart complained to Charles H. Tweed, president of the Southern Pacific Railroad after the death of Collis P. Huntington, that Mackay supported Newlands "on account of Mrs. Newlands," since he held Edith McAllister Newlands in high esteem.

For whatever reasons, Sharon's strategy at the Central Committee meetings of the Silver and Democratic parties in Reno worked. On April 12, Sharon joyously telegraphed Newlands that "Silver Party State Central committee appointed Committee of Conference [to] meet with Democrats Saturday to select time and place for holding joint conventions." The following day Sharon reported that the Democratic Central Committee appointed three Silver party men and three Democrats to the national convention: Silver, Judge Charles E. Mack, Governor Reinhold Sadler, and Newlands; Democrats, John H. Dennis, C. H. Belknap, and P. C. Weber. Also, the Silver party primaries were scheduled for July 28 and the Democratic primaries for August 25. The two parties agreed to meet in two conventions set for Virginia City, September 5, 1900. The two days of meeting in Reno looked like a victory for the fusion forces. And Newlands was anything but a "dead duck."[4]

Wallace was not happy. The work of months fell apart when he saw the silverites pass motions to join with the Democrats in sending a delegation to their national convention and agreeing to hold virtually joint Silver and Democratic conventions. He still could count on the majority of the good Republican silver men in the Silver party, but he pressed Stewart to return to Nevada as soon as possible to join the campaign and urged Jones to oppose Newlands if he hoped to retain his Senate seat two years hence. "If you folks don't show up in season,"

Wallace warned, "I will throw up the sponge and attend to my railroad matters. I am not going to make a losing fight." But on second thought his P.S. to the letter read: "I have had offers made to me to walk off and leave the fight alone, but I am not built that way." Newlands controlled most of the newspapers of western Nevada. He followed the practice of paying from $5 to $10 a column for favorable tracts about himself and the suppression of speeches by the opposition. There were protests, but financially beleaguered editors welcomed the opportunity to be of service.[5]

Sharon's energy in following up the advantages gained in Reno with trips throughout the state, promises, and liberal treatment of newspapers prompted speculation that a Newlands political machine had arrived. Sharon offered assurances that local politicians on the county and state level welcomed. They had enjoyed this under Wallace's "bad political machine," but one admirer wrote Newlands, "Now let there be a good Newlands machine. . . . Sharon's presence throughout the state is an assurance . . . there is to be a Newlands machine [that] stimulates your strength." Advised to meet Sharon in Salt Lake City right after Congress's adjournment for a swing through Lincoln, White Pine, Eureka, Elko and Lander Counties before July 4th, Newlands telegraphed Sharon on June 1 that he would not return to Nevada until after the Democratic National Convention in Kansas City in the first week of July.[6]

This did not mean that Newlands was ignoring Nevada politics. During the summer he launched his own private offensive into the heart of the railroad hierarchy in San Francisco. "Wallaceism" had to be defeated and the best way to effect this was to go to the source of its power. Newlands wrote to his old friend and former law partner in San Francisco, William F. Herrin, who was now "the chief counsel and political adviser for the Southern Pacific" that "there should be harmony between the transportation line and the interests it served." He denounced Wallace as "a low political schemer" and requested his removal from Nevada. If the railroad felt its interests should be represented, it should appoint a Nevadan who commanded respect and who could work for the welfare of the state. If Wallace remained, he suggested there could be unforeseen consequences. Herrin may have been sympathetic to Newlands's request, but Stewart and Wallace for the moment still had the ear of the company hierarchy.[7]

On the national scene Republican President William McKinley prepared to do battle once again with Democratic challenger William

Jennings Bryan in the 1900 elections. As in 1896, this would also be a battle of the gold standard versus the silver standard, but it would be further complicated by the imperialism issue. When he returned from the Democratic National Convention in mid-July, Newlands declared his acceptance of the 16-to-1 declaration (the free coinage of silver at the ratio of 16 parts silver to one part gold) in the Democratic platform. He was also pleased to announce that he converted Democrats to a program of national reclamation for the arid lands of the West. This, in Newlands's view, was a major accomplishment for a party that many regarded as the party of the South, big eastern cities, and opposed to the expansion of federal power. Actually, the Democratic platform said only that the party was in favor of "an intelligent system of improving the arid lands of the West," whereas the Republican plank was more explicitly national when it said, "we recommend adequate national legislation to reclaim the arid lands. . . ."[8]

Bryan decried imperialism in the Philippines and the gold standard at home. Newlands faced the challenge of uniting the silverites and the Democrats. With the Democratic party holding to silver, Newlands had to cement local rifts between it and the still committed silver men in the state. This was no mean task since most silver men were ex-Republicans. After the primaries, delegates from both the Silver party and Democratic conventions convened in Virginia City on September 5, 1900. The conventions met in adjacent buildings and negotiated through conference committees that finally struck an acceptable agreement. Both parties endorsed Bryan for president, called for a union of the "reform" forces within the state, cheered the cause of silver, and denounced imperialism in the Philippines. Newlands obtained the joint endorsement of the parties for the congressional race. The Wallaceite faction within the Silver party was smashed. The Silver party was gradually absorbed by the Democrats, confirming predictions that it would soon die in the embrace of the Democracy. If the fusion continued, the Democratic party could look forward to victory in state elections in 1902. The silverites called for the resignation of Senator Stewart because of his return to the Republican fold and struck from the record words condemning W. E. Sharon and Newlands in the 1899 convention. Newlands had turned what was a bleak political situation into one with bright prospects, not only for the upcoming congressional race but also for his senatorial ambitions in the 1902 legislative elections.[9]

The political cadre functioned smoothly, giving Newlands an impressive Fusionist victory over his Republican rival. Stewart was quick to point out that he spent an embarrassing amount of money for it. Despite his congressional win, some observers believed Newlands faced a heavy fight for the Senate, when he would not have the assistance of the national Democratic ticket and its prominent support of silver. The old-line Republican Yerington did not believe Bryan helped Newlands, but rather that Newlands's well-financed campaign "carried the state for Bryan, otherwise it would have gone Republican surely." This was sour grapes, no doubt, on Yerington's part but he recognized that, "Newlands was laying pipe for the senatorship in the recent election." But "even he won't have a walk over."[10]

Senator Stewart lost no time in trying to block Newlands's efforts in state and national politics. Senator Jones, concluding thirty years as a senator, told Stewart that he would not seek reelection. Stewart, desperate to find a candidate to oppose Newlands, turned to southern Nevada mining entrepreneur Joseph R. DeLamar. As early as November 17 he wrote to DeLamar telling him that Newlands, "after the expenditure of vast sums of money," was reelected to Congress. But nationally Bryanism was buried forever and that Newlands had made his bed in the Democracy "which since the silver party is dead, will again be the minority party." This was a fatal mistake on Newlands's part, which cleared the way for DeLamar to have the senate seat if he wanted it as a Republican.

Stewart continued to urge the DeLamar candidacy. He told DeLamar, "the mere suggestion of your name has made Newlands wild and desperate. He is now equipped for folly." He believed that DeLamar had a better claim to residency than did Newlands. Stewart's task was to defeat Newlands's bid for the Senate, to encourage DeLamar, and to urge railroad support for DeLamar. On the latter point he reported that the railroad people looked favorably on DeLamar's candidacy.[11]

While the enemy camp talked of Newlands's demise, "the man from Chevy Chase" returned to Washington to take up the challenges of the new century. As business revived at decade's end, Newlands paid discreet but noticeably less attention to silver, turning his eyes to more enduring national questions. He addressed issues relating to the place of the corporation in American life and turned his attention to a program for national irrigation development—the subject that first drew his attention in Nevada.

By 1899 Newlands received on a regular basis invitations to national conferences on trusts because of "the general interest you feel in the subject matter. . . ." Progressive editor E. Rosewater of the Omaha *Bee* kept Newlands informed on various conferences on the problems of trusts. The 1899 conference, sponsored by the Chicago Civic Federation, was purely educational. Newlands, invited to share his views, argued that since the corporation is the creation of the state, "it is the right of the state to limit and control it." He dismissed attempts at state regulation of corporations: "The only adequate remedy is through Federal legislation, the operation of which will be uniform throughout the Republic." He suggested creating a Bureau of Industry that would register every corporation in the country and require annual reports to help guide legislation. This was a forerunner of the Bureau of Corporations established in 1903. The 1899 conference was a predecessor to a series of conferences that emphasized the need to regulate large corporations rather than accepting a strict "literalist construction of the Sherman Act" that attacked all combinations in restraint of trade.[12]

On January 26, 1901, Newlands introduced a national irrigation bill. His speeches ridiculed plans for ceding lands to the states for this purpose and described the ineptitude of states in administering such plans, resulting in the monopolization of land by large interests. "Now," he said, "I ask, who should undertake this work? Who can undertake the work? The view of the people of the arid region is that this is a public work of internal improvement which ought to be undertaken by the Government of the United States." He made the point that the work resembles "those improvements that have been made for a number of years in dredging our rivers and improving our harbors—public improvement intended for the general welfare; improvements from which the Government does not expect a direct reimbursement, but simply the general advantage that comes to the entire country and the general welfare from the promotion of enterprises of this kind." The demand that the federal government spend a proportion of its revenues on water conservation and reclamation proportionate to the money it spent in other states for river and harbor improvements had been sounded in Nevada and other arid states for at least two decades. Ever since Newlands had attempted to organize the Truckee River resources into a comprehensive system of reservoir storage, he recognized the necessity to have broad authority that extended beyond the boundaries of states. In some ways his suggestions reflected Colonel John Wesley Powell's *Report on the Lands of the Arid Region of the United States* (1878) that the river basins were the natural political units of the arid West. Newlands too believed, "The arid region must be considered as a unit, regardless of state lines. Each unit should be a main river and all its tributaries." Speaking from his Nevada experience he noted, "The plains to be watered may be in one state; the sources of the river which is to water them, and the only available sites for reservoirs, may be in an adjoining state. No state can act outside of its own boundaries nor can it clothe its citizens with sufficient power so to do." Little wonder he took the position that "The National government, by reason of its national character, is alone capable of taking hold of this interstate question and solving it." In his opinion private capital could not do the job because "The speculative element must be entirely eliminated; the purpose is to create homes for the people, to make the waters of the West available for the reclamation of arid lands by actual settlers, and to eliminate entirely the speculator and the capitalist."

Finally, Newlands appealed to science. Irrigation was the "most scientific method of agriculture." Under irrigated agriculture water "taken from a stream by a ditch, and distributed over lands at lower level, there can be an absolutely scientific adjustment of the moisture to the requirements of the soil." Newlands rhapsodized about this kind of farming: "40 acres of land properly irrigated will sustain a family better than 160 acres of land in the Middle or Eastern States; and under certain characters of cultivation 10 or 15 acres of land will support a family."[13]

Newlands's remarks represented a decade of reflection and not a little romanticizing of the advice of hydrographical engineers.[14] The Newlands speech echoed recommendations from George Maxwell's National Irrigation Association, which foresaw nationally backed irrigation in the West. For a decade irrigation advocates Maxwell and publicist William E. Smythe had sought a workable avenue to achieve development of the West's remaining arid lands through irrigation. In addition Newlands capitalized on back-to-the-land themes urged for the restless masses of America's cities.

Newlands's ambition required that he get government action. He needed to achieve something in irrigation matters to boost him into the Senate in the 1902 elections. His ceaseless activities for national aid to western irrigation after 1900 indicated that he had much at stake in this fight—the ultimate ambition of his public life, a Senate seat from Nevada.

In 1901 death proved Newlands's ally. Wallace died on January 31, 1901, in Mariposa, California. The Wallace-Stewart alliance was broken. Stewart wrote Herrin nominating Nevadan Charles A. Norcross to fill Wallace's position, but Herrin refused. The railroad would now delegate those duties to its land agent in the state, Robert Fulton, longtime friend of Newlands. Yerington felt that political duties would fall to Will Sharon and Newlands would have railroad support in his election bid for the Senate.[15] Death also cut short President McKinley's second presidential term, and Theodore Roosevelt became president of the United States. Creative, energetic, decisive, and bombastic as president, he was a far cry from McKinley's more subdued style. Moreover, he had an abiding interest in the West and in an activist federal government.

Long before Roosevelt's advent to the presidency, Newlands in December 1900 was at work with Frederick H. Newell, hydrographer of the Geological Survey, devising a national irrigation bill that could be funded from the sale of public lands. In his view he was acting as a responsible political figure when he consulted experts in the field on the shaping of legislation. The funding provisions of this bill that called for the expenditure of monies received from the public lands in the western states eliminated the process of explicit appropritations from Congress. This was particularly offensive to the older leadership of the House.

Newlands was not the only congressman to seize the irrigation issue. There were many irrigation bills afloat in Congressional committees. Senator Francis Warren of Wyoming sponsored many bills and was so vocal that he succeeded in making irrigation the leading western issue from 1899 to 1902, superseding the silver crusade. But Warren's measures, embracing both state control and private enterprise, were well within the West's traditions of local control and private development. Newlands broke with those traditions. Partisan politics underlay much of the jockeying for position on the issue. The party that could claim credit for such legislation could appeal to voters of the entire region. Beyond partisanship the issue was whether local, states, and private enterprise should play major roles in reclaiming the American West.[16]

In debate in the House on January 30, 1901, Congressman William H. Moody of Massachusetts said that Newlands's rejection of state management of the irrigation projects seemed to be a "reflection upon the gentleman's own state." Newlands denied this, but his experience there revealed how close to the truth this charge appeared. The real problem was the nature of the West's geography. Newlands recognized the interstate nature of rivers throughout the arid regions: ". . . sources are in an adjoining state, and thus beyond its jurisdiction and control . . . ." Therefore the national government "dealing with the entire public domain regardless of state lines, is better equipped to carry out a comprehensive plan than the state. . . ." Finally, Newlands replied that the national government was the proper director of these projects because it alone possessed the scientific experts to plan and execute projects. The federal government for twenty years had been training scientific men in the Geological Survey, "a corps unsurpassed in the world so far as regards education, scientific knowledge and practical experience, and that it would be a blunder amounting to a crime to substitute for the accumulated experience and intelligence and comprehensive work of this corps the inexperience of individual states and territories operating under the most embarrassing limitations."[17]

But Newlands was not to have his way in 1901. In the House the Newlands bill was referred to the Committee on Irrigation of Arid Lands on March 1, 1901, and there it remained. Longtime Republican House Speaker "Uncle Joe" Cannon was happy to see the bill turned back in 1901 when he remarked:

> I will not vote, as I am now informed, to pay by grant from the Federal Treasury, for the irrigation of 600,000,000 acres of land. It would breed maladministration; it would be a great draft upon the Treasury; it would breed great scandal in the public service and destroy the manhood of the very constituents that the gentleman represents.

Later criticisms of national reclamation echoed these warnings, but in 1901 the attitude and the power of the speaker meant that the Newlands bill would not reach the House floor unless something persuaded the speaker otherwise. In the Senate, also on March 1, 1901, the same bill introduced by Senator Henry C. Hansbrough of North Dakota was defeated for consideration by the entire senate.[18]

In late December 1901, Newlands hosted a large dinner at the New Willard Hotel in Washington whose guests included both proponents and opponents of the national irrigation plan. Addresses were delivered by Secretary of Agriculture James Wilson, George H. Maxwell, executive chairman of the National Irrigation Association, Gifford Pinchot, head of the Forestry Bureau of the Department of Agriculture, Charles D. Walcott, director of the Geological Survey, and Newlands himself. The Washington *Times* reported that Representative Newlands explained his national approach to the project, but a rival bill, prepared by Senator Warren of Wyoming, provided for irrigation under state control. "A division of forces results upon the issue of Government and State control," reported the *Times* and concluded, "It is reported that a bill, which will probably be known as the 'compromise bill' is being prepared. . . ."[19]

With both major parties declaring in favor of arid land irrigation, there would be some type of irrigation legislation coming from Congress in 1902. Wyoming's Senator Warren was determined that it would be his style of legislation, based on cooperation between state and federal government and private enterprise. Warren backed what was known as a "State Engineer's Bill" that provided for state control, federal financing of reservoir building, and private ownership of the irrigation delivery system.

In the end the western irrigation bill assumed much of this shape, although Senator Warren is generally portrayed the loser in his promotion of greater state control and private enterprise. The chief opposition to Newlands's viewpoint came from easterners who were rightly concerned about bringing into production at high cost unneeded agricultural lands in the West. Some sources argue that Warren interests would have won the day in the irrigation struggle had it not been for a streak of "freakish developments" that compelled the West to accept the kind of nationally controlled development that Newlands advocated. Senator Warren was called away to the bedside of his dying wife. His absence took from Congress "the one politician influential enough to resist the tactics of Roosevelt and Newlands." This cleared the way for Roosevelt to convince western Republicans (and some eastern ones) to change the Warren bill so that it really was transformed into the Newlands bill that pointedly nationalized the building of western irrigation systems.[20]

Newlands described the changes as "safe" and "conservative" while Roosevelt twisted arms. Newlands continually scoffed at arguments that the bill would water acres at public expense which would compete with the crops of the midwestern states. Watering western lands simply continued the policy of the government to administer the public domain as a great trust for the settlement and development of the country. He echoed the words of his friends in the hydrological sciences when he advocated planned development of entire watersheds or river basins. A state, he said, cannot operate outside of its own boundaries, and it will be impossible for it to treat the river as a unit and develop every one of its tributaries for the purpose of preventing the torrential floods, creating a constant flow, and thus securing the highest beneficial use of the water.

The bill passed the Senate with the national provisions included. The government would construct reservoirs and highline ditches from a national reclamation fund created by the revenues from the sale of public lands in the arid states. Roosevelt persuaded the House leadership to let the bill reach the floor. It passed the House with more nay votes and abstentions than yea votes, but nonetheless passed. Newlands later pointed out that more Democrats voted for the bill than Republicans, as he tried to make the point that the National Reclamation Act was more strongly supported by the Democratic party than the Republican. Yet Roosevelt was crucial to its passage because it was he who convinced the key Republicans to switch their votes to the national bill that both he and Newlands supported. Certainly this would have been beyond the powers of a lone Democratic representative from a small western state and a member of the minority party. President Roosevelt signed the bill on June 17, 1902. The western press hailed the bill as the salvation of the region and a measure that would ensure the future economic stability of the arid states.[21]

Both Republicans and Democrats rushed to take the credit in the western press. More than the Republican party, the figure of Roosevelt emerged as the hero in the eyes of westerners in the struggle for arid land reclamation. The Denver *Post* said: "For the happy termination of an endeavor which in its incipiency appeared almost hopeless, the people of the West are very largely indebted to President Roosevelt without whose influence the passage of the bill would have been practically impossible." Even Newlands's own Democratic mouthpiece, the *Nevada State Journal*, announced it in headlines as the passage of the Hansbrough bill for national irrigation. Senator Hansbrough of North Dakota, a Republican, had originally introduced the Newlands version of the House bill in the Senate. The commanding figure of the president and prominent role of Republican Senator Hansbrough all tended to obscure Newlands's role in the passage and forced him to go on the offensive to keep his name associated with the measure; he believed the Republican members of Congress only came to support the bill under duress from the president. In the West this question was to remain a point of controversy between Newlands and the president in the upcoming 1902 elections and the presidential contest in 1904.[22]

The controversy began almost immediately in Nevada. The anti-Newlands Republican Reno *Evening Gazette* editorialized : "Mr. Newlands has been the Congressman from Nevada for ten years, during which time the State needed irrigation quite as badly as it does now, without having scored such a success. The secret of its passage was President Roosevelt." The *Gazette* did grudgingly accord some acknowledgment to Newlands when it said "there is glory enough for all," but Roosevelt deserved the greater share. No doubt, it said, Congressman Newlands has done what he could to help the bill, but it saw no need to give him any extra credit or praise for "performing his plain duty." After the passage of the reclamation bill the pro-Newlands *Nevada State Journal* said that it was about time this column dealt with Mr. Newlands in an honest fashion and report that within the last three weeks he secured passage of a $400,000 war claims bill that had been pending for nearly a quarter of century; he steered the Reno public building appropriation into the Omnibus Appropriation Bill and most of all was "the recognized leader in the contest for the irrigation bill which will benefit our State more than all other previous congressional legislation. . . ."[23]

Suffice it to say that Roosevelt's presence in the White House was the catalyst for the passage of the national approach to arid lands irrigation. To ballyhoo one side at the expense of the other smacks of a puerile partisanship both among politicians and historians. More important, the legislation was national in scope, gave great authority to federal project engineers, and placed government in the role of shaping the character of rural western society with the ideals of a small farmer democracy well in mind, and "in conformity" with local water law. The law made water rights "appurtenances to the land irrigated, and beneficial use . . . the basics, the measure and the limit of the right." As a shaper and subsidizer of the West the National Reclamation Act takes its place alongside the Homestead Act of 1862 and even the original Land Ordinance of 1785 with its bequest of grids, townships, and ranges.[24]

Newlands prided himself on the acreage limitation clause for "it provided that no one owner of lands could get water for more than 160 acres." The act, according to Newlands, prompted the breakup of "the existing land monopoly which has been so bothersome in California and the inter Mountain states. . . ." He believed this would occur "without injury and I say with benefit to the owner, for land heretofore unsaleable would be made available." He forthrightly claimed to a constituent that, "I prided myself upon this feature of the bill. . . ." For Newlands its implications were far wider than a regional domestic aid package. Speaker Cannon still believed the bill represented destructive charity that would rob westerners of their free-born manhood.[25]

For Newlands the passage of the National Reclamation Act came at an opportune moment. Throughout the year Will Sharon moved to line up support for Newlands in the upcoming legislative elections, tightening his grip on the holdover legislators and generally creating a good impression about the congressman's loyalty to silver, his anti-imperialist views, his sympathy for workers, and his heroic battle for national irrigation.

Newlands had problems winning labor support. He at first opposed the eight-hour-day law because he claimed that states without this law could more favorably attract industry. Labor was also aware that the Sharon estate had in the past employed cheap Chinese labor. In the Reclamation Act Newlands could now point to its requirement of the eight-hour-day in construction projects and the banning of "Mongolian labor." Labor support became more critical by 1902 because Nevada's mining population zoomed upward with the development of new mines in southern Nevada. A Reno newspaper said Tonopah was attracting attention from all parts of the world: "This morning fifty passengers alighted from the east bound trains . . . bound for Tonopah, the Eldorado of Nevada. It is said that two or three hundred additional people are headed this way and that Tonopah is the most talked of place on the Pacific coast." Nearly 50,000 came into the state between 1900 and 1910 as part of Nevada's twentieth-century mining boom, centered around Tonopah and Goldfield. Copper mining experienced rapid development at the same time in White Pine County near Ely. Most of these newcomers voted Democratic, further vindicating Newlands's efforts to build a Fusionist Democratic party in the state.[26]

Mining unions made demands that shocked employers, who had become accustomed to the acquiescence of labor during twenty years of hard times. Labor unrest occurred even in Nevada's traditional mining center, the Comstock in Virginia City. The community survived by eking out a living by reprocessing tailings left from the bonanza days with the V&T railroad faithfully serving what remained of the town. In January 1902, the general manager of the V&T reported trouble from "some smart allechs" who claimed labor was paid half its worth and given no rights. The local labor union demanded three dollars a day, forcing section men, yardmen, and engine wipers to join "for fear of their lives," according to Yerington. But Yerington believed the ruckus was closely tied to the upcoming elections. He told Newlands that the affair was "nothing but a political Peace Club and of course the intention is make you and other candidates 'put up' for the benefit of labor." The seasoned manager of the V&T could see no way out but to pay the three dollars and "throw in the sponge" to prevent disruption of the railroad's "perfect service," avoid violence, destruction of property, and "kindred troubles." Reassuringly, he wrote Newlands, "consider the affair settled although a bitter pill to me I trust that it will prove to be water on your wheel." By early March Yerington publicly accepted labor's demands and grudgingly informed Newlands that, "The Union then held a jubilee meeting and passed a vote of thanks, giving you and 'Billy' Sharon credit for the victory—'such is life'."[27]

Unfortunately for Senator Stewart, DeLamar declined all urgings to announce for the Senate against Newlands. By late July the Republicans settled upon the candidacy of former Nevada Supreme Court Judge Thomas P. Hawley, who served on the U.S. Circuit Court. Republican newspapers reported that "Judge Hawley's candidacy created wild excitement among the Republicans and great dismay in the ranks of the Dem-Silverites." Judge Hawley, fresh from court decisions against the State Board of Taxation and Equalization and in favor of the Southern Pacific Railroad, declared that the board made rulings that unfairly singled out the railroad for increased taxes while exempting other classes of property. Senator Stewart hoped this would tempt the railroad to become involved in the contest to elect Hawley. But even stalwart Republicans could not foresee this outcome. Yerington conceded that, "Judge Hawley is popular but it must be remembered that Mr. Newlands and his party have been in power for many years, held all the offices and got things fixed generally."[28]

Newlands took no chances. He liberally funded the entire state Democratic ticket, especially those legislative candidates from whom he could expect support and who would offer him the senatorship. Yerington, always the shrewd observer, reported that Newlands was in town in January 1903 for the opening of the legislature and expected to be elected senator by the end of the month. On January 27, Newlands's senatorial dreams had finally been realized. He could point to his legislative record that brought benefits to the West and to Nevada in the Reclamation Act and to his loyalty to silver, but still it was clear that he committed heavy sums to the campaign to ensure his election. Beyond the election, Newlands and his supporters turned to shaping events in the Nevada legislature. Now the opportunities opened to build the kind of state he had been talking about since the 1890s. Obviously, the time was at hand to push through legislation enabling Nevada to utilize the provisions and benefits of the National Reclamation Act. Beyond this, more far-reaching reforms were needed in the state to build in Nevada what Newlands liked to call a "model democracy."[29]

IX

NEWLANDS
"A MODEL DEMOCRACY"

Newlands took an almost proprietary interest in the affairs of the legislature. At several points his watchful eye mapped out legislative programs designed to create the "model democracy." His influence was crucial to the development of a state-based Progressivism. Without him there were few voices in the state with the kind of resources and commitments he could make to legislative reform. His new senatorial position made him a powerful voice in state politics.

The 1903 Nevada legislature was clearly under the influence of Newlands's political network. The legislation that came out of it might even be termed "progressive" although there is no evidence that Newlands employed that term in describing the legislature's accomplishments. Not surprisingly, in view of the expanding ranks of labor, demands for an eight-hour-day law and prohibition of yellow-dog contracts received favorable attention by the legislature. In Nevada the ban on yellow-dog contracts took the form of an anti-card law that made it illegal for an employer to require an employee to carry a written pledge not to join a union.

The 1903 legislature also took up the water issue. The move was urgent. The Reclamation Service could only consider projects in states where an adequate water administration system existed. This meant the appointment of a state engineer as chief administrator and registrar of water rights. Newlands spearheaded the effort to bring Nevada's water administration in line with the expectations of the Reclamation Service. He coaxed through the legislature a bill "providing for the cooperation of the State of Nevada with the Secretary of the Interior of the United States in the construction and administration of irrigation works for the reclamation of arid lands."[1]

After the passage of water legislation that created a rational system of identifying and assigning water rights through a state engineer's office, Newlands proudly reported the events to the National Irrigation Congress in Ogden, Utah, on September 18, 1903. Nevada, he said, had extended the hand of cooperation to the national government by shaping "friendly" state legislation to receive the initiatives of the federal government in the construction of storage reservoirs and irrigation works. He wanted the region and even the nation to know of the advanced legislation being passed in Nevada. Cooperation must be foremost in water projects: "Such is the spirit in my own state," he proudly asserted. He applauded the fact that Nevada's state engineer under new legislation must be virtually approved by the federal agency before appointment. "And so under this act," he said, "the State of Nevada, through its governor, appoints the state engineer upon the recommendation of the Secretary of the Interior. The governor can reject the nomination of the Secretary of the Interior and compel another nomination, but the man when finally appointed must be recommended by the Secretary of the Interior. We thus obtain a man upon whom the judgment of both the National Government and the highest state official has united as the man best fitted for the place."

The act provided for the appointment of district water commissioners, also nominated by the Department of the Interior. They were to begin their activities after water rights were ascertained; to supervise on each stream the use of water according to a list of priorities, to serve each the water according to the established right, "and to serve the government and its grantees their water according to their rights." Newlands said, on the Truckee, "the existing settlers have water for the use of 40,000 acres; the Government is about to create water there that will supply seven or eight hundred thousand acres." He asked in his support of increased federalization of water resources, "Would it not be colossal effrontery upon the part of the owners of that 40,000 acres to demand that they should have the absolute control over the stream; that Uncle Sam should be compelled to spend millions of dollars in storing water and absolutely lose all control of it as soon as it disappears from the reservoirs?"

The law, he said, was drawn with two purposes in mind:

> One was that it was but just to give the creator of the majority of the water something to say regarding the administration of it, and the other was we felt assured it would be for the benefit of our own people to have such men as are in the geological service—trained engineers, experienced men, and, above all, impartial men—administer the control of the stream.

Newlands was well aware that many had already worked through trial and error various means of stream control administration, but he did suggest "that there are many things in this act, and particularly in the spirit of this act, that can be emulated by our sister states and territories." He noted that President Roosevelt on a recent visit to Nevada referred to this act as "a model of legislation for other states. . . ."[2]

By consolidating water rights with a state engineer under federal scrutiny, Newlands risked touching the sensitive nerve of state sovereignty, but he was willing to take the risk in state politics. Besides, that nerve had been considerably dulled by twenty years of depression. The measure was insurance against future ill-considered policies arising out of the poverty of Nevada politics that might destroy the special relationship established with the federal government in the area of water resource development.[3]

In Washington by early 1904, Newlands could report: "I am immensely interested in my senatorial work." He also indicated a growing interest in foreign affairs that included the Cuban and Philippine questions. Although he was critical of the expansionist policies embarked upon after the Spanish-American War, he was particularly critical of Roosevelt's acquisition of the Panama Canal Zone in November 1903, and the affront to Columbia. "This Panama business of Roosevelt's," he wrote, "is one of the most disgraceful periods in our diplomatic history. Cunning-sharp practices, force all combined to get what we could with a little more time have secured peaceably and humbly." His disagreement with the president's policies in foreign affairs contrasted sharply with his general agreement with him on domestic issues, especially those related to western conservation.[4]

For Newlands, the Spanish-American War was a diversion from more pressing domestic problems, with the peace settlement leading to continued foreign complications. Early on he was confident of victory in the war but believed the business community was too cautious about the future, with the result that the war postponed "the era of realizations." As a heavy investor in the American future in the early 1890s, Newlands was eager to recoup some of those investments as prosperity began to return in 1897 after the disastrous depression that began in 1893. The war, he feared, would merely postpone this recovery by inspiring too much caution in the business community. Finally, he sorely wished (as he put it) that the government would stop irritating foreign lands and get on with the business of irrigating domestic lands.

The new horizon of foreign affairs required a Democratic party response. The Republicans took the initiative with the war and accepted the burdens of victory that involved occupation of the Philippines and the determination of Cuba's future. Newlands opposed the continued presence of American authority and armies on foreign soil. He endorsed William Jennings Bryan's anti-imperialist position.[5]

He believed imperialism could be rejected, but at the same time expansion overseas could be accepted. The answer was the extension of the American territorial system and the right of statehood to new lands. Additions should be made on an equal footing with the older states, but not all lands should be eligible for acquisition. He saw this as possible for Hawaii, whose annexation in 1898 by joint resolution he had sponsored in the House, and also for Cuba, but not for the Philippines. Political incorporation into the nation as new states could only be extended to those possessions whose population and cultural institutions closely resembled the United States. Newlands sought both racial and cultural homogeneity in the new territories to be added. The Philippines was not a candidate for annexation because of its predominantly racial difference from the United States, but Hawaii, if further Asian immigration could be curtailed, was a candidate.[6]

The Democrats abandoned their peerless leader Bryan in the 1904 presidential campaign for the conservative gold Democrat Judge Alton B. Parker. Parker simply offended too many western Democrats who had been attracted to Bryan because of his stand for silver and the Great Commoner's appeal to the underdog in American society. Still, Newlands tried to influence Parker's views on the tariff question and the passage of the national irrigation act. He urged that the Democrats not take a traditional stand that the tariff is robbery —"an old shibboleth which ought to have been relegated to the limbo of worn out phrases that tend only to arouse old prejudices and contentions." Newlands urged the party to give business and labor assurances that Democratic tariff reform meant "progressive reform that will benefit not destroy." Republicans were using this phrase against Democrats effectively among workingmen by telling them the difference between labor wages in Europe and how such Democratic policies would bring wages to European levels.[7]

Newlands was outraged at the "mendacity of the Republican party and Republican press" in the intermountain region on the origins and passage of the irrigation bill. Everyone should know that the irrigation movement had Democratic origins and that a new Democratic administration would promote it.[8] He had occasion to trace the rise of this Republican critique of the origins of the irrigation bill as early as the 1902 campaign for the Senate in Nevada. He told George Maxwell, head of the National Irrigation Association, that Republicans first attacked him on his support of the irrigation measure in his campaign for the senate in 1902. He said the limit of "malevolence and falsehood was reached here in the last campaign. . . ." The Republican press gave him full responsibility for the act which, it said, gave Nevada only the proceeds from public land sales within Nevada for irrigation projects. This they laughingly pointed out was only $7,000 a year. Then when the large irrigation project began in Fallon, they hailed it as a Roosevelt measure and characterized Newlands "a mere passenger in the boat," having little to do with the passage.[9]

In Nevada, the Stewart forces collapsed and Stewart retired from his long political career. Newlands seriously considered a Will Sharon candidacy as his power and influence grew in Nevada politics after the turn of the century, but as he wrote Fred Sharon about his nephew, it would take at least $35,000 to effect his election in 1904. Such a move would have to be carefully considered. But before the campaign came to a head in the fall of 1904, two other possibilities loomed. Popular cattleman turned politician, John Sparks, had been elected governor on the Democratic ticket in 1902. When he indicated his desire to seek the senatorship, Newlands and his brother-in-law decided against the Will Sharon candidacy for financial reasons. Sparks received the Democratic nomination and Newlands's open support. This included some financial aid; in fact, Newlands advanced him $5,000 as a contribution to the senatorial campaign fund.

On the Republican side, George Nixon sought the party's nomination. Nixon, Newlands said, was invited by Republicans to seek the nomination "with a view to breaking up the Silver Party. . . ." They induced Nixon ". . . who has been cooperating with the Fusion forces as a member of the Silver party for the past ten years to return to the Republican party." Nixon was "an acute, adroit politician" who had represented the Southern Pacific Company in matters of taxation and in a quiet way in matters of legislation. His appointment was a result of an outbreak against the political domination of both parties by the Southern Pacific. Newlands identified himself with this movement and denounced the constant interference by the previous Southern Pacific agent in the affairs of the state. The result was the substitution of a businesslike, instead of a political, management of the Southern Pacific in Nevada. Since Nixon's appointment, Newlands declared the railroad had never had such a peaceful relationship with the state.

Clearly Newlands's praise of this situation was genuine. A closer look at the situation suggests that the Nixon candidacy suited Newlands better than support of Sparks. Nixon could pay his own way in politics, for he and his partner, George Wingfield, were developing Goldfield mines and negotiating loans from New York financier Bernard Baruch.

Nixon could remain close to Newlands and at the same time stabilize the Republican party in the state and ultimately offer the Newlands network some influence over the Republican party. The beginnings of a bipartisan political machine can be seen in this arrangement. Nixon's partner, Wingfield, later gained notoriety for his alleged bipartisan machine that ruled Nevada after the deaths of both Nixon and Newlands. For Newlands, Sparks would take constant support and would not have the long-established working relationship that he and Nixon enjoyed. Sparks suspected this secret acquiescence on Newlands's part toward the Nixon candidacy and when the legislature overwhelmingly elected Nixon in January 1905, all seemed confirmed. Certainly $5,000 was not enough to elect a Nevada senator. There was not a good deal that Sparks could do and he outwardly maintained good relations with Newlands, although his wife became "an open enemy for life." Some press reports asserted that Newlands personally favored Will Sharon but dropped him in order that Sparks might suffer such a complete defeat that he would give no thought to running against Newlands in 1908.[10]

Newlands was quite satisfied with the retirement of the Southern Pacific from politics in the state. He asked Mr. Harriman in New York and other leading men of the Southern Pacific that "it maintain its policy of hands off." He felt that the state and the railroad were now uniting for the development of Nevada. Meanwhile, both the increased mining activities and the recent irrigation project expanded the number of voters in Nevada. The majority of the newcomers were Democrats, but they required organization to bring them to the polls. Ultimately Newlands hoped that the next election would be won on the basis of "the efficient administration we have given in state and county government in which we have been in complete control for years. We have sought," he said, "to indoctrinate all our party managers, officials and candidates with the view that whilst we demand thorough party loyalty and activity, we also require the best service that can be given the public. Many Republicans agree that the state has never been so well governed."[11]

While Newlands tried to put the best face on the election results of 1904, he could not help notice that some of his control over Nevada affairs had slipped away. Governor Sparks was sullenly resentful of his perceived mistreatment. Nevada broke ranks from the Democratic party and voted for Roosevelt, and the legislature (Republican in the lower house and Democratic Fusionist in the upper) behaved in an erratic and disappointing manner on all sorts of progressive measures after it elected Nixon in 1905. Governor Sparks was a wildcard from Newlands's point of view. He could never have any confidence in

Sparks. All in all it was a rather checkered political picture Newlands faced in Nevada. Luckily, he did not face reelection until 1908. Still, he was aware that Nevada matters demanded serious attention.[12]

He was dismayed at the inattention of the legislature to many pieces of legislation. The legislature either refused or joined with Governor Sparks in vetoing measures essential to the Newlands reform agenda. At the beginning of the legislative session he accepted Republican domination of the lower house as consistent with the decision to let Nixon move easily into the senatorial seat. But this meant that many in the legislature were not beholden to the Newlands machine and would have virtually no purpose and direction after electing Nixon. Away in Washington, Newlands did not initially suspect the mischief and neglect in the legislature. He pressed for the building of a stronger Democratic party through the voice of the Reno *Nevada State Journal*, edited by E. L. Bingham and subsidized by Newlands. He urged Bingham, as a representative of the party Central Committee, to contact Democrats in local, state government and in the legislature pressing upon them, "the importance of raising the whole standard of public service and making a model commonwealth of Nevada through the action of the Democratic party." Newlands obviously understood the institutional nature of the party over individual ambition when he told Bingham: "In all things political you should act as the representative of the state central committee and in the general interest of the party with a view to securing a strong party press and thorough organization and not as the representative of any candidate."

Newlands authorized Bingham to obtain another linotype and to employ William E. Smithe to write articles, especially editorials on the "New Nevada" for the Sunday edition. He said Smythe's books, *Constructive Democracy* and *The Conquest of Arid America*, should be sold directly by the newspaper at a profit. He offered to pay for Bingham and Smythe to meet in San Francisco to talk over matters. It was important that Bingham should act quickly on these matters because, "My most important work is being done now and proper attention should be called to it in Nevada," but he was quick to add, "as an element of party organization." Clearly Newlands saw the necessity of building a Democratic party in Nevada, but his support of Nixon would belie this intention unless he believed Nixon could be the nucleus for a viable and safe Republican party in the state. He feared the prospect of randomly electing people to sit in the legislature and in local government. They should be tied by a common purpose and philosophy, and the political party was the cement of this bond.[13]

Newlands's vision of Nevada as a model commonwealth conflicted with the disappointing performance of the 1905 Nevada legislature. The Fusionist-controlled senate had failed to pass initiative measures or strengthen the referendum law. He immediately demanded the voting records of individual legislators. He wanted to know how consistent their actions were with the platform adopted by the party. In addition to initiative and referendum legislation, Newlands was interested in why a law creating a tax examiner had failed and also, inquiring in a priggish tone typical of the progressive reformer of his class, the failure of a measure against the sale of liquor near irrigation construction sites. The Reclamation Service objected to these places it called "Deadfalls."[14]

The replies to Newlands's questions suggested the breakdown of party discipline in the legislature. One old-time Democrat said that there was no "boss" among the Fusionist Democrats. The head of the Democratic Central Committee, Nate Roff, complained there were "anarchist elements" within the party that offended conservative, intelligent men. Moreover, he claimed that Sparks was "probably the most unpopular man in Nevada today." Bingham of the *Nevada State Journal* confirmed that the Fusionist party fragmented when it confronted issues and was a far cry from the well-oiled machine of the 1903 legislature. James G. Sweeney, another Democratic Central Committeeman, disagreed. He believed Sparks was "never stronger politically" and believed he would be reelected two years hence. Furthermore, his trips to Tonopah, Goldfield, Columbia, and Bullfrog districts in the south revealed that the political makeup of the new population was three-to-one Democratic over Republican. "According to the influx of people into the southern country, I predict that southern Nevada in the next election will practically decide the future political destiny of the state," he wrote, "and that we will have an overwhelming political majority not withstanding all the reports that you may hear." He believed that the party would be in good shape after the next election with Sparks leading the ticket.[15]

By the adjournment of the legislature in March, the *Nevada State Journal* pointed out that after the election of Newlands to the Senate in 1903, he had remained in Nevada to help guide actions on water and tax legislation. His efforts ensured that Nevada was the first state to profit from national reclamation legislation. "How much better it would have been," mused the paper, "had Mr. Nixon pursued the same policy instead of rushing on to a Washington tailoring shop to have his toga fitted." It blamed the failure of the session on "a hoodlum element . . .

unfitted in years, experience or judgment to appreciate the importance of the questions submitted to them." They were not representative of the people and were selected solely on "how they would vote on the senatorship." This, concluded the paper, was an indictment of the present system of electing U.S. Senators. Until this system was abolished, the state could look forward to many such legislatures.[16]

Events indicated that, without Newlands's close involvement, the party mechanism did not yet function in Nevada. Much work, cajoling, and an open purse were still needed. Important as local politics were to his continued success, Newlands was a United States Senator and he was ready to speak out on national issues. His position on the Senate Commerce Committee drew his attention to the role of the corporation in American life. Disputes persisted between railroads and state government over the right to regulate interstate trade. Newlands, seeking a national solution, proposed that railroads be incorporated by the national government and be regulated by the Interstate Commerce Commission. Newlands explained his ideas in an article in the *North American Review*. His proposal, praised by a railroad official, was roundly criticized in state circles because it exempted the nationally incorporated railroads from state taxation as well as regulation.[17]

Newlands also spoke out on foreign policy. The Spanish-American War increased national involvement in the Caribbean and the Philippines. Newlands became concerned about the political crisis on the island of Hispaniola. The island's troubled history touched the United States first when Napoleon decided to abandon it as the key to his plans to build a New World empire. The island's people eventually divided into the nations of Haiti and the Dominican Republic. President Grant determined to annex the latter in 1870, but Congress rejected the move. By the end of the century a series of corrupt governments left the small country hopelessly in debt to foreign creditors, both European and American. Roosevelt, to avert European intervention and to assert American interests under the Monroe Doctrine, moved to place the customs service and financial affairs of the republic in U.S. hands with a plan to retire the debt to foreign interests.[18]

Newlands linked the Santo Domingo question to what he called the "race question" in the United States. This island and others in the Caribbean, including Cuba, offered the opportunity, not at an overwhelming cost, to remove the African American population from the United States. On this issue he revealed himself as an old-line Democrat, who never accepted the citizenship of blacks as defined by the

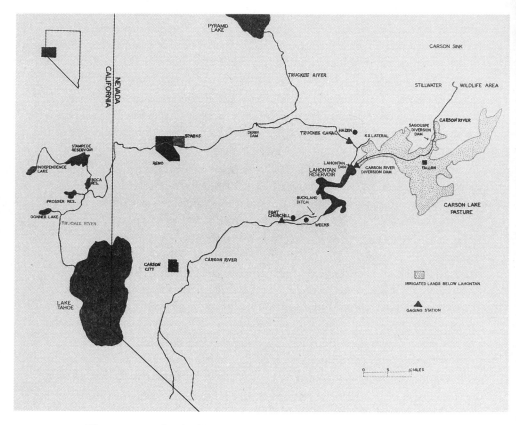

Water sources for the Newlands Project showing the Derby diversion dam
on the Truckee River and the Lahontan Dam on the Carson River.

Radical Republicans and the Fourteenth and Fifteenth Amendments
to the Constitution. He saw no place for blacks in American society,
except under a segregated arrangement. Preferably, he looked to the
removal of blacks from the society to avoid a future "race war." If a path
of action were not developed soon on this issue, he feared, "race
massacre or the inferior race [black] being subjected to a condition
approaching slavery ... the subjection of the Negro would simply renew
the conditions which prevailed before the Civil War." He noted that
prior to emancipation black colonization had been suggested by African
Americans, philanthropists, and politicians. "Here we have in the
Caribbean Sea an island of unsurpassed fertility of soil and richness of
resource, admirably adapted to the black race." But he knew the
president to be a man "intent upon doing things, and who likes to do
them quickly. . . ." He regretted that Roosevelt linked this issue only to

5. Senator Newlands addresses the crowd at the opening of Derby Dam, east of Reno on the Truckee River. This ceremony occurred on June 17, 1905, three years to the day after the passage of the National Reclamation Act of 1902. Photograph courtesy of the Nevada Historical Society. Used by permission.

the question of debt payments and the discouragement of European interference in this hemisphere. Slower and more thoughtful action could make Santo Domingo the beginning of a solution to what he saw as the great race problem in the United States.[19]

While his views were expressed in the *North American Review*, Newlands and his wife prepared for a vacation in the Orient. But before Newlands left he made it a point to be on hand to conduct ceremonies at the completion of the Derby diversion dam on the Truckee River, marking it as the first completed national reclamation project. The event, held with great local fanfare, included a visit from the prominent members of the House and Senate Irrigation Committees. Newlands captured the spotlight on June 17, 1905, just three years to the day after President Roosevelt signed the National Reclamation Act in 1902. One observer writing in a local publication gave all the credit to Roosevelt and called it, "the day of Nevada's emancipation." When Newlands spoke at a banquet of the Congressional Irrigation Committee in

6. Newlands assists Edith McAllister Newlands in breaking a bottle of
champagne on the opening gates of Derby Dam, June 17, 1905.
Photograph courtesy of the Nevada Historical Society. Used by
permission.

Sheridan, Wyoming on June 30, he underlined his and his party's role in
the passage of the Reclamation bill. "Yet," he did say, "this bill was
passed by a union of Democracy with president Roosevelt and his
Republican friends of like faith," but he insisted, "that history records
that the bill, in all its essential features, was framed by a Democrat and
was passed in the House of Representatives by a vote, the majority of
which was Democrat." Afterward he rushed to San Francisco to meet
Edith for the sailing date of July 8, to inspect the much-deplored
Philippine involvement.[20]

This trip was to be one of the high points of his life. A great deal of
glamour, rumor, and gossip was associated with it because the
president's outspoken and unconventional twenty-one-year-old daughter, Alice Roosevelt, signed on for the voyage. She also invited her
friend, Congressman Nicholas Longworth of Ohio to join her. According to the custom of the day Edith Newlands was to be her official
chaperon, and Secretary of War William Howard Taft, who was also
from Ohio, was to keep a watchful eye on Congressman Longworth.
Alice drew the never-ceasing attention of the press, who referred to her

as Princess Alice or Alice in Wonderland. Her antics overshadowed the serious nature of the "inspection tour," whose purpose was also to assure the Japanese that the United States presence in the Philippines was no threat to their security. But according to the outspoken Alice, "It was a huge Congressional party, a 'junket' if ever there was one."

Secretary of War Taft had been civil governor of the Philippines, appointed by President McKinley in 1900, and recalled home in 1904 to serve as secretary of war in Roosevelt's cabinet. He had promised to return to observe the operations of its elected legislature, and this trip was a fulfillment of that promise. In early July nearly eighty congressmen, their wives, friends, and servants boarded the steamship *Manchuria*, scheduled to depart on July 8. The press previewed Alice Roosevelt's trip to Asia with stories headlined: "Alice in Wonderland: How First Maiden of the Land Will Travel in Orient and Tropical Romance Anticipated." While in the city, Alice evaded the supervision of the Newlandses and visited the forbidden streets, shops, and dens of San Francisco's fabled Chinatown.[21]

Both Newlandses must have known when they boarded ship that "Princess Alice" and Longworth would test the conventional standards of the day. At one point Taft was compelled to ask Alice, "I think I ought to know if you are engaged to Nick," to which her reply was, "More or less, Mr. Secretary, more or less." Alice recalled that Mrs. Newlands was "my own particular chaperon and there never was a more charming, sympathetic, and gay one." During the first stop of the voyage in Hawaii Alice spent long hours on the beach with Longworth, took a great interest in the hula dance, and caused a small party, including the Newlandses, to miss the scheduled departure of the *Manchuria* with the tides from Honolulu harbor. All was saved, Alice remembered, when she, Longworth, the Newlandses, and a few others boarded a fast launch, "leis about our necks, regret in our hearts at leaving, . . . pursued the *Manchuria* out into the open Pacific."[22]

From Hawaii the "Inspection Tour of the Philippines" steamed on to Japan. There Alice was indeed received as a "princess," for the Japanese hoped that her father would award them spoils of the Russo-Japanese War at the upcoming Portsmouth Peace Conference over which Roosevelt was to preside. "No people have ever been treated with greater consideration and kindliness than we were by the Japanese, not only Mr. Taft and myself, but the entire party," Alice Roosevelt recalled. The party then went on to Manila.

From the Philippines Alice, Congressman Longworth, the Newlandses, and a few others took transport up through the Yellow Sea to the port of Tientsin and then overland to Peking. In the ancient Chinese capital they stayed in palaces and eventually received an audience from the Empress Dowager herself. Alice writes, ". . . though at the time we met her she was over seventy, one felt her charm. She by no means looked her age; her small, brilliant, black eyes were alert and piercing; they and her rather cruel, thin mouth, turned up at one corner, drooping a little at the other, made her face vivid and memorable." From China the party left for Korea aboard the battleship *Ohio,* and from Korea they departed for Yokohama, Japan. From Yokohama they boarded the ship *Siberia* and joined the railroad magnate E. H. Harriman on the return voyage. At the insistence of Harriman, the ship made the trip from Japan to San Francisco in ten days, "bettering the previous record only by minutes."[23]

Little wonder that Newlands almost felt like Marco Polo. Newlands took time to write aboard ship because in December the *North American Review* published his "A Democrat in the Philippines." He believed the possession of the islands was a mistake and saw no hope of fostering democracy there because he did not think the people "fitted for democratic methods of government, nor that they could quickly develop into a homogeneous people, or act with unity of purpose." Newlands thought it probable that left to themselves the islands would fall into chaos, a military dictatorship, or fall prey to another foreign power. While deplorable, the U.S. had no obligation to prevent it. He argued for hands off: "if the Filipino people were to be killed, it were that they should kill each other than that we should kill them or if they were to be conquered by a foreign power, that some other country should undertake the destructive task." Although his views might square with Democratic party positions on imperialism, they contrasted sharply with those of William Jennings Bryan, who also visited the islands on his world tour of 1905–06. Bryan, overwhelmed with his reception in the Philippines, found the people fully capable of self-government.[24]

In his article for the *North American Review,* Newlands hoped to present "a common sense argument against the Philippine War without the . . . invective of the Anti-Imperialist League." Newlands deplored the desire of American business to exploit Philippine products. The American government in the Philippines, he insisted, should function to protect the people from an overzealous and "frenzied commercialism." Later, Newlands described Taft's policies toward the islands as "paternalistic, socialistic, and unanarchistic . . . which is only an adaptation of [an] altruistic policy to the gradual abandonment of an imperialism accidentally forced on a Democracy." These views came forward as he addressed the issue of establishing an agricultural loan bank in the islands: "let it be a government bank not a government aided bank. The one is as paternalistic as the other and I would rather trust the commission with its management than the representatives of frenzied commercialism." In a later article Newlands called for a twenty-year training period in self-government for the islands to be followed by complete independence, after provisions for the retention of a coaling station for the navy.[25]

If Newlands deplored paternalism in the Philippines, he conducted his own light-handed variety in Nevada. After the struggle with Stewart, he avoided direct confrontations and when Will Sharon did not undertake them, they did not occur. Neither did he choose to punish those who did not take his orders or conform to his views, nor did he exert a python-like grip on state officials and events. His position and refinement could not allow the degree of desperation that at some points drove the lives of the latter-day kingpins of Nevada life and politics. As a director of a quasi-political machine, Newlands, in comparison to George Wingfield of the 1920s or to Pat McCarran of the 1940s, appeared weak and vacillating.[26]

Newlands was much influenced by William E. Smythe, who waxed eloquently and unrealistically about the future of Nevada and its irrigation society. He said colonization efforts, reclamation, and progressive political institutions could make Nevada an example to the nation. Newlands was committed to help underwrite the publication of Smythe's second visionary work about arid America, *Constructive Democracy*. Smythe believed that somewhere in the arid West there would be created the highest conditions of life for the common man that the world had known. He declared:

> Nevada offers the best field for such a movement because it is conceivably possible that within ten years a majority of its people may reside upon lands now vacant, but in process of reclamation by the Government. Hence the institutions established there may dominate the life of a Commonwealth, and so challenge the attention of the world.

Then he asserted that opportunity for Nevada lies in two directions: First, in developing political institutions which shall represent the purest democracy to be found in any modern state, and second, in developing social and economic life that will offer masses living on the land the highest standard of living to be found in any part of the world. When this effort is even partially successful, "the contrast between a new and redeemed Nevada and its old reputation as a worthless, sagebrush waste, a rough mining camp, a rotten political borough will challenge the attention of the nation and the world." Smythe believed that W. R. Hearst's recently announced Independence League in New York advocated many of the reforms he envisioned: direct nominations by a primary system, direct legislation, initiative, referendum and recall, public ownership and operation of utilities, abolition of monopoly, and just wages and fair hours for labor. He urged the establishment of a Nevada Constructive League that might be a branch of Hearst's Independence League. Smythe said:

> At first blush it looks to me as if we had everything to gain and nothing to lose by this alliance, for the Independence League seems pretty certain to supply the nucleus of the coming radical party. So far as I am concerned, 'it looks good to me.' But if Bryan returns and tries to keep the Democratic party away from Hearst, so that the latter is driven into forming a new party with Watson, the situation might become embarrassing for you.

Smythe wanted a national weekly under his editorship, funded by Newlands and named *Nevada Nation*. It would take money (Newlands's money) but it would advocate the Nevada situation nationally.[27]

Newlands listened to Smythe's ideas with more than a passing fancy. Later, he urged Bingham not to attack Hearst's *Examiner* and pointed out that it was the leading Democratic paper on the Coast. He believed that Hearst was in line for the Democratic nomination in 1908 and that he stood on the people's side on most issues. He should be appreciated, wrote Newlands, as a man who conducts a newspaper in the interests of popular rights at a time when "the system" controls most newspapers of the country. He should be excused for his occasional sensationalism and flamboyance. Moreover, the paper had a wider circulation than any other in Nevada, and it should be borne in mind that "there will be blows to give as well as blows to take," if Hearst thought that the *Journal* was unfriendly.[28]

X

THE ROAD AHEAD

If the Nevada Democracy needed rebuilding, the same was true for the national party after the disaster of 1904. Hope arose from the ashes. The 1906 congressional elections cut the Republican majority in the House from 112 to 55, giving Democrats greater opportunities for building the strength of the party on a national basis. In the face of President Roosevelt's overriding partisanship and popularity this was a major challenge. But Newlands believed that the political trend pointed to reform of "the system" and toward a greater role of government at all levels in American life. The passage of the National Reclamation Act convinced Newlands that many aspects of American life should be planned at the national level. The problem facing him within the Democratic party was its states-rights orientation. To modernize the party, much of that doctrine had to be abandoned. He saw evidence of this, especially as Democrats became more committed to the path of reform. Like Bryan, he believed that Democrats were more consistent in the support of Roosevelt's reform programs than were most of the members of the president's party.[1]

The road ahead was by no means clear. Roosevelt had already announced that he would not seek a third term. Unfortunately for progressive Democrats, the party had many conservative liabilities. It was still the party of the rebel South and of urban political machines built on immigrant votes. This meant that Republican power rested on a deep reservoir of suspicion about the character of Democrats, tainted with the blood of secession or carping voices of immigrant groups. The party's enemies often referred to its three R's, "Rum, Romanism, and Rebellion." Given these handicaps, few believed the party could tap into the mainstream of the American electorate and become a dynamic reform element. Drawing strength from third parties in American politics was a possibility, especially on the state level. In Nevada, Newlands had done as well as Bryan in luring third-party adherents into the ranks of Democrats in fusion movements. In most western states Democrats had to develop these tactics to forge majorities.

The spectacular development of Nevada mining placed the Democratic party in a stronger position than it could have hoped for ten years earlier. The population of the state by 1910 was 82,000, almost double the 42,000 in 1900. Practically a new electorate voted in the state by the end of the first decade in the new century. But it was an unstable, volatile electorate. The threat of a third party loomed with the rise of the Socialists. Uncertainty about this new electorate stirred the Newlands camp in Washington to carefully monitor all news from Nevada.

National issues also demanded attention. As he had earlier championed a bureau of corporations, now Newlands pressed for the national incorporation of interstate railroads. He laid out these plans in an article, "Common Sense of the Railroad Question," and at Roosevelt's request forwarded copies to the White House. When he returned to Washington in January, he felt it was "the psychological moment to press such legislation." He termed his plan the "nationalization of railroads," which to him did not mean ownership but management. Newlands saw opponents in both parties to his plan, but he believed it could be achieved with "the combined action of members of both parties to secure legislation just as it was required with reference to the nationalization of irrigation."[2]

Roosevelt was less inclined to speculate than was Newlands. For him, the immediate question in 1906 was how to enhance the powers of the Interstate Commerce Commission and overcome the weaknesses of the 1903 Elkins Act that had not prevented rate discriminations. A strong bureau of corporations directing national railroads could perform this function under the Newlands plan. But Newlands's proposal also raised the issue of local and state taxes on railroad property. Their abolishment in favor of a national tax on gross receipts to be redistributed to the states was preferable. This might entirely eliminate railroads from state politics. Newlands acknowledged that the railroad monopoly "has come in the course of natural evolution," and such monopoly "is inherent in our modern method of transportation"; it should now be welcomed and made legal through national incorporation. An arrangement with generous provisions for workers would end the constant agitation between railroad workers and their employees.

The Newlands proposals were radical. They would have rocked Congress had they come from the president. To supplant the private railroad system of the nation, although large and monopolistic, for a "national machine" essentially run by the government was completely beyond achievement. It took from early 1906 to late spring before the Hepburn bill emerged intact from both the House and Senate. It was an important part of the Roosevelt agenda for bringing railroads under effective government supervision. It also provided a model for other regulatory legislation promoting the national welfare. In the debates Newlands wanted more. He believed that there are but two propositions before the country: "either a complete control of the railroad system of the country by national incorporation or national ownership." The Roosevelt solution was one of government regulation and not of quasi-government ownership and certainly not nationalization.[3]

Newlands persisted in his belief that government could be a more positive force through ownership, but he held back from advocating it "because of the complexity of our government and its weakness in points of administration." He noted that the government was already in the construction business in four areas: improving harbors and rivers with engineers of the War Department; building the Panama Canal under a commission appointed by the president; constructing public buildings under the direction of the Treasury Department; constructing irrigation works under the direction of the Interior Department. He noted that the Geological Survey started the work of irrigation with a body of hydrographers, topographers, geologists, and hydraulic engineers to which were added construction engineers. "We did everything that legislation could do to make the Reclamation Service effective," declared Newlands, but the same had not been true for the improvement of harbors and rivers, the construction of the Panama Canal, and the erection of public buildings. He complained that river and harbor improvements and the construction of public buildings had been a matter of pork barrel politics among members of Congress. He looked to the correction of the system in the future by the establishment of commissions to receive appropriations and carry out projects in accordance with efficiently developed plans instead of the whims and deals struck in Congress.[4]

In Washington theory ran far ahead of practice, but in Nevada Newlands had to match theory with practice. True, there would be no legislative session in 1906, but the congressional elections were coming up and the party had to be put in order for the legislature of 1907 and his reelection campaign in 1908. His pronouncements about the Philippines, Santo Domingo, and the incorporation of railroads carried little weight in a Nevada undergoing its most hectic mining boom since the Comstock. Will Sharon's health required him to remain much of the winter and spring in San Francisco, causing Newlands to reach out for help from other members of the Democratic Central Committee.

Nevada politics challenged Newlands to become an outright political boss, but he disdained the role. Nevada revealed a poverty of political talent. Building a party structure required money upfront before people would step forward. No party pride, loyalty, tradition, or principle existed according to state Democratic party chairman Nate Roff. Even after the money was dispersed, loyalty could not be assured. Others believed that a number of so-called leaders stood between the people and political action. Many had no regard for the public interest, but simply desired to hold office or to make money out of politics.

Although he did not like to think of himself as a "slate maker," Newlands said he would not oppose Sparks's renomination for governor. If Newlands's counsels were to prevail he must, in the words of Nevada's longtime editor of the Carson City *Morning Appeal*, Sam Davis, "limber up" or more bluntly "pay up." Most always the news from Nevada said things looked good with the influx of the new mining population and workers in the irrigation project, but inevitably the message at the end of letters said "we have the fight of our lives on our hands" without lively candidates to inject cash into the campaign.[5]

On April 18, 1906, the San Francisco earthquake and fire struck an immediate blow at Newlands's cash reserves. Devastation in the city caused enormous losses to the Sharon estate. Insurance coverage, defaults, and even federal funding and supervision of the rebuilding of the city occupied Newlands in the weeks following the quake and fire that left 200,000 homeless and the business section of the city in charred rubble. In an article in the *Independent* barely a month after the earthquake, Newlands outlined the possibilities for federal aid to the city and the reform of its politics along progressive lines, such as the city of Galveston adopted after it experienced a destructive hurricane. Newlands's financial picture brightened when Yerington told him that D. O. Mills had authorized a V&T dividend of $50,000, payable to Newlands immediately.[6]

Fortunately for Newlands, despite the ominous reports from Democrats, the Republicans were ill prepared to fight. By August Yerington bemoaned the sorry state of the Republican opposition and believed that the Democrats would carry the state in the fall. Senator Nixon, perhaps because there was an unspoken agreement with Newlands that he would not build a serious Republican opposition to the senior senator, did little. In 1906 the Democrats won a six seat majority in the State Assembly and retained seven holdover state senators. This placed Newlands in a good position for the next elections in 1908. If the decision were confined entirely to the legislature, he could be confident of a second term. But as Newlands championed the will of the people in direct primaries, he pledged to follow the results of popular election and requested that the legislature do likewise.[7]

Newlands had high hopes and deep concerns about the 1907 Nevada legislature, both of which he explained to State Senator James T. Boyd. He hoped the legislature would fund the office of tax examiner as an aid to the State Revenue Board which could apply uniform tax assessments and result in "the equalization of burthens." Newlands also feared that the legislature would act intemperately and establish a rate-making commission. Although the Hepburn Act of 1906 was not everything that Newlands wished for, it did strengthen the hands of the Interstate Commerce Commission and committed the commission to deal with discriminatory rates. He believed Nevada could seek adequate redress without establishing its own state railroad commission. He worried that hasty action by the legislature with so much talk nationally about controlling railroads would bring the railroad back into Nevada's politics. He did not want the railroads "to collect a lobby at Carson and . . . dismember the Legislature." He saw the railroads in other states controlling both parties and felt that "instead of dominating the railroads, the railroads, with their immense resources and power, will dominate us." Moreover, "There is hardly a State Commission in any of the Western States that I know of that is not under the control of the railroads," he declared. But if the legislature wanted a commission, he recommended consulting the laws of Massachusetts, Texas, and Minnesota, the only states he knew in which railroad commissions had been of any service.[8]

The 1907 legislature did not act as Newlands hoped, but as he feared: it established a railroad commission. A railroad commission clearly worried V&T manager Yerington, but he believed that Newlands would have much influence with the commission. He told D. O. Mills that "we can get a reasonably fair freight tariff. . . ."

The Southern Pacific in northern Nevada was the largest line in the state with the Salt Lake and Los Angeles railroad having a line connecting those two cities through Las Vegas by 1905. The Southern Pacific determined to fight, and lawyers arrived to obtain an injunction against Nevada's Railway Commission. The Eureka & Palisade and Tonopah & Goldfield railways also brought suit. For Yerington, "the war is fairly on" and he felt that the roads were bound to win. He accordingly delayed the decision on the V&T rates until September, "for by that time the Court would decide as to its legality" and until that time the road could continue with its present tariffs. In court the railroad lawyers failed and the commission became a fixture of Nevada state administration until it was merged into the new Public Service Commission in 1912.[9]

On the reclamation front in Nevada, the Reclamation Service continued building ditches and dams at the Carson-Truckee site in the Lahontan Valley at Fallon and urged settlers to take up homesteads in the project. On much of this land Indian allotments already had been made, posing problems for the Reclamation Service's land distribution office. In an agreement signed between the Service and the Bureau of Indian Affairs, Indians near the Stillwater settlement were offered 10-acre reclamation farms. Nearly 350 persons signed trust deeds for irrigable farms. All of this occurred in exchange for reduced Indian claims to large portions of the irrigable acreage in the Lahontan Valley.[10]

In March 1907, President Roosevelt appointed an Inland Waterways Commission and asked Newlands to be a member. Newlands came to regard the commission as one of the most significant assignments in his career. Later he proposed major legislation to carry on centralized water planning and development, which he believed was the vision of the commission. He liked the president's proposal that it look to "broad considerations of National policy." The commission should consider "the full and orderly development and control of the river system of the United States. . . ." Up to now works to control waterways usually addressed a single purpose, "The time has come," declared the president, "for merging local projects and uses of the inland waters in a comprehensive plan designed for the benefit of the entire country." Roosevelt asked the commission to consider the relations of the streams to the use of all the great permanent natural resources and their conservation for the making and maintenance of prosperous homes.

Mid-May 1907 found Newlands and other members of the Inland Waterways Commission on the Mississippi River enroute to New Orleans. Afraid the trip would be seen as a junket, Newlands asked the *Nevada State Journal* to explain that he was involved in the work of the commission. "I am not simply away on pleasure. Those who are hostile to me take advantage to misrepresent every absence as proof of my non-identification with Nevada." Upon arrival in New Orleans on May 22, Newlands made a major speech on the future work of the commission in the absence of Chairman Burton to the Progressive Union Club. He emphasized the national legislation that was necessary regarding inland waterways and urged southern men to abandon their contention for

7. Newlands with members of the Inland Waterways Commission
on Lake Superior, Duluth, Minnesota, 1907. Photograph
courtesy of the Francis Griffith Newlands Papers, Manuscripts
and Archives, Yale University Library. Used by permission.

"state's rights" in matters clearly national in scope. After New Orleans
he found himself characterized in the national press as a "central-
izationist." The New York *Sun* declared: "President Roosevelt, Mr.
Bryan, Secretary Root, Senator LaFollette, and Senator Beveridge are a
most notable galaxy of centralizationists, but they are magnificently
eclipsed by Senator Newlands." The Washington *Post* described him in
similar terms. He protested to the *Post* that he believed in true Democracy. The people, he believed, would demand that more national
government power be exercised in the interest of the entire people,
"regardless of state lines." States'-rights men and Wall Street, he
predicted, will be the opponents of the exercise of national power out of
jealousy and economic selfishness.[11]

In Nevada the expansive mining developments in Tonopah and
Goldfield since 1901 and the beginnings of serious copper mining and
smelting near Ely in White Pine County ushered in a new era. The
threat of conflict was not between country and industry over water, but

between capital and labor over wages, working conditions, and union-ization. The workers in Nevada's twentieth-century boom carried a different mood than the laborers who went down into the depths of the Comstock thirty-five years earlier. Western hard-rock miners emerged from the depression of the 1890s with a new consciousness about their need to have power in order to fight the mine owners, who were in league with government to lower wages, neglect working conditions, and disallow the formation of labor unions. One expression of this new consciousness was the formation of the Western Federation of Miners in 1893.

The more radical Industrial Workers of the World (IWW), organized in Chicago in 1905, were also active in Nevada. Any labor dispute could easily call forth the reservoir of ill feeling in miners built up during years of repression in other states and fanned now by IWW labor doctrines. Nevada had escaped the labor strife of the 1890s principally because the industry was totally in decline, if not nonexistent. But with 50,000 new miners in the state after 1903, warnings about a Socialist third political party appeared ominous, considering the latent militancy in the labor force.

George Wingfield and George Nixon succeeded in organizing the Goldfield Consolidated Mining Company in 1905 after obtaining financial backing from eastern sources. They were heavily in debt. The company had to produce big profits. Put in this vulnerable position and facing a militant labor force, the ingredients of an explosive labor struggle leading to a dramatic showdown emerged.

Newlands, absorbed with politics and the impact of the San Francisco earthquake on estate finances, gave little attention in 1906 to a labor dispute in Goldfield between the well-organized Local 220 of the Western Federation of Miners and the company over working condi-tions. By the spring of 1907 there were general strikes and lockouts. Wingfield was instrumental in forming a local employers group, which met at the Montezuma Club, to combat labor, especially the IWW during a company lockout, aimed to rid the community of the IWW. Goldfield became virtually an armed camp, but negotiations put work-ers back on the job with concessions from both sides.

During August the company announced plans to crack down on the widespread and common practice of highgrading: workers taking rich ore rocks from the mines. This practice enraged Wingfield, who saw it as outright theft by miners of the highgrade ore. Local juries did not convict miners for the offense and merchants accepted the ore as a medium of exchange in the community. To end the practice the company introduced change rooms. The company instructed miners to place their street clothes in a locker in one room and walk in underwear to another room of lockers and put on their work clothes. In leaving work, they must reverse the process so that they would not have the opportunity of carrying ore unobserved. Infuriated, union members called a strike. A compromise agreement was reached, placing lockers side by side. Labor peace was being achieved through negotiations, but in November the financial panic of 1907 forced or encouraged companies to stop cash (gold money) wage payments. The company offered scrip that would be accepted in the local community. By voice vote, not written ballot, the work force voted to strike. The failure to take a written ballot violated the agreement between union and management that such would be taken before another strike could be called. There was little doubt that the written ballot would have produced the same results, but the mine owners seized this opportunity to charge that the strike was in violation of earlier agreements, if not illegal. In one important respect, the strike was welcomed by mine owners who no longer had to meet a payroll.[12]

What they did not welcome was the militant unionism in the labor force. The strike offered an opportunity to smash union power in Goldfield. The stakes were high and Wingfield, in a meeting with the governor on December 2, 1907, convinced Sparks to cooperate in plans for the destruction of unionism in Goldfield.

In most states this could be accomplished with the use of the state militia, but Nevada maintained no military organization. This meant that federal troops must somehow be brought into the state. What followed was an exchange of telegrams between Governor Sparks and President Roosevelt. First came an inquiry from the governor about under what circumstances he could request the aid of federal troops within the state. The president replied that the Constitution guaranteed protection of life and property and if a state could not provide this, then the state might request the intervention of federal troops. After this Governor Sparks requested troops to put down impending violence in Goldfield. On December 5, Roosevelt ordered two companies of troops from the San Francisco Presidio by rail to Goldfield.

Overnight, the Nevada political situation changed. Newlands's "model commonwealth" turned into an armed camp with troops behind Gatling guns keeping organized labor from attacking both property and scab labor, which arrived almost simultaneously with the troops. Sena-

tor Nixon, with an obvious conflict of interest as an owner of the
company, and Nevada Congressman George A. Bartlett supported the
call for troops. Newlands denied that he joined in the request. He did
join with Nixon and Bartlett on December 10 in requesting Roosevelt
to send representatives to Nevada for an investigation. Roosevelt
maintained that the troops were sent at the request of the governor, the
two senators, and the representatives. Newlands insisted that the
president mistook his requests for an interview, "that I wished to urge
the immediate sending of troops as requested by Governor Sparks." He
did not want to charge the president with "any intentional misstate-
ment." But Newlands did admit that, ". . . if I had seen him I would have
stated . . . that in my judgment an outbreak was imminent against which
the State authorities would be powerless. . . ." The acts of both the
governor and the president boded ill for the Democratic party in the
next election. Newlands had an awkward choice. He wanted neither to
offend labor votes nor the head of the Democratic party in Nevada, the
governor.[13]

The president sent a three-man commission to Goldfield made up of
Commissioner of Corporations Herbert Knox Smith, Assistant Secretary of Commerce and Labor Lawrence O. Murray, and Commissioner
of Labor Charles P. Neill. Their report, delivered by December 30,
virtually condemned the actions of the governor and made the president look embarrassingly imprudent. The report stated:

> no public intimation was given in Goldfield that troops had been asked
> for or were expected. Neither the county commissioners, the sheriff,
> nor the district attorney were consulted, nor had any one of them even
> a suspicion of the action which had been taken. The first news that the
> city had that it was in a condition of lawlessness and disorder, requiring
> the intervention of the federal government, was when the dispatches
> appeared in the papers that the troops had been called for and were
> then on their way to Goldfield.

"Honest" John Sparks did not appear so honest in the national press
when it told the Goldfield story. The big winner was Wingfield. His
gamble destroyed the union, made the governor the servant of the mine
owners, and duped the president of the United States. Wingfield
boasted, "the Western Federation of Miners are now eliminated from the
camp of Goldfield and always will be as long as I am identified with it."[14]

Where did all of this leave Newlands? As a Democrat he counted on
the labor vote in the upcoming election. Newlands realized that with
the president eager to extricate himself and federal troops from Nevada

that the state must assume the responsibility for law and order. The legislature must come into session and create an adequate law enforcement arm. Two days before the Presidential Commission's report, Newlands telegraphed Sparks insisting that the state organize its own peacekeeping force.[15]

Newlands's undoubted sympathy with capital and property reflected his social and economic status in society. But he would have been surprised if someone accused him of this because he believed his views also served the interests of labor. Foremost in his thinking was that a state police force could offer services in the interests of peace, harmony, and state-wide growth in mining, agriculture, or any other industry drawn to the New Nevada. Under pressure from Roosevelt and Newlands, Sparks capitulated and called a special session of the legislature. On January 27 the legislature approved a Nevada State Police Bill.[16]

Its form followed lines recommended by Newlands and was guided through the legislature by his supporters. By late February, a Nevada State Police force started replacing federal troops in Goldfield. If the entire affair had been avoided he could have looked forward to his reelection campaign more confidently. As it stood he could be attacked by the anti-police bill forces as a backer of capital and persecutor of labor and by Republicans for not coming immediately to the support of the call for federal troops. Mostly, he feared a group of Democratic legislators led by Assembly Speaker John Skaggs, who opposed any police bill. They could launch a splinter party that could cut into the regular Democratic vote. The Democratic party stood for the police bill and it might be roundly punished by labor in the upcoming election. There was also the slight possibility that Republicans might condemn the intervention and the Democratic police bill to win labor votes.[17]

To a great extent Newlands had played the intermediary throughout the entire affair. Governor Sparks grew increasingly aware, even though his judgment was impaired by alcoholism, that Newlands had saved him with both the president and the people. He would be solidly in the Newlands camp in the upcoming election, but the big question for Newlands was if he had saved the governor, had he in the process lost the labor vote? He hoped that he had saved himself.[18]

Nevada Republicans too faced the unknown. The events of December 1907 and January 1908 offered Republicans a chance to get rid of Newlands. A Republican, who might turn events to his advantage was Tasker Oddie, a young lawyer from New Jersey who came to Nevada to make his fortune. Oddie, already a legend, was only thirty-eight years old. He had made a fortune and lost it and was now "worse than broke." But as one of Newlands's observers in Nevada wrote, ". . . with the rapidity with which fortunes are made and lost in the southern portion of the state, one cannot tell three months ahead what the financial condition of one may or may not be, and this applies to Oddie more than to any other man in the state." By late February he believed that Oddie would be Newlands's Republican opposition in the senatorial election. His candidacy appeared very dangerous for Newlands. Aside from Oddie's personal charm and charisma, there were indications that the Southern Pacific Railroad saw him as a "very compliant man" and it was likely that he could obtain necessary campaign funds from railroad sources.[19]

On March 7, 1908, Oddie made public his candidacy for the Senate. He pictured himself as the miner's candidate who shared every miner's dream of striking it rich. He had done so once and lost it in further adventures. He was not afraid to take a gamble and risk all. He believed it important to speak out against Newlands's role in supporting the police bill against the hardworking union miners of Goldfield. But first he had to capture the Republican party leadership from Nixon. To Wingfield and the party's central committee chairman in Reno, P. L. Flanigan, Oddie's bid for the Senate was unthinkable. It would threaten not only their control of the state Republican party, but also of management control of labor in Goldfield. Newlands probably convinced the railroads to stick with the status quo policy in Nevada politics.[20]

The state political arena became more volatile when Governor Sparks died in June 1908. Suddenly, in the state's official grief over his death, even in the bungled Goldfield affair he assumed a dimension of statesmanship. If any Democrat was to be criticized Newlands was the proper object of scorn. This could hurt Newlands, if Goldfield became a major issue in the senatorial campaign. Only Oddie could raise this question. But this was not to occur. The *Nevada State Journal* reported that "when the heavy contributors were approached with Oddie's name and were asked to put in their usual little amount, they balked like a sheep in the snow and couldn't see Oddie at all." The sheep metaphor was a direct reference to state Republican leader, a sheep rancher and possible candidate for the nomination, Patrick L. Flanigan. A month later Oddie abandoned his candidacy. One newspaper simply explained, "Mr. Oddie found it impossible to make the campaign owing to pressing business reasons. . . ."[21]

Newlands must have watched with satisfaction the collapse of the

Oddie candidacy. The opposition would have to turn to a candidate whose position on the Goldfield incident and the police bill was more vulnerable to labor attack than his own. At the Republican state convention at Goldfield in August, Patrick Flanigan received the Republican nomination for the fall senatorial elections. Newlands joined with Flanigan in an agreement to submit the senatorial election to popular election with the legislature pledged to honor the choice of the voters. A direct primary law went into effect in 1910 for state elective offices. The fall senatorial battle early on assumed the traditional mode of two wealthy men opposing one another for a Nevada senatorial position, but neither, much to the relief of the Newlands forces, chose to make the election a referendum on the Goldfield settlement.[22]

But events in the southern mining camps demanded a watchful eye. Would a socialist party emerge or, more dangerous, would William Randolph Hearst see opportunity for his Independence League movement to make a splash in the state and before the national audience that had followed the events in Goldfield? The first indications that Hearst would enter the fray in Nevada came when the Sparks *Forum* attacked Democrats with the headlines: "Democrats Desert Workingmen, Labor Left without Political Affiliation." Without the Democratic party workingmen were left as "helpless prey to the plotting money class" whom the Republicans always championed. Two days later Hearst's San Francisco *Examiner* stated that the "Independence party is the hope of the honest voters of Nevada to break the combination which long is alleged to have existed between the Republican Senator Nixon and the Democratic Senator Newlands."[23]

In the following weeks the Newlands forces took countermeasures by buying up hostile papers. The Sparks *Forum* suddenly became a pro-Democratic sheet, receiving almost $1,000 from Newlands's campaign fund. No Hearst candidate stepped forward. Apparently Hearst did not wish to buy into the Nevada campaign to this extent simply to play the role of spoiler. Oddie remained in the shadows, suggesting that Hearst did not make the type of serious effort in Nevada that could have brought a man of his talents back into the running. Newlands breathed easier about the Hearst threat.[24]

Hearst's reference to the Newlands-Nixon combine in Nevada did touch a sensitive nerve in Nevada's political structure, with personal relationships forming the underlying and real structure of politics rather than party or ideology. Certainly Senator Nixon could not have been ardently committed to the defeat of Newlands, although on the surface he played a loyal party role by supporting the Flanigan candidacy. In his few appearances in the campaign, he always prefaced his remarks with, "No one has any higher regard personally for Senator Newlands, . . . " and then moved on to discuss the need for more Republicans in Congress. The tacitly understood nonpartisan arrangement between the two Nevada senators was no particular secret, as the San Francisco *Examiner* noted.[25]

Flanigan's campaign against Newlands became a comedy of errors. He claimed to be loyal to Roosevelt but he was a member of the unprogressive majority of the Republican party. The Republicans assailed Newlands as a carpetbagger who wore clothing made in England and detested the smell of sagebrush. Cartoons appeared to this effect, much like the cartoons Stewart had published in the late 1890s, characterizing Newlands as an un-Nevada-like effete English aristocrat. In addition the party hired the services of Thomas Fitch, an aging congressman. As a seasoned politician Fitch realized that Flanigan was going nowhere unless he could seize the labor vote by opposing Newlands's role in the passage of the police bill. Without warning, in an introduction of Flanigan in Goldfield, he let loose an attack that scorned the police bill and Newlands's support of it, imploring the house of labor in Nevada to return to the Republican party. Flanigan, almost speechless when he rose to speak, tried to undo the thrust of the Fitch remarks. Two days later the Republican Reno *Evening Gazette* announced:

> The Republican party in Nevada stands for law and order, and it has placed itself squarely on record as being in favor of the police bill. Fitch, in his speech at Goldfield a few nights ago, denounced that measure, and that speech was the last one he will ever deliver under the auspices of the Republican committee. . . . [26]

In contrast the Newlands campaign delivered hard hitting consistent messages about Democratic accomplishments in Nevada. Newlands spoke throughout the state recalling his previous campaigns and joined in the planned revelry at the saloons to assure voters of his strong ties with Nevadans. His speeches emphasized that the Democratic party possessed an impressive record of Progressive legislation, including an eight-hour-day law and an Employers Liability Act. He said, "We have declared that the great public corporations are public servants subject to public regulation"; reduced taxation; had passed an irrigation law giving the Reclamation Service encouragement to build Nevada projects; and finally, the power of the Southern Pacific Railroad had been bridled in this period of reform and "the State has been free from corporate interference in the control of its politics. No corporation and no special interest has ever contributed during that time one dollar or one ounce of effort to the Democratic cause...."[27]

On national issues he hammered away at the further development of water resources. Newlands emerged as the leading voice that mapped new directions in natural resource policies. He addressed one of his favorite topics: the development of American waterways. He wanted the nation to develop comprehensive plans for the development of natural resources relating to water, "with the primary purpose of facilitating water transportation." The plan should embrace the treatment of forests, the irrigation of arid lands, reclamation of swamp lands, bank protection, and clarification of rivers. This would make available hydroelectric power and flood control that would make possible the tillage of more productive land. Through inland waterways projects and canals, Maine could be connected to Texas and Texas to the Great Lakes. Also, rail transportation must be coordinated with water transportation. As in the building of the Panama Canal and the creation of the Reclamation Service, Congress should give this work over to an independent administration and avoid the inefficiency that had marked work authorized by the perennial rivers and harbors legislation in Congress. The development of an Inland Waterways Commission remained a passion of Newlands's public career until his death amid the turmoil of World War I.[28]

The Newlands organization gave every sign of delivering a victory for the senator in November. Flanigan's campaign was in shambles after Fitch's misstatements and dismissal from the Republican campaign trail.[29] Then came a bombshell. On October 29 the Republican mouthpiece, Goldfield *Tribune*, blared:

SENATOR NEWLANDS A.P.A. ATTACK ... CALLING FOR FLANIGAN'S DEFEAT BECAUSE HE IS A CATHOLIC

The story reported that thousands of bills were in the mail and being handed out in Reno declaring that Patrick L. Flanigan was unfit to be a U.S. Senator because of his Roman Catholic religious beliefs. They called for all non-Catholics to vote for Newlands. The paper said Catholics and non-Catholics deplored this tactic and intended to vote for Flanigan in reprisal. It was a last-minute attempt to smear the Newlands campaign and deny him the large number of Irish and Italian votes.

Newlands's supporters moved swiftly against it. In Goldfield, H. A. Dunn, editor of the Goldfield *Chronicle*, saw Father J. B. Dermody of that town, who was also convinced that the handbills were a political dirty trick. He gave the *Chronicle* a statement deploring these attacks against Newlands and praising Newlands's character and broadmindedness. On November 3, Newlands walked away with the election. He received 12,473 votes to Flanigan's 8,972 and the Socialist candidate, T. C. Lutz, received 1,389.[30] Never again would Newlands receive such a decisive majority in a Nevada election. It was a testimony to his and Will Sharon's attention to detail in building their political network throughout Nevada based on prominent editors and loyal individuals who responded to Newlands's leadership and liberal spending. The Newlands press admitted "he hated the smell of sagebrush" as the opposition charged, but the Newlands press asserted this caused him to work all the harder for reclamation in order "to make the desert of Nevada bloom and bear as a fertile valley."[31] The $45,000 campaign budget of the Democratic State Central Committee came almost entirely from Newlands. Publicity costs to newspapers totaled $11,000. Newlands could congratulate himself on the local campaign and take satisfaction from the national attention he had gained by speaking out on prominent issues of the time from his now secure position in the Senate. He had traveled well the road to power, security, and influence.[32]

XI

RACISM AND REFORM

Newlands made the race issue into a special political hobbyhorse. He rode it repeatedly, weaving it into his general views on the future of American political culture. Like many Progressives in both political parties who espoused political democracy, he believed in the exclusion of nonwhite people from the political process. In Newlands's view the modern Democratic party should seek to disfranchise African Americans in the interests of efficient, workable government. As were many educated Americans of his era, Newlands was heavily influenced by popular social theories that saw the American future in terms of whites only.[1]

Excluding nonwhites from the political process was, in Newlands's view, essential to making the Democratic party progressive and modern. The bridge between Newlands's progressivism and racial policies rested on his view that nonwhites had no aptitude for democracy. As a result of racial diversity in society Newlands saw complications: industrial disturbance, and hostility repugnant to the efficient, modern state. Therefore the national government should restrict immigration on the foreign front and eliminate black men from the domestic political process. Newlands openly called for a repeal of the Fifteenth Amendment to the Constitution and sought a plank favoring the elimination of black suffrage in the Democratic National Platform of 1912. In a preliminary draft of a disfranchisement resolution Newlands termed the Fifteenth Amendment "poison in the Constitution" and called for its repeal.

Newlands's statements demonstrate a link between western and southern Progressivism. Progressive Senator John T. Morgan of Alabama, defending the disfranchisement sections of the 1900 Louisiana constitution, stated: "It is not necessary to go into the details of history to establish the great fact that Negro suffrage in Louisiana and other southern states has been one unbroken line of political, social, and industrial obstruction to progress, and a constant disturbance of the peace in a vast region of the United States." Newlands believed southern idealism could shine forth if national policies removed blacks from the political process.[2]

In the same breath that Newlands spoke of "a national negro policy," he swiped at unrestricted Asian immigration. This was a sore point because the press never let Newlands forget that the Sharon estate had employed Chinese labor. Asian immigration was far more relevant to Newlands's political career than black suffrage, which was hardly of concern to Nevadans. Still he could not resist it.

His service on the Senate Committee for the District of Columbia with its large black population and his roots in the old-time Democratic party pushed him forward. But his policies toward African Americans reinforced his Progressive ambition to streamline democratic government, to free it from tensions, and to promote its efficient operation. Still, some charged that his purpose was entirely political; that he intended to fuse the anti-Oriental West with the anti-black South in the cause of white supremacy for a presidential bid. Publicly Newlands rejected the idea as far-fetched: Nevada presented a weak springboard for any presidential candidate no matter how popular his national views.[3]

Newlands fitted in well with a coterie of other West Coast Progressives such as Hiram Johnson, James D. Phelan, and Chester H. Rowell who believed that government in the twentieth century was for white men only. For Newlands, one way to open the doors to reform was to ban nonwhites in government. One authority has emphasized that in the Far West and South "reform thinking accommodated itself to race-thinking." In Newlands's case "reform thinking" not only accommodated itself to race-thinking, but partially inspired it.[4]

Newlands's position on the Senate Committee for the District of Columbia gave him the opportunity to influence the education of African American children. Predictably, he advocated training for manual service occupations: "My idea," he said, "is that the District of Columbia should furnish a model system to all the southern states for the training of colored children." Booker T. Washington, president of Tuskegee Institute, much to the disgust of northern black intellectuals such as W. E. B. DuBois, espoused similar ideas.

Like others of his generation and reinforced by an emerging school of southern historians who romanticized plantation life, Newlands proposed an educational system to substitute for the discipline that the plantation had once demanded of slaves in the antebellum South.

"Under the old system of slavery," he reasoned, "every plantation was a training school, in which discipline was maintained. The colored race has lost this training, and no adequate training has been substituted for it." The best education for "an inferior race," he argued, was training in industrial trades. The practical training schools in the District of Columbia would fit "colored children with their present intelligence" to the proper vocations. From his position on the Senate's Committee for the District of Columbia he continued to offer advice on the course of black education for the District and the nation until his death.[5]

The Atlanta *Constitution* complimented him on his "familiarity with the race problem as it exists today in the south." The paper said Newlands's system of education for the District of Columbia was identical to its remedy for "solving the domestic servant problem, and partially, the industrial labor problem," and concluded, "It is encouraging that the exigencies of the situation, as they actually exist are being recognized by men of influence outside of the southern states."

As Newlands spoke out on African American education, California's anti-Japanese movement received national attention because of the San Francisco school board's attempt to institute a segregated school system. The state also attempted to deny aliens land ownership. The protests by Japan against what it considered discrimination prompted President Roosevelt to pressure California to ease the anti-Japanese policies.

Nevada's 1909 legislature moved to pass resolutions in support of California's right "to enact such stringent measures as will absolutely stop forthwith the encroachment of the Japanese." President Roosevelt called Nevada's senators to the White House, hoping they could influence their legislature not to issue inflammatory statements about Japan. Strong resolutions from Nevada, the president feared, would encourage Californians "to take drastic measures." After the conference, Senator Nixon telegraphed the president of the Nevada senate and speaker of the assembly that "the very object of the resolution may be injured by radical action at this time."[6]

Senator Newlands took similar action in a long letter to Nevada Governor Denver Dickerson. He suggested a plan of action to preserve friendship between Japan and the United States but would "mark clearly our purpose to maintain this country as the home of the white race. . . ." He chided the legislature for its threats, which would be ineffective and possibly harmful. The surplus of all peoples must be stopped from coming to the United States, said Newlands. Such a

policy would not offend the Japanese. A declaration must come from
the federal government and through "statutory enactment that it would
not tolerate further race complications." He pronounced, "Our country,
by law to take effect after the expiration of existing treaties, should
prevent the immigration into this country of all peoples other than those
of the white race. . . ."

Japanese exclusion revealed only one side of Newlands's overall
racial policies. He declared the race issue to be "the most important
question confronting the Nation." On the "Negro Question," he reas-
serted his belief that the nation had "drifted regarding the black race
into a condition which seriously suggests the withdrawal of the political
rights heretofore mistakenly granted. . . ." He had for three years urged
"a humane national policy which, with the cooperation and aid of the
southern states, would recognize that the blacks are a race of children
requiring guidance, industrial training and development of self-control.
. . ." His plan was aimed at reducing "the danger of race complication
formerly regional, but now becoming national."[7]

Southern newspapers saw Newlands's statement and his subsequent
press releases as a move toward a national race-purity policy, since he
had said the race question was not regional but national. The Atlanta
Constitution of February 9, 1909, believed that Newlands's statements
suggested an alliance between the South and the West on the race issue.
"The overtures of Senator Newlands of Nevada, indicate that the anti-
Jap west is yearning to have the anti-Negro south pull the exclusion
chestnuts out of the fire for it," the Atlanta paper concluded, but at the
same time refused to accept that the racial problems on the West Coast
were comparable to the southern racial crisis. The Macon *Telegraph*
welcomed Newlands's statements as a sign of a growing "bond of
sympathy with the West." It congratulated Newlands's "sane policy"
with regard to the Japanese question: "it has opened the eyes of the
West to the necessity of race integrity and purity in which the South has
so vital an interest."

Some westerners were not as concerned with creating a sectional
alliance on the race issue as they were with making the anti-Japanese
movement "respectable." Senator Newlands served this purpose, according to the Santa Cruz *Sentinel*, and it applauded his letter to the
Nevada governor not because of its service in forming a national race
policy, but because the letter outlined a reasonable argument against
Asiatic immigration. The paper added that he presented the problem
without "that sensationalism in which writers who discuss the 'yellow

peril' are wont to indulge." Newlands warned, "the brown races of Asia would quickly settle up and take possession of our entire coast and intermountain region." The *Sentinel* insisted that Newlands was no rabble-rouser who appealed to marauding street crowds, and it declared, "This is not sand-lotism." Rather, his statements reflected truths "that are fully recognized by most persons who have studied the race question in general, and especially on the Pacific Coast, where it has phases that are almost unknown in other parts of the country." His statements, the paper suggested, were the opinions of an informed expert and not a political opportunist.

Newlands's racism was respectable whereas lower-class "sand-lotism," which combined anti-Asian agitation with attacks on capitalism, was not. His respectable racism, Newlands argued, sought to preserve, strengthen, and equip American society for the challenges of the twentieth century. An old-line Republican paper, the Washington *Bee*, classified Newlands with southern politicians whose chief whipping-boy and claim to fame was their persecution of African Americans. Newlands was compared to "the old Southern Cracker" who by tradition took "the Negro as his text." Newlands may not have appreciated the comparison, but in the opinion of the *Bee* he ranked alongside Senator Benjamin Tillman of South Carolina and James Vardaman of Mississippi as demagogic racists.[8]

In 1912, Newlands spoke of denying the vote only to unborn blacks to avoid "the appearance of injustice." He continually argued that the black's "sudden transformation from slaves to 'sovereigns' as the greatest cruelty that could be inflicted upon them, as well as the whites." "Freedom," he said, "was a right; suffrage was a privilege." By denying this privilege the nation and the states could cooperate "for the real—not the sham—betterment of this unfortunate race."[9]

As the movement to prevent nonwhite aliens, principally Japanese, from owning land gained popularity among Progressives in California by 1913, Newlands commented that, "We should confer citizenship upon no one but people of the white race" and "we should write the word white into our constitution." In 1916, just one year before his death, Newlands was asked to give his views on the life and work of Booker T. Washington. He warned, sensing even by this time the archaicness of his position, that "True humanity to the negro demands today that the right of suffrage in this country should be limited to the white race." If blacks should later "insist upon participating in the government," because of their development, this would present a difficulty that could be met by transporting these people in a humane manner to African soil where they could enjoy political rights. "But the only sure development of the black race in this country depends not upon the grant of political rights but their denial."[10]

Newlands's views reflect not only his devotion to white supremacy and the popular racial myths of the day but also demonstrate how the political, social, and intellectual currents afoot in America affected racial ideas.[11] He believed that he stood for progress and that his racial policies were an expression of his Progressive program. They reflected confidence in both material and social engineering schemes. If the reclamation engineers could successfully bring water to the Nevada desert, proper Progressive legislation could also engineer a viable and homogeneous society, avoiding the costs and complications of racial and cultural diversity.

Newlands, fresh from his victory in the senatorial election of 1908, moved aggressively to set what amounted to a Progressive agenda for the state and hoped that 1909 would see a "banner legislature."[12]

While he used the word "Progressive," he stuck to identifying his program with the Democratic party and the prospects of "good government." The party's support of the referendum, first passed in 1903, and its support of a constitutional amendment for the initiative and the recall demonstrated the party's commitment to "government by the people." He supported easier methods for amending the constitution, especially to ward off the possibility of a constitutional convention that might put into the constitution an entire code of laws, as in the case of Oklahoma. He called for increased compensation for legislators and deplored the fact that there were no lawyers in the legislature because they could not afford it. The governor needed at least an $8,000 salary. Adequate compensation for elected officials opened officeholding to a wider number of people in a democracy. Newlands recommended the legislature create a Wisconsin style legislative reference bureau "to keep in touch with current movement for progressive legislation. . . ." He also called for more sweeping powers for Nevada's governor because the public was generally accepting the view "that the proper service of the people demands the concentration, and not a division of responsibility, and that the Governor of a State should be charged with full responsibility in order that he may render a just account to the people for his service without being compelled to plead as an excuse for bad government that, owing to the division of executive power, the responsibility rests upon others rather than upon himself."[13]

Several of Newlands's suggestions came to pass in 1909, but not all. The legislature did become involved in a highly controversial move supported by Reno progressives to make gambling illegal. The press, the Protestant church community, and the professional community, including the University of Nevada, combined to urge the legislature to remove this blot on the state's character. Under these influences, the legislature passed one of the strongest antigambling laws in the nation. Although Newlands does not appear directly involved in the passage of the measure, after the session he noted that a bipartisan opposition to gambling was the best approach. Clearly he feared alienating the saloon crowd, where gambling was popular, from the Democratic party and himself. He wanted the question out of politics, "for it would prove a most disturbing element, and I do not see how any one could profit by bringing it into politics." By 1913 Newlands did speak against weakening the antigambling bill and retreating from the high moral position taken by the 1909 legislature.[14]

Newlands also had an agenda, which included conservation, the proper integration of large corporations into American institutions, and the modernization of the Democratic party. Increasingly he voiced interest in the multifaceted nature of the conservation movement and the far-reaching implications of the Rivers and Harbors Commission in the multipurpose river development schemes.[15]

Giant strides had already been taken in the bureaucratization of major resources on public lands in terms of forests and range, and Newlands hoped for further achievements in land, water, and mineral policy. Because Nevada welcomed federal reclamation, it appeared pro-conservationist at a time when other states complained of thralldom under the federal yoke. It even welcomed the establishment of National Forests after 1906 for watershed and grazing controls that from the view point of local cattle ranchers excluded sheep. Newlands did not live long enough to witness the growth of a deep-seated opposition to federal conservation agencies. Already the Cattle and Wool Growers Associations and the Elko Chamber of Commerce protested proposals by Chief Forester Gifford Pinchot that land leasing programs occur outside National Forests. By 1914 Newlands conveniently supported state control of public grazing lands and took pride in the completion of Lahontan Dam and Reservoir on the Carson River.[16]

On water issues Newlands endorsed multiple purpose dam building for irrigation, water power development, and flood control. But, like fellow conservationist Pinchot, he believed that government encouragement should be coupled with rate-making and rules to prevent water power monopoly. Northern Nevada's Truckee-Carson Irrigation Project faced some embarrassing problems. Engineers overestimated the number of farmers the project could accommodate, soils proved too alkaline, with drainage problems, and water rights on the Truckee and Carson were not secure in the face of upstream demands. There was also objection among project settlers over the 160-acre restriction on individual land ownership. Some charged that the Reclamation Service under the direction of Frederick Newell was an arrogant bureaucracy that pursued its own interests rather than protecting the welfare of settlers. They denounced the idea that their farms should simply produce "a living." They asked: "Will a national government ask that men abandon home, and friends, and go into another newer land, and upon a conquest of a virgin prairies, toil for its development for a mere living?" These restrictions flew in the face of "the pure and typical American, the man of pluck, of energy, of resources, and, if you please, of speculative tendencies." The Reclamation Service shot back with counterarguments, but theorizing engineers and experts left settlers bereft of enthusiasm. As the Service under Newell's leadership waged a campaign against these criticisms, he told Newlands, "every opportunity should be seized to educate the public along important lines."[17]

Newlands knew full well the problems faced by Nevada's irrigation project. Still, he felt the Truckee-Carson project reflected all the hopes and goals of national conservationism. To achieve these hopes, cooperation of the nation, states, municipalities, corporations, and individuals must occur. This policy required the national government to take the lead. On navigable rivers the power of the national government was supreme. He believed it could "do anything in the way of irrigation, forestry, prevention of soil waste, and reclamation of swamp lands, that will aid in maintaining an equal flow of the river, in preventing obstructions, and in promoting navigation." This power, he said, extended to the remotest sources of a navigable river.

But in his view the Truckee and Carson Rivers were neither navigable nor tributary to navigable rivers. With these rivers the power of the national government rested "upon its ownership of the public domain and its right to prepare it for settlement by the scientific utilization of waters which would otherwise go to waste. . . ." There was no doubt in his mind, as he told President Taft: "the nation has the constitutional power, in the construction of its irrigation works, to develop water power and utilize it by sale, rental, or otherwise in such

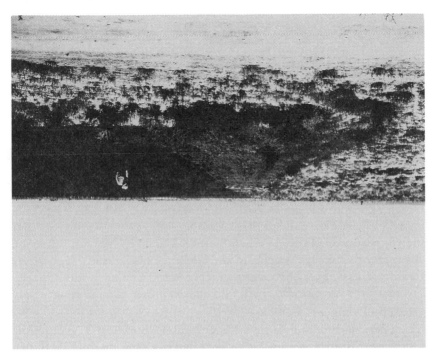

8. The irrigated land in the Newlands Project raises alfalfa while the non-irrigated land barely supports sage brush. Photograph courtesy of the Nevada Historical Society. Used by permission.

a way as to reduce the cost of irrigation." The building of such dams could be seen as a part of the conservation policy and should be included in the comprehensive plans. Irrigation and power development should "fit into the ultimate development of these rivers for every civilized use" including the conservation of forests as the sources of water supply, and the storage of the waters for power, irrigation, and flood control.

The creation of hydroelectric power raised the complicated question of government versus private power development. Newlands's first thought was how to protect the public from oppressive charges: "These works will necessarily be monopolistic in character and we must have either a governmental monopoly or a private monopoly."

This posed a problem. The national government could not regulate intrastate companies that were outside of the flow of interstate commerce. Nevada had no commission to regulate a powerful private monopoly. Inevitably, these great works would require a public service commission manned by men of ability and character. Newlands did not emerge as a single-minded advocate of public power. He desired to accommodate the interests of private corporations, if they could be properly regulated by public commissions. By 1910 the concept of the public utilities regulatory commission became a prominent element in his progressive rhetoric.[18]

Nevada in 1910 faced its first gubernatorial election where Progressivism was an issue. Newlands himself asserted: "Insurgency is in the air." He urged Nevada Democrats to recognize that Progressives were making headway in both parties and the party that could convince the voters of its Progressivism would win the election. He believed that Progressives could all unite in the Democratic party, if Democrats could present a Progressive ticket that reflected their accomplishments since they took control of the state. Under the Democrats Nevada surpassed all other states except Wisconsin and Oregon in Progressive legislation. California was lagging in comparison. He noted that even the Republican platform promised to maintain the Railroad Commission established by Democrats in 1907.

But Nevada's politics were still personal. Republican Tasker Oddie waged a low-budget campaign for governor from his automobile traveling throughout the state, proclaiming his Progressivism and identifying with the working miner. Democrat Denver Dickerson went down to defeat, believing Newlands had not done enough to squelch factionalism in the party. There was also a lingering suspicion that his close ties to George Nixon dampened his enthusiasm for the challenge of Democrat Key Pittman for the Senate seat. The Democrats, however, still controlled the legislature and Newlands kept his lines of communication open.[19]

No matter how distinguished his national reputation as a Progressive, he still represented the desolate stretches of Nevada—a state that could barely support a population of 80,000 as the Tonopah-Goldfield mining boom declined. He emphasized the growing Progressive record of Nevada and occasionally embellished it.

Meanwhile, he continued to identify himself with major issues of the day, urging cautious reform that led to the greater authority of the national government. There were issues on which he resisted centralization, when it worked against local interests. He feared uncontrolled centralization of banking because it drained the country's banks of capital and made them subject to demands they could not immediately meet. He took exception to the Postal Savings Banks on this same ground. The real purpose of the Postal Savings Bill, he said, was to "coax money from the pockets of the wage-earning class, and particularly laborers of foreign birth who are accustomed to paternalism in Government." Once in the postal depository the funds would go to local banks, from where they would go to the great banking centers to be used for promotion, speculation, and floating large issues of watered securities. All this only served "exaggerated fortunes that were the characteristic of our times," he said. This was prostituting the thrift among wage-earners "to a base commercial use."

He was convinced that ever since the financial crises of 1893, the goal of the Republican party was not to the security of bank depositors, but the promotion of speculation by the withdrawal of money from the country to the great financial centers. The Postal Savings Bill, even though deposits were guaranteed by the government, was another example of this. From the vantage of 1910 he did not expect banking reform to come soon because "the great interests have too firm a control upon the leading committees of Congress to promise hope."[20]

According to a contemporary in the Senate, Charles S. Thomas of Colorado, Newlands viewed himself, his role in the Senate, as well as his social position with a high degree of seriousness. His life, according to Thomas, he believed was about great work and to the future of the nation as it moved into the new century. Thomas termed him "a very prosy and indifferent speaker and when he took the floor the galleries soon emptied and senators retired to their cloakrooms. If he felt insulted he did not reveal the fact. Perhaps it was obtuseness," recalled Senator Thomas. "Time was of no consequence to him when holding forth to a deserted Senate." He had the habit of speaking just as the Senate was ready to vote on a bill. He hammered away for hours on the themes of conservationism, cooperation, and correlation of the various government bureaus to be charged with these duties. His speeches appeared in pamphlet form for distribution, but it was the guess of his colleague that few if anyone read them because they were so long and involved. Yet many westerners agreed that the subjects he spoke on were noteworthy and were a call for government action in the field of resource development and protection.[21]

Newlands's private secretary, Millard F. Hudson, was also critical of his elaborate speeches to Congress. Newlands, asserted Hudson, should quit devoting so much time to Congress and channel his energies outside of it. He should understand that Congress was really not a deliberative body and that he could not make it into one. Cynically Hudson said, "It is today unless I greatly err, just as much of a huckster-shop as the day you entered it." Furthermore, since Newlands had few electoral votes to offer and served no great business enterprise, he had nothing to sell in Congress and he could not be bought. Without these qualities his influence was limited. Hudson believed the passage of the reclamation law "merely a fluke." He could not foresee a Democrat or an Insurgent Republican being permitted to sponsor such legislation of importance. He saw no hope of an alliance with the Insurgents. They were only friendly because they needed help, but "They are partisans, like the others," he warned.

Hudson urged Newlands to emulate Senator LaFollette's example and go to the people. He told Newlands that his most effective addresses were those made outside of Congress. Newlands should "accept every opportunity possible, and never hesitate to leave Washington for the purpose." He should be like other Democratic senators who had long ceased to expect the passage of important legislation. He might push a bill for national incorporation through a committee, but the Senate would never seriously consider it. Newlands should realize the truth that Senator Nixon spoke when he asserted before the voters that only a Republican can accomplish anything in Congress. Newlands should go more directly to the people who in turn can pressure Congress into passing "advanced" legislation. Hudson endorsed a plan to write a book describing the changes and reforms Newlands had worked for since he came to Washington in 1893. It is difficult to assess the impact of Hudson's candor.[22]

The year 1912 was a presidential election year. The era of the Bryan candidacies had passed and the party faced a crossroad. Newlands feared the influence of the conservative wing of the party. In his opinion, by the end of 1910 "the great interests" planned to control the candidates of both parties in 1912. Already they were discrediting Roosevelt as they had previously attacked Bryan. The people, he believed, demanded Progressive legislation and they would cross party lines to obtain it. At this point, however, there was a great distrust of the Democratic party. Newlands frankly told Charles Bryan that his brother William Jennings could not be elected, just as Roosevelt would not be able to be elected again. Other Democrats also did not inspire confidence. Newlands came to the conclusion that "the one man outside of Mr. Bryan who today has opportunity, the talent, the genius, and the disposition to constitute himself a national voice is Woodrow Wilson."

Newlands urged Progressive Democrats to bide their time before choosing a candidate and to lay out certain Progressive principles against which prospective candidates could be tested. State Democratic organizations should concentrate on party organization and orientation toward Progressivism, thereby assuring the public that the Democratic party stood for gradual reform that would not involve violent business adjustments. A group within the party committed to Progressive measures might ultimately select "not only the most progressive but the most available candidate."[23]

Newlands himself received invitations to bid for the nomination. William C. Liller, president of the National Democratic League of Clubs, urged him to get in the race with others, to which he replied that, "Should my record regarding the constructive and administrative policies result in any demand for my candidacy, it will be time enough to consider the matter." Later his replies became more negative, noting that the party would not "go so far west or to so small a State for a candidate," as he put it to Walter Hines Page. He expressed surprise that suggestions for his candidacy for the presidency started among eastern newspapers, "where it would have seemed that my chief difficulty would lie." Newlands did believe that the Pacific Coast and intermountain states should maintain a solidarity in every presidential contest. He wrote Clay Tallman, chairman of the Nevada Democratic Central Committee, "I am, therefore, not discouraging the movement, and if it takes any considerable proportions I may avail myself of it."[24]

In 1910 Newlands was criticized for failing to support conservation measures in the eastern states. At issue was the Weeks bill, which authorized the government to buy watershed lands in the eastern states and exercise the same protection of them that it provided for government forests in the West. The bill failed in the Senate principally because of a filibuster led by Newlands. Newlands opposed the bill because it did not go far enough in applying the conservation policy. To him this meant "the development of rivers for every useful purpose," including protection of forested watershed, the use of flood waters for irrigation of arid lands, the protection of the lowlands against the floods below, the intermediate development of water power, and the promotion of navigation. All of this meant the development "of our waterways for every useful purpose to which civilization can put them," including also teamwork on the part of the various scientific services. The bill did not meet these goals. "I am," he said, "for big plans, big work, big experts and constructors, and big powers." But he was against pork barrel and piece-meal legislation. The Weeks bill only provided for the purchase of forests and had no provision whatever relating to the real promotion of navigation. Newlands sought to add a major feature like the creation of a conservation commission to command overall planning and direction.

He did not characterize his opposition to the bill as a "filibuster" but rather honest debate in which these broader issues could be discussed. He contended the purpose of "the Appalachian and White Mountain bill" was to protect and enlarge the existing water power development, a subject which does not come within the jurisdiction of the nation. The following year Gifford Pinchot wrote Newlands asking him not to oppose the bill if it did not include a conservation commission. Pinchot was much in favor of a commission but he did not want to see the Weeks bill defeated because of that omission. Newlands relented and the bill passed in 1911.[25]

Newlands and wife Edith departed for Europe on August 22, 1911, aboard the *Crown Princess Cecelia* in this age of luxury liner steamship service across the Atlantic. Their visit lasted into October, while the jockeying for presidential nominations took shape at home. Fellow Democrat Franklin K. Lane of California, who had earlier urged Newlands's name upon the Sacramento *Bee* as a possible presidential nominee, kept Newlands apprised of the maneuverings of the various candidates. Clearly Democrats sensed opportunity as Taft faltered in the face of Roosevelt's grassroots campaign for the Republican nomination. Lane detected insurgency among Republicans throughout the West and even a breakdown in party loyalty as voters sought more Progressive candidates. Old-line Republican newspapers threatened to bolt the party if Taft again received the nomination. Lane expected Taft's renomination, but only after a desperate fight in the convention that would leave the party weakened. The prospect, he believed, was favorable to Woodrow Wilson on the Democratic side.

California and Washington, Lane asserted, were leaning toward Wilson, but the rise of Missourian Champ Clark's candidacy presented a serious threat to Wilson in the Midwest and the South. Clark's strength, according to Lane, was that the House of Representatives under his leadership acted sanely during the last session. It remained to be seen whether Hearst would create enough of a following in the western states to give himself leverage that he might eventually throw to Clark. Bryan, Lane acknowledged, would loom large in the convention, but he was convinced that Bryan did not have a veto over the convention even with his large personal following. Wilson's recent denunciation of the money trust surely endeared him to Bryan, but Wilson's attitude was aloof to the point of his refusal "to do as much as write a letter to those who ask his guidance or direction in the matter of making a campaign for him." Lane as well as Newlands's sympathies were with Wilson. Newlands correspondence with Wilson became more frequent at the beginning of 1912.[26]

A month before the Democratic convention Newlands's political future in Nevada was clouded by the death of Senator George Nixon. Newlands accompanied the body home for the funeral in Reno. The trip removed him for the moment from the presidential politics in the East and made him look more carefully at the growing dangers to his own political base in Nevada. George Wingfield, business partner of Nixon, had recently declared himself a Republican. Republican Governor Tasker Oddie offered the empty Senate seat to the thirty-six-year-old Reno millionaire. All of this pointed to a revitalization of the Republican party. Much to everyone's surprise, Wingfield declined the appointment, citing his continued devotion to his business interests in Nevada. Still, his energy and money could mean that Newlands faced a more difficult reelection challenge in 1914.[27]

Newlands laid plans to influence both selection of the Democratic presidential candidate and the party's platform. By early 1912 he found local Democrats organizing Wilson Clubs with little interest in nonpartisan Progressive groups. Newlands announced his support of Wilson and Wilson requested his counsel on national questions. But in many states, with the help of Hearst's San Francisco *Examiner*, Champ Clark gained support as the convention approached. For Newlands, the *Examiner*, which enjoyed a large circulation in Nevada, "had poisoned the minds of the people" against Wilson. Unfortunately, Wilson also made it clear that he did not support Bryan's ideas about silver.

Despite these currents, Newlands was surprised and embarrassed when Nevada Democrats in primary elections chose Clark to receive Nevada's convention votes. He wrote Wilson that he regretted the outcome and could only describe it as a groundswell among the rank and file Democrats. He had been invited to go to the Baltimore convention instructed for Clark, but had declined because his loyalty was still with Wilson. Nonetheless, Wilson urged him to be a delegate. Newlands became a National Committeeman by proxy. In that role he told Wilson he could support the Bryan forces in demanding a Progressive platform. By July 1 he related that Nevada delegates, restless with their pledge to Clark, recognized it as a mistake, but were bound by their pledge. Newlands was optimistic about Wilson's nomination. He wrote:

I have found a very fruitful field of effort here in disarming the
conservative forces, with which I happen to have some degree of
influence, of their distrust of your candidacy. Throughout I have
endeavored to impress them with the view that inasmuch as they
cannot hope to get a reactionary, they should welcome the success of a
progressive who, whilst determined upon a radical cure, will apply all
the palliative remedies necessary to save the life of the patient. I had an
opportunity of urging this view today with great force upon a man who
stands in a position of exceptional strength with the Illinois delegation,
and he promised me that he would take immediate steps to bring that
delegation into line.

At the same time that he sent encouraging words to Wilson, he had
prepared a detailed two-thousand-word biographical sketch of himself.
There was still the possibility of a deadlocked convention; he would be
available. When the convention finally turned to Wilson, Nevada's
delegation remained with the "hound dog" statesman from Missouri,
much to Newlands's disappointment. But this disappointment was
overshadowed by Wilson's nomination. He told Wilson, "I am looking
forward with the most confident hope to cooperation with you in the
future in the interest of real progressive action." [28]

In the struggle over the platform Newlands argued for a Progressive
document. It was difficult for Newlands to obtain the specifics of his
own proposals in the document. The party platform would not support
a Federal Trade Commission; it merely denounced private monopoly
and promised vigorous enforcement of an enhanced Sherman Anti-
Trust Act. He also worked for a moderate tariff policy, not a free
proposal to dispose of the protective tariffs which many Democrats
advocated. He supported equal franchise for women.[29]

The issue that brought Newlands the most publicity in the platform
debates was his proposal to disfranchise blacks through a repeal of the
Fifteenth Amendment, which guaranteed protection of all rights regardless of race or previous condition of servitude. He saw it as "poison
in the Constitution."[30] The New York *Times* for June 17, 1912, reported
the Newlands white plank in full:

> Experience having demonstrated the folly of investing an inferior race
> with which amalgamation is undesirable with the right of suffrage, and
> the folly of admitting to our shores peoples differing in color, with
> whom amalgamation is undesirable, we declare that our Constitution
> should be so amended as to confine the right of suffrage in the future to
> people of the white race, and we favor a law prohibiting the immigra-

tion to this country of all peoples other than those of the white race, except for temporary purposes of education, travel, or commerce.

The measure, the *Times* noted, would appeal to the South and meet the views of the Pacific Coast on Chinese and Japanese exclusion. The Democratic party would lose no votes by putting it in the platform because "in the North the negro vote is practically all Republican; that in the South it is suppressed, and nobody ever sat up nights trying to corral the Chinese vote or the Japanese vote."

The reaction to Newlands's proposal was not entirely favorable even in Nevada. The generally pro-Newlands *Nevada State Journal* saw it as out of step with Progressivism, declaring, "It sounds funny coming as it does from a senator of Nevada—a state wherein suffrage has been a plaything in the hands of millionaire politicians." The Tonopah *Bonanza* denounced Newlands's ideas and declared them an injustice to the "colored race." It believed that Democrats would prevent the insertion of any such plank in the platform. The *Western Nevada Miner* believed that Bryan stopped the proposal. Some California newspapers concluded that Newlands was "undoubtedly entering his dotage." A midwestern conference of the African Methodist Episcopal Church urged Newlands to forget the politics of the "bloody shirt" and accept the conclusions of the Civil War. The Sacramento *Bee* denounced this proposal as "one to make politicians grin from ear to ear." Whatever the national and local comments, the resolution did not pass in committee.[31]

In Nevada, Governor Oddie appointed W. A. Massey to the unexpired term of Senator Nixon, who now faced election. Key Pittman was the Democratic nominee. Newlands did not like Pittman in the past, but he was willing to let "the embers of old contentions" die. He wanted to promote Democratic sentiment throughout the state. For these reasons he thought it would be a mistake to embarrass Pittman's candidacy by bringing out rival candidates. The party should concentrate its efforts on Wilson and Pittman in order to achieve complete Democratic success.[32]

With Theodore Roosevelt bolting the Republican convention and running for the presidency as a nominee of the Progressive party and Taft remaining the Republican nominee, the majority Republican party faced a split vote in the November election. The election of the first Democratic president since Grover Cleveland appeared likely. Newlands hoped a Democratic president would be an ally on water programs and quickly drew Wilson's attention to the National Irrigation

Congress in Salt Lake City and hoped Wilson would telegraph encouraging words to the Irrigation Congress. Newlands wrote that ever since "my irrigation bill" became a law, "I have been intent upon a general and comprehensive plan and organization for the development of our rivers, not only for transportation but for other useful purposes through the cooperation of the nation with the state, each acting within its respective jurisdiction." All of this was part of an "enlarged policy" that went beyond developing rivers by bank protection and channel improvement to a policy of the control and beneficial use of flood waters in the development of irrigation, hydroelectric power, and the prevention of floods. Mention of the enlarged policy, Newlands insisted, occurred in the comprehensive declaration on the 1912 platform because of his efforts. He hoped Wilson's message would embrace "a broad waterway policy." In his own speech to the Irrigation Congress Newlands asserted, "In the building of the Panama Canal and the carrying out of vast irrigation projects, the efficiency of a democratic form of government as a constructive force in the world is on trial."[33]

During the election campaign Newlands contributed $4,000 to the national and state campaign and was pressed for more from local officials. In his judgment his contribution was more than any American citizen should be allowed to make in an election. He spoke of a system of "Democratization of Finances by the Democratic party, so that any man, however poor, who has the character and ability, may be able to run for any office in this state from United States Senator down." He then struck at what he considered the evil of Nevada's political life to which many considered him a subscriber. That was the custom of permitting rich men and large interests to finance party organizations. He termed this "the very root of all the evils of which we complain" and said that if the people of Nevada were in earnest about establishing "a real democracy," they will end this practice. What Newlands looked forward to was further legislation limiting campaign expenditures by individuals and corporations that would relieve him of the constant pressure of supporting Democratic campaigns.[34]

Wilson's election victory was sweet but did little to secure Newlands reelection in 1914. To this end he prepared a reform agenda for the upcoming legislative session.[35] The inauguration of a Democratic president by no means gave Newlands a green light for his national reform program. He still saw immense difficulties with the states-rights Democrats that had emerged during the campaign. Both Wilson and Roosevelt outlined roads to Progressive reform. Wilson's New Freedom, masterminded by Louis Brandeis, saw the breakup of the great conglomerates and the restoration of freedom of competition for American business. Theodore Roosevelt's New Nationalism first espoused by him in 1910 and put forth by Herbert Croly in his 1909 book *The Promise of American Life* embraced the business conglomerate as the wave of the future. But it was a future dominated by the large hand of federal regulation of corporate America. There was little doubt that Newlands stood in sympathy with the New Nationalism and there was little doubt too that he would exert his energies to prevent the Democratic party from following the "radicalism" of the New Freedom.

XII

VISIONS WON AND LOST

One of Newlands's primary visions for the future rested with the so-called second Newlands bill. His "enlarged policy" went far beyond the original Reclamation Act in terms of water utilization. He began to shape this second effort after the Inland Waterways Commission and later the National Waterways Commission went out of business in the Taft administration. He now proposed a permanent commission to oversee, plan, authorize, and implement river development in aspects of irrigation, dam building, flood control, navigation, forest and soil conservation, and hydroelectric power. This sweeping proposal that gave so much power to an appointed commission met opposition within and outside of government. In the War Department the Corps of Engineers saw its authority threatened by plans for centralized overall planning, direction, and selection of projects, as did those in the Interior Department with the Reclamation Service. Most of all Congress recognized that its control over pet projects for constituents stood in peril if authority escaped to the all-powerful commission. Outside of government private power resisted the idea of strong government authority over river systems because it might be crowded out of the picture if the hand of government was omnipresent. Finally, the demands of the war effort in Washington offered little hope for such a scale of internal development and planning.

Surprisingly, a Newlands Waterways Amendment to the Rivers and Harbors Bill of 1917 passed in the summer of 1917. By providing for an oversight commission, the objectives of Newlands's long-proposed river regulation bill seemed within reach. A press release by the Department of Commerce in September 1917 said that in the amendment Congress created a "cohesive, constructive, and continuing national policy of developing and using the now wasted forces of nature for the promotion of agriculture, soil conservation, forestry, and transportation." Newlands took satisfaction in these late years of his life that one of his primary visions might be fulfilled and spoke with great hope for this measure throughout the fall of 1917 as being the key that would link the nation together in a vast web of production, distribution, and efficient use of natural resources. Most of all the system could serve the war effort and provide the foundation for prosperous growth in the peacetime years to follow. But President Wilson never appointed the commission. With Newlands's death at the end of 1917, the amendment lost its spokesman, and much to the relief of many inside and outside of government, it was repealed by the Water Power Act of 1920. The second Newlands bill became a failed vision at the end of two Democratic administrations.[1]

At the beginning of these administrations in 1913, when Woodrow Wilson came to the presidency, he offered a Progressive agenda, but not all of the Wilsonian program conformed to Newlands's vision of the future. Moreover, the issues the president considered most urgent sometimes directly affected the economic welfare of Nevada. Although Newlands spoke often for the general welfare, he chose not to vote against what he thought were the best interests of his constituency. For example, Newlands faced a dilemma over the tariff. For decades traditional Democrats denounced protection, but Newlands was not so enthusiastic. Prior to the election, he declared that Democrats should oppose "radical readjustments" in tariff policy. For Nevada, this especially meant the protection of wool and sugar. By June 1913 Newlands and a group of other western senators voted against "free wool and sugar," while Key Pittman, the junior Democratic senator from Nevada, voted for it in what was emerging as the Underwood Tariff Bill of 1913. Newlands predicted that if the party did not remove wool and sugar from the free list, it would lose some of its fourteen senators from west of the Missouri.[2]

When Democrats berated him for this lack of party loyalty on the tariff issue, he replied that he could not support measures detrimental to the interests of important economic groups in Nevada. On closer analysis Newlands would have done well to sidestep this issue in Nevada. Key Pittman made a splash in the Nevada newspapers by his criticism of the sheep industry and the Basque herders who worked for cheap wages with no thought of becoming American citizens. Newlands placed himself in the position of supporting the interests of larger sheep outfits, sometimes owned outside of the state, who employed foreign labor. Hard-line Democrats, cattle people, and nativists all opposed Newlands on this issue.[3]

Support for Newlands came from the Republican press and from none other than Goldfield mining entrepreneur turned Reno banker George Wingfield, who had invested in sheep and sugar beets. Wingfield urged him not to vote in favor of the tariff on the final vote, although it included many features Newlands favored, including an income tax to make up for lost tariff revenue. At the same time Wingfield argued that zinc dust, lead acetate, and sodium cyanide should be on the free list because these were used by the mining industry.

As the tide of tariff reform swept him along, Newlands observed that, "There seems to be an overwhelming disposition to follow Wilson's lead in everything. I think with entirely good motives he has made a mistake regarding these industries." The Democratic Central Committee in Nevada, under Newlands's control, tried to explain that Newlands stood with the people on the tariff issue. Ironically the Republican press agreed. Newlands deserved the esteem of Nevadans for standing by the interests of sugar and wool and with Republicans. Newlands's Democratic friends in Nevada concluded that criticism of his stand on the tariff was "only a pretext for an attack by your enemies in your own party headed by Dickerson and his followers."[4]

Ultimately Newlands voted for the "radical" Underwood Tariff. He could see virtue in the bill if it emerged from conference with a Tariff Board or Tax Commission, which, Newlands believed, would "take away from both the Republican and the Progressive parties their chief contention" that the bill was a mindless attempt to slash tariffs by doctrinaire low-tariff Democrats. Even with the inclusion of a tariff commission with the power to move tariffs upward or downward, Newlands still believed that Democrats had lost an opportunity of attracting progressive Republicans had they distributed many of the reductions in the bill over a period of three years.[5]

Another troubling issue was the bill to create a Federal Reserve banking system that emerged with administration support in 1913. Oddly enough, given his reputation as "a centralizer," Newlands saw it as too radical. He advocated state reserve associations, not large regional reserve districts. Even Nevada's Republican press feared the domination of currency and the banks by a board composed of presidential appointees. It asked how Wilson's "new Freedom of business" was consistent with the domination of this board and asserted that the "new freedom" appeared to be the offspring of the "old paternalism." It was as intrusive upon property as any measure of "Bryanesque finance." As with the tariff bill, after much soul-searching Newlands remained loyal to the party in the final votes.[6]

One of Wilson's programs won Newlands's enthusiastic endorsement—the Federal Trade Commission Act. For years he had supported the commission concept in keeping with his admiration of government by experts. This was the best method to deal with the confusing demands of antitrust legislation. He believed there were two views of the commission. One saw the role of the commission as regulating monopolistic industry in the public interest. The other thought private monopoly intolerable, unscientific, and abnormal, and saw the commission as essential to the enforcement of competition. The Trade Commission, empowered to play either role, offered new certainty and freedom to business by replacing the capricious interpretations of the Sherman Anti-Trust Law by the courts. Furthermore, the Trade Commission possessed the power to investigate compliance with its rulings. Newlands also welcomed the passage of the Clayton Act and endorsed the idea that labor organizations were not illegal combinations.[7]

As the European war erupted in August and September of 1914, Newlands told President Wilson, "The conduct of America is an inspiration in the midst of all this carnage, and I have the greatest admiration for the serenity, wisdom, and sensibility with which you appeal to the best judgment of the country and the world." These words revealed Newlands's attachment to the inner workings of the administration as a leading Democrat in the Senate. The president introduced him to his confidant on foreign policy, Colonel Edward M. House. It was no surprise that Newlands supported the president's foreign policy, including the occupation of the port of Vera Cruz and the refusal to recognize Mexican strongman Victoriano Huerta's government.[8]

In his fall 1914 campaign for the Senate, Newlands tried to relate local to national affairs. "If you want a representative at Washington to be serviceable to you," he told a Fallon audience, "by all means make him serviceable to the country and to the world." These were the true dimensions of his senatorial office. But he knew full well that state elections were rarely won on national or international issues and in this campaign he returned to the theme that Nevada was no longer a "controlled state" where the railroad bosses directed political life. The Democratic party under his leadership had put an end to this.

Early on Newlands recognized the threat that the Socialist vote presented to his election. The Socialists drew many more votes from Democratic ranks than from Republicans. Senator Pittman demonstrated this in 1912 when he won by 7,942 to 7,853 (an 89 vote plurality) for his Republican opposition in a field that also gave 2,740 votes to the

Socialist candidate and 1,428 to the Progressive. The Socialist vote almost handed the election to the Republican. Newlands understood that a similar danger awaited him. The threat was even more pressing because the 1914 election was the first in the state to be conducted under the 1913 Amendment of Article VII of the U.S. Constitution that required a popular election instead of election by the legislature. The threat was greater because there would be no Progressives to take votes away from the Republican candidate. The necessity of winning only the popular vote drew Newlands's attention away from legislative affairs. This became evident in the 1913 session. When the legislature revamped the 1903 Water Act it dropped the requirement that the Reclamation Service approve the appointment of the state engineer and gave the all-important water office over to the complete control of the state.[9]

Newlands befriended the women's suffrage movement and other causes of interest to women. In 1913 he told Anne Martin, head of the state's Equal Suffrage Association, that he supported the submission of the issue to the voters and that "the social and moral conditions of Nevada would be vastly improved by the aid of women's votes." The Nevada Association of Women Opposed to Equal Suffrage protested any movement toward suffrage because it would undermine "the strength of the nation which lies in the home and the family." Newlands rejected these views and told Martin in 1914 that "I am becoming so firm in this view [for suffrage] that any denial of it based upon the old fashioned arguments rather irritates me." When the club women in Nevada expressed concern with the hardships of the local Washoe Indians, Newlands introduced legislation for homes for Native indigents. When women's groups supported the creation of a Children's Bureau, he lent his support to the bill's passage in 1912. Finally, the General Federation of Women's Clubs announced support of the Newlands-Broussard bill for river regulation. Little wonder Newlands looked to women as a major force for Progressive improvement.[10]

But supporting women's causes could not help as his career teetered on disaster. Factions within the party wanted him out of state politics. Denver Dickerson threatened a challenge in the primary, and Pat McCarran also had ambitions. Newlands's friends in Reno "did some very agile and effective work in procuring McCarran to lie down." Not only were the rising ambitions of new arrivals in Nevada politics a threat to Newlands but also there were disgruntled reactions to various Progressive reforms in the state. Utility companies complained of regula-

tion and ranchers objected to the more efficient tax assessments required of the counties. The Cattlemen's Association centered in Elko
was determined to force the legislature to abolish reform. Joining them
were the big mining companies and the utility companies. The Nevada
Industrial Commission, established by the 1911 legislature to provide
insurance for workmen's injuries, escaped criticism, probably because
it protected companies against workmen's suits for on the job injuries.[11]

Newlands's old political allies urged him to come out to Nevada soon
because the election would not be "any cinch for you." One Newlands
backer estimated that the Socialist candidate Grant Miller had 5,500
socialist votes at the outset and the Republican enemies would play
their strongest candidate against Newlands. Others urged him to be in
Nevada at least directly after the party primary in early September and
to lend his support to the nomination of Emmett Boyle as the Democratic candidate for governor. One supporter described Boyle to Newlands as "a clean, well educated, progressive gentleman" who would
immeasurably strengthen the Democratic ticket. This would make for
a strong local ticket because a weak ticket would be "a menace to your
reelection." The Boyle candidacy would be "progressive in everyway"
in contrast to the other Democratic candidate, Lem Allen, who opposed
all the Progressive commissions that had become a part of state government. Furthermore the state's Democratic attorney general, George
Thatcher, argued that Boyle's success was essential to Newlands's
victory in the election.[12]

Before Newlands left Washington he prodded the Reclamation Service to issue a statement about its future plans in Nevada as he returned
"to give an account of my stewardship" to the people of Nevada. This
required "a report to them regarding the progress in my propaganda for
the enlargement of government cooperation in the development of the
Humbodlt, Walker, and Upper Carson rivers in Nevada" and the
cooperation that it had enjoyed with Boyle as state engineer in Nevada.
Newlands could then use this in the campaign to encourage the election
of Boyle, whose presence in the governor's office would no doubt
facilitate future reclamation development in the state. Previously Newlands announced that he envisioned the harnessing of the Colorado
River by the Reclamation Bureau for the building of the West and
Nevada. "Dam it, we must," he declared. While announcing himself in
favor of water utilization, he also offended nature lovers who saw other
qualities in rivers besides economic utilization. Dr. J. E. Church of the
University of Nevada urged Newlands to support John Muir's opposi-

tion to the damming of Hetch-Hetchy Canyon within Yosemite National Park, despite Newlands's devotion to the doctrine of "beneficial
use." Newlands rejected Church's advice and announced his full support
of Hetch-Hetchy, endorsing the victory of use over aesthetics and parks.[13]

Not only did Newlands have to give an account of "his stewardship"
to the voters of Nevada, he had to do it within the spending limits of
campaign expenditure laws. Federal law permitted him to spend up to
$10,000, but state law in Nevada permitted him to expend only 40
percent of his first year's salary in the elected office. Newlands had for
many years stood for limitations on campaign expenditures to prevent,
as he said, great wealth from monopolizing offices and to restrain the
demands made upon his purse by Democratic candidates. In this
election he may have regretted the limitations, which he himself
imposed.[14]

The Republicans were well organized. Their candidate, Sam Platt,
argued that Newlands was so wrapped up in his schemes for western
development, trust regulation, and world events that he had forgotten
Nevadans. Republicans cast him as a relatively powerless figure in his
own party because of his disagreements with the president over tariff
and monetary policy. Pro-saloon Democrats were clearly upset with
Newlands's stand against the sale of liquor in the construction camps
building the irrigation works at Derby Dam, the ditches in Fallon, and
at Lahontan Dam. This latter point might have been overlooked, if the
pro-saloon crowd in Reno had not become frightened by the reform
element in the town that attacked gambling, saloons, and legalized
prostitution.

A major reform came when the legislature abolished gambling in the
state effective October 1, 1910. Another extended the divorce residency from six months to one year. Business groups in Reno especially
felt the sting of these measures and feared the ultimate arrival of
prohibition. On one point, during the final stages of the campaign that
would surely identify him with these forces, he wished to remain mute:
women's suffrage. He pledged Anne Martin's Equal Suffrage Association $1,000, but asked that it remain a secret until after the campaign.
Martin in return pledged to respect this confidence until Newlands
gave his leave to make his support public. She did note that, "Mr.
Wingfield is opposing us in every way possible, but there is every
prospect of winning with good thorough work."[15]

Unfortunately for Newlands's reelection drive the "New Day in
Nevada" had not totally arrived. In Fallon, on the reclamation project,

settlers were restless under the "excess lands" restriction of the reclamation law. It forbade owners from using reclamation project water for more than 160 acres. Many possessed only 40 acres and feared increased water assessments under the new Reclamation Extension Act. They blamed the Reclamation Service for restricting them to "just making" a living and suggested that the Service was in the process of making "serfs" out of them. The Socialists made severe inroads in the irrigation community, and Newlands had old Democratic enemies in Fallon who believed they had been insufficiently rewarded by his patronage. This sharply cut the Newlands vote in Churchill County, where he believed his greatest strength should lie as a tribute to his campaign for reclamation. One man who supported Grant Miller, the Socialist candidate, later regretted it because his vote almost elected the Republican.[16]

The Socialist campaign against Newlands was no joke. Their newspaper, *The Socialist* described Newlands as an aging senator and painted his career in terms of treachery and betrayal. It charged that Newlands cooperated with the Southern Pacific Railroad and that, although he was due some credit for securing the Truckee and Carson irrigation project for Nevada, he profited through his ownership of large tracts of land within the project. It recounted how Newlands changed political loyalties and asserted that he actively opposed Wilson's policies on the tariff and currency and only voted for them when it became apparent they could not be defeated. These were "his old familiar tactics of playing both ends against the middle." It asked that no Democrat vote for Newlands because he was "the constructor of the bi-partisan machine that has disorganized the Democratic party in Nevada." It sneered at the idea that he was the father of the Federal Trade Commission bill as chairman of the Interstate Commerce Committee. His original bill was rejected by the administration because "it had no teeth in it."[17]

To counter these attacks from both the Socialists and the Republicans, Newlands made good use of an editorial in *The Commoner* by the secretary of state and champion of the silver cause, William Jennings Bryan. Bryan recommended Newlands to the voters because of his service to the cause of Progressivism, to the cause of irrigation in the West, and his role in creating the Federal Trade Commission Act, marking "a new epoch in the effective regulation of trusts." Bryan praised his advanced ideas on banking, his support of the eight-hour-day law for railroad telegraphers, for safety devices, and employers' liability. He pointed out that Newlands had consistently opposed the movement of goods made by convict labor through interstate commerce to compete with the products of free labor. Bryan continued:

> Mr. Newlands belongs to that class of men who, having imagination and the constructive faculty largely developed, are often in advance of their times; but he has had the good fortune to see many of his ideas enacted into law and others on the highroad to enactment, thus proving his claim to practical constructive statesmanship.

Bryan believed Newlands's national water policies were on the verge of enactment and noted he had long stood for the scientific coordination of the work of river regulation and flood reduction, by putting the work on a national, instead of a local footing. The achievement of this is on the high road to enactment and will prove his claim "to practical constructive statesmanship." *The Commoner* concluded, "The nation can not afford to lose the services of such a public servant."[18]

Newlands squeaked through the election. Final results showed Newlands with 8,078 votes to Republican Samuel Platt's 8,038 votes. Socialist Grant A. Miller commanded an impressive 5,451 votes. The closeness of the vote and the belated report of favorable returns from Nye County led many of Newlands's friends to believe he had lost the election. Secretary of the Interior Franklin K. Lane, believing Newlands defeated, called it discreditable that, "after twenty-two years of loyal and distinguished service, your people have failed to realize what honor you brought them." Senator Pittman at first thought the returns discouraging, but as the election day wore on he became more confident of a Newlands victory. He was happy to report that Nye County gave the senator 214 votes over the Republican candidate. Newlands believed that Pittman played a large role in delivering his largest plurality in the state from Nye County. President Wilson's private secretary, Joseph P. Tumulty, telegraphed Newlands asking for news of the election results because, "The President and I are deeply interested in your contest."[19]

Following the election Newlands wrote exhaustively analyzing his near defeat. The letter to President Wilson went into particular detail. He charged that the Republican party financed the campaign of Socialist candidate Grant Miller. This was done by ensuring that Miller won a fee of $5,000 in a lawsuit against the Pittsburgh Silver Peak Mining Company at the outset of the campaign. This money was then used to great effect in the mining centers of the state. In addition the banking interests of the state, under the control of George Wingfield, stood solidly against his reelection, largely because Wingfield and his followers, so Newlands believed, resented his final vote on the tariff bill. Newlands was also greatly disappointed with Churchill County. It was the chief beneficiary of the Reclamation Act, "of which I was the author." But apparently they forgot this fact "in resentment regarding free listing sugar as the beet sugar development was the main hope of that project." The county only gave him a seventeen-vote plurality. The vote in the county gave the Socialist candidate nearly 2,500 votes: more than the vote for Socialist presidential candidate Eugene V. Debs two years before, and almost all of this increase came from Democratic ranks.

Newlands explained that he based his campaign largely on the achievements of the national Democratic administration and only the president's policy of "watchful waiting" regarding the European war was "immensely popular." Newlands said, "I believe we would have lost the state had the contest taken place before the European war." The war theme was crucial to his victory. The war persuaded voters to stay with those who supported Wilson's safe and cautious policy.

Newlands explained that the Democratic congressional seat had been lost to the Republicans, but he assured the president that his personal popularity was "very great." Yet, he thought, "We are still . . . a merely plurality party, but I hope that our actions will be such as to win to us the progressive element of the Republican party which is now adrift and likely to float either way."[20]

Newlands told his old friend, Senator C. S. Thomas of Colorado, that he had "never known a more defamatory campaign upon the part of Republicans," and Socialists conducted "an insinuating one with the entire fight concentrated on myself." He concluded, "Altogether I am quite lucky to have gotten out of the woods at all." He noted too the defection of Reno's nominally Democratic *Nevada State Journal*, despite his $3,221.53 of advertising in it. This paper demanded $15,000 as its price to support Newlands, and when this was declined, the paper threw all of its force against him but generally supported the rest of the ticket. After the women's suffrage measure passed in 1914, he told Anne Martin that she "will have much influence in the line of social betterment."[21]

This was Newlands's last political campaign. As he entered his third term, he assumed the mantle of elder statesman and Key Pittman extended to him every form of cooperation as they moved as a Democratic team in the state and in the Senate. Democrats in Nevada, of course, continued to look to Newlands for financial support, and he parsimoniously doled out his contributions in each campaign.[22]

There was growing awareness that this was his last term. His health, always fragile, became a subject of concern among his friends. His political influence in the state waned after his near defeat. The chairman of the Democratic Central Committee asked him not to appear too frequently in support of Pittman's reelection campaign in 1916, although he did make appearances speaking on behalf of President Wilson's reelection. With the passage of the Reclamation Act in the distant past and its achievement in Nevada less than millennial in scope, the biting words of one critic from the Carson City *News* rang louder than ever that Newlands's Nevada career "was more constructive than real."[23]

As the senior senator he regularly gave speeches that drew the larger picture of the world and the development of natural resource use in the West. His appearance at the University of Nevada in October 1915 took on the air of an elder statesman offering advice and wisdom to youth. He was described by the student newspaper as "a constructive statesman in the development of the natural resources of the West." His speech was in part a sentimental journey. He reiterated his advocacy of legislation to capture and distribute the snowy waters of the high mountains for beneficial uses in irrigation, water power, flood control, and navigation. Currently he had legislation pending to take and manage all the large rivers of the country from the point "they fall until they reach the ocean." Especially should the water of the Colorado River be tamed for use in Nevada, Arizona, and Utah. As Newlands looked back he noted the progress of Nevada over the past twenty-three years. He saw a state that once languished in the grips of railroad political bosses to one that now eagerly adopted "methods of popular government." From the past Newlands turned to the present. He foresaw the need of an international police force to keep order in the world. More immediately in the United States education and military training could become one and the same beginning in the land-grant universities.[24]

When Newlands advocated "preparedness" by dovetailing military defense with education and employment in constructing public buildings, regulation of rivers, in forestry activities, reclamation projects, and other scientific services, he foreshadowed the Civilian Conservation Corps established under the New Deal in the 1930s. With this combination of peacetime services under military regime and training, Newlands believed the nation could afford a large military establishment in time of peace.[25]

9. United States Senator Francis G.
Newlands. Photograph courtesy
of the Nevada Historical Society.
Used by permission.

Newlands squarely supported Wilson on foreign affairs. But the resignation of Secretary of State Bryan because of Wilson's strong stand against the German government's employment of submarine warfare in the sinking of the *Lusitania* in 1915 shocked the Progressive western wing of the party. Could it remain loyal to the president now that the old standard-bearer of reform and silver broke with the president? Newlands, eager to heal the rift, saw Bryan's action growing out of personal conviction, but he knew Bryan would support the president in any conflict with the Germans. He wanted the German ambassador to know this and suggested that Germany should now seize the moment to settle the war without indemnities in territory or money. It was the best time "for getting out of this scrape with honor and without humiliation," he declared. He was convinced that the allies would win the war but, "it will be at a cost to civilization and prosperity that no one can measure." In the presidential campaign of 1916 Newlands urged Nevadans to support the president because it was his courageous leadership that had kept America out of war.[26]

After the *Lusitania*, it became clear that American policies could lead to war if the Germans resumed unlimited submarine warfare. The Wilson administration's attention turned to preparedness and when the Germans opened up their submarine warfare on a wide range of commerce in early 1917, America intervened in the war. For Newlands, with an enemy this diabolical there could be no compromise or quarter given. In the midst of war Newlands spoke of a "Teutonic dream of world conquest" and demanded the dismemberment of the old Austro-Hungarian Empire to break the cohesion of the Central Powers from the North Sea to the Mediterranean. He said no peace should be negotiated on the basis of the maintenance of this power bloc because it would in a short time rebuild and threaten the stability of Europe and "be a constant menace to the states on the fringe of Europe surrounding it and to a disorganized Russia."[27]

Newlands achieved the promises of American life—wealth, family, and wide-ranging political influence. What he realized personally, he saw for American society as well. His record, however, strikingly indicates that people of color were excluded. His vision of a modern racially exclusive future was not uncommon to people of his background and class at the turn of the century. That it was the wrong vision would have come as a surprise to him.

Blue prints for the nation's future abounded at the beginning of the century. In 1909 Herbert Croly, author of *The Promise of American Life* and founding editor of the *New Republic*, charted a Progressive path in terms of a larger, more dynamic activist national government that intervened positively in American society and economy. Theodore Roosevelt took up these themes in 1910 and called them the New Nationalism. Government would replace Adam Smith's regulatory "invisible hand" over the affairs of the business world. Newlands's political and economic thinking reflected Croly's Progressive view of the future.[28] His support of the Adamson Act of 1916 with its close government supervision and mandated eight-hour day for some railroad workers was an example of government exerting its larger economic powers.

A summation of Newlands's career must reflect this broad national perspective and the grand, sweeping strokes in which Croly painted the future of the country. Newlands was one of the insurgent voices in the West to which the noted American historian Frederick Jackson Turner referred when he wrote that they were demanding an "increase of federal authority to curb the special interests, the powerful industrial organization, and the monopolies, for the sake of the conservation of our national resources and the preservation of American democracy."[29]

Newlands was one of the few Democratic liberal nationalists at the beginning of the century. He sought national solutions to problems at a time when that viewpoint in his party was extraordinary. *Town and Country* magazine in 1916 said he had, "Truly a national record," and, "Although a Democrat by inheritance, instinct and training, Senator Newlands is also a nationalist." Visualizing solutions to many problems through actions by the national government, he differed markedly from southern states-righters. He was more a New Nationalist Republican than an old-time Democrat, except on questions of race, and in some respects he was more of a national senator than he was a representative of Nevada. His Reclamation Act of 1902 nationalized the tasks of irrigating arid America. For him the Reclamation Act was merely one aspect of his general view that the power of the central government should be utilized to bring efficiency and greater opportunity to American life.[30]

Senator Newlands's career captured many of the central tenets of the Progressive movement. The main theme of his thought was the rational utilization of natural resources, especially water. His interests in economic organization and the role of the corporation in the nation also dominated his thinking. He embraced government and legal action against concentrated wealth and excessive competition. On balance his attention focused more quickly upon excessive, chaotic, destructive competition than on the evils of concentrated wealth, unless that wealth was lawless in its conduct. The concentration of capital and magnitude in enterprise he accepted as the hallmark of modern America and the wave of the future that could not be reversed. His views put him at odds with his own party. As such, Newlands simply believed that he was a more modern Democrat.[31]

Long an advocate of what the press called "the Great West," Newlands made his last trip to Nevada and the Pacific Coast during the fall of 1917. The war especially weighed upon him. In a long, rambling, detailed speech to the Reno Commercial Club, Newlands addressed its implications for the future role the United States in world affairs. He saw the war presenting itself "in so many protean forms" with reference to the future of Russia, the dangers of consolidation of power in central Europe, and the growing importance of Washington as a world capital to which all countries look for leadership. Increasingly his pronouncements during the last months of his life echoed the Wilsonian internationalist rhetoric about the nation's destiny as a world power. American participation in the war made Washington the clearinghouse of world ideas: "it is one of the most interesting places one can imagine." After his appearance in Reno and San Francisco, he returned to the nation's capital busy with the war effort. There he continued to push for water, navigational, and power development.

In the midst of preparing for hearings by the Senate Interstate Commerce Committee on impending railroad legislation, he died suddenly of a heart attack on Christmas Eve, 1917. He was 69 years old. With President and Mrs. Wilson attending the funeral services, Newlands was buried three days later in the Oak Hill Cemetery in Washington, D.C. His eulogists in Nevada spoke of his legacy of progressive legislation and that the state was a better place because he had lived. But some noted that because he was "engrossed in the larger things of national legislation [he] did not generally cultivate personal contact." Nevada Congressman George A. Bartlett said the state and the nation had "lost a broad-minded constructive statesman" who fathered the reclamation policies and inland waterway developments.[32]

During the war, Newlands felt vindicated as he saw the president abandon the New Freedom and accept the regulation of large business concentrations instead of their dismantlement. The organization of American businesses on a gigantic scale during the war bespoke efficiency and the new realities of American economic life and, of course, of a developed modern economy. Newlands also welcomed the growth of big government.[33]

These views revealed a Newlands who was conversant with the prevalent ideas in the ruling circles of the country. They also revealed a sophisticated view of power realities in the world geo-political picture. Newlands's life over the years became the embodiment of sophistication, from the clothes he wore to the elegant, tasteful homes he chose in Reno and in the nation's capital. Likewise, his ideas and plans for an improved modern America and his Wilsonian ideals about America's role as arbiter of Europe and its future reflected the kind of cosmopolitan sophistication he believed a progressive and internationally responsible America must embrace.

Washington as the nerve center for a new international community captured his imagination just as his imagination had been excited with the possibilities of Washington directing the development, especially of water, and conservation of the natural resources of all of the West. Yet Washington was a far leap from the arid West and certainly the Nevada of 1917, although both in Newlands's view had come a long way toward modernizing and moving in the direction of economic, political, and even social reform. While strong forces nationally and internationally changed the nature of life in Washington, of which Newlands felt privileged to be a part, marked changes also occurred in Nevada and the West since 1900. In the transformations that helped move the region beyond its rough mining-town past, Newlands saw the beginning of a "new day" and the Nevada experience was a good example. While Newlands welcomed the twentieth-century mining boom in southern Nevada, like all mining he regarded it as a short-lived event that did not represent the future.

But what did? Forces within Nevada turned it against the social reform of the Progressive period as it adopted the economics of a vice-related economy, in part to compensate for its failure to develop an economy based on its own limited natural resources. While Newlands saw himself as always looking toward the future, he seriously misread the future of the moral side of Progressivism in the state and even the future of a small-farmer society based on irrigation. All of his work for reclamation and Progressivism did not bring the promise of American life to Nevada.

Newlands did have faith that events were vindicating his policies on the national scene and he was confident in an ultimate allied victory because the United States acted as the make-weight in the balance of power. But the course of his own state's development within the context of the Great Basin environment remained elusive to him. No matter how hard he strove to establish his local credentials, in truth he

remained an outsider and a symbol of a rich Comstock interloper from
an era when San Francisco–Nevadans dominated the state. Nevada's
rejection of Progressive social and moral reform ultimately confirmed
that much of what Newlands foresaw for the state's future simply would
not occur. As such, Newlands's memory in the state, but not necessarily
in the arid West, became increasingly blurred with the distance of time.

NOTES

1. SENATOR NEWLANDS

1. Jeanne Elizabeth Wier, "The Mission of the State Historical Society," from an address to the Nevada Academy of Sciences in 1905, *First Biennial Report of the Nevada Historical Society* (1907–1908), 66; *Nevada State Journal*, June 17, 1905; Donald J. Pisani, "Federal Reclamation and Water Rights in Nevada," *Agricultural History* 51 (July 1977), 541.
2. *Nevada State Journal*, June 17, 18, 1905; Reno *Evening Gazette*, June 17, 1905.
3. William E. Smythe, "When the Gates Were Lifted on the Truckee," *Out West* 3 (August 1905), 101–12.
4. Reno *Evening Gazette*, June 17, 1905; *Progressive West*, 1 (June 1905), 1–2; *Nevada State Journal*, June 17, 1905.
5. Samuel P. Hays, *Conservation and the Gospel of Efficiency: The Progressive Conservation Movement, 1890–1920* (Cambridge: Harvard University Press, 1959), 109; Stephen Skowronek, *Building a New American State: The Expansion of National Administrative Capacities, 1877–1920* (Cambridge: Cambridge University Press, 1982), 13; Newlands to Dent H. Roberts, September 17, 1904, Newlands Papers (Sterling Library, Yale University [hereinafter cited as Newlands MSS]); Newlands to Leslie M. Shaw, January 20, 1906, Newlands MSS; William Lilley III, "The Early Career of Francis G. Newlands, 1848–1897" (Ph.D. diss., Yale University, 1965), 16.
6. Carson City *News*, March 18, 1913.

2. TOWARD THE PROMISES OF CALIFORNIA

1. William Newlands to Betsy Moffat, January 13, 1846; William Newlands to Betsy Moffat, July 21, 1851 (Barland-Newlands Papers, State Historical Society of Wisconsin [hereinafter referred to as Barland-Newlands MSS]).
2. William Newlands to Betsy Moffat, July 21, 1851, Barland-Newlands MSS.
3. Lilley, "Early Career," 6; George Barland to Francis G. Newlands, February 27, 1903, and March 12, 1912, Barland-Newlands MSS.
4. Lilley, "Early Career," 8–9, based on Barland-Newlands MSS.
5. Jessie Moore to Betsy Moffat, December 30, 1866, Barland-Newlands MSS.
6. Newlands to Betsy Moffat, August 29, 1868, Barland-Newlands MSS.
7. Theodore C. Pease and James G. Randall, eds., *The Diary of Orville Hickman Browning*, Collections of the Illinois State Historical Library, vol. XXII (Springfield, 1925), 235.
8. Albert W. Atwood, *Francis G. Newlands: A Builder of the Nation* (n.p.: Newlands Company, 1969), 7; Lilley, "Early Career," 18, based on correspondence of Jessie Moore to Betsy Moffat, 1866, in Barland-Newlands MSS.
9. D. W. Cheeseman to Hon. Lorenzo Sawyer, n.d., 1870, Barland-Newlands MSS; "Biographical Sketch of Francis G. Newlands," by George Morrison

and Alfred Bates, c. 1891, MSS in the Bancroft Library, University of California, Berkeley.

10. Morrison and Bates, "Biographical Sketch"; Lilley, "Early Career," 24.
11. Jessie Moore to Betsy Moffat, May 21, 1871, Barland-Newlands MSS.
12. Jessie Moore to family, July 1, 1871, Barland-Newlands MSS.
13. Jessie Moore to family, July 1, 1871; Lilley, "Early Career," 30, 29 n.24 for description of his lifestyle; Betsy Moffat, July 6, 1871, Barland-Newlands MSS.
14. B. E. Lloyd, *Lights and Shades in San Francisco* (San Francisco: Bancroft, 1876) in the chap. "The Elite: Who They Are," 108; William H. Chambliss, *Chambliss' Diary, or Society as It Really Is* (New York: Chambliss, 1895), vi. Oscar Lewis, *This Was San Francisco* (New York: McKay, 1962), 192; Samuel Williams, "The City of the Golden Gate," *Scribner's Monthly*, 10 (July 1875), 266–85; Jessie Moore to family, July 1, 1871; Jessie Moore to Betsy Moffat, n.d., 1873, Barland-Newlands MSS.
15. Jessie Moore to Betsy Moffat, October 5, 1871, Barland-Newlands MSS.
16. Jessie Moore to Betsy Moffat, September 1874; April 3, 1874; July 1874.
17. B. E. Lloyd, *Lights and Shades in San Francisco*, "A Wedding in the Upper Ten," 108; Jessie Moore to Betsy Moffat, October 24, 1873.
18. Amelia Ransome Neville, *The Fantastic City: Memoirs of the Social and Romantic Life of Old San Francisco* (Boston: Houghton Mifflin, 1932), 206.
19. San Francisco *Chronicle*, October 10, 25, 1874.
20. Jessie Moore to James Newlands, September 1874.
21. San Francisco *Chronicle*, November 20, 1874.
22. Lewis, *This Was San Francisco*, 184; Lloyd, *Lights and Shades in San Francisco*, 108–10.
23. San Francisco *Chronicle*, November 20, 1874; Jessie Moore to Betsy Moffat, November 29, 1874; October 24, 1874; William Newlands to Betsy Moffat, February 1, 1874, Barland-Newlands MSS.
24. San Francisco *Chronicle*, November 20, 1874.
25. Jessie Moore to Betsy Moffat, November 29, 1874, Barland-Newlands MSS.

3. IN DEFENSE OF PROPERTY

1. Historians disagree over the circumstances of Ralston's death. See Cecil G. Tilton, *William Chapman Ralston: Courageous Builder* (Boston: Christopher Publishing House, 1935), 391–93, 422–23, who is critical of Hittel and Bancroft, who accept the suicide view; Amelia Ransome Neville, *The Fantastic City: Memoirs of the Social and Romantic Life of Old San Francisco* (Boston: Houghton Mifflin, 1932), 204; David Lavender, *Nothing Seemed Impossible: William C. Ralston and Early San Francisco* (Palo Alto: American West, 1975); William Issel and Robert W. Cherny, *San Francisco, 1865–1932: Politics, Power, and Urban Development* (Berkeley: University of California Press, 1986), "probably from a stroke while swimming," 28.
2. Lavender, *Nothing Seemed Impossible*, suggests that Sharon welcomed the departure of Ralston, as do other sources, i.e., Tilton, *William Chapman Ralston*, 358; Julian Dana, *The Man Who Built San Francisco: A Study of Ralston's Journey with Banners* (New York: Macmillan, 1936), 366, 370–71.
3. Charles A. Murdock, *A Backward Glance at Eighty* (San Francisco: Paul

Elder, 1921), 138–39; Lilley, "Early Career," 62–63; San Francisco *Bulletin*, October 10, 1884; Issel and Cherny, *San Francisco, 1865–1932*, 117–38.

4. Murdock, *A Backward Glance*, 138–39; see also comments by James Bryce, *The American Commonwealth* on the ill-gotten, ostentatious wealth of California, vol. II (London: Macmillan, 1891), 387; Peter R. Decker, *Fortunes and Failures: White-Collar Mobility in Nineteenth-Century San Francisco* (Cambridge, MA: Harvard University Press, 1978), 250–60; Philip J. Ethington, *The Public City: The Political Construction of Urban Life in San Francisco, 1850–1900* (New York: Cambridge University Press, 1994), 259–60.

5. Newlands, *Spring Valley Water* v. *San Francisco*, Petition for Rehearing, 29–30; Ethington, *Public City*, 274.

6. Theodore H. Hittel, *History of California*, vol. IV (San Francisco: N. J. Stone, 1898), 594–95; Issel and Cherney, *San Francisco*, 125–30.

7. H. M. Yerington to William Sharon (H. M. Yerington Papers, Bancroft Library, University of California, Berkeley [hereinafter Yerington MSS]). In 1880, Nevada's population was 62,266 and in 1890 it was 47,355; see Elliott, *History of Nevada*, appendix, table 1.

8. Jessie Moore to Betsy Moffat, November 28, 1877; Spring 1878; June 7–22, 1878; November 26, 1878, Barland-Newlands MSS. The contemporary name for this condition was neurasthenia, as described in George Miller Beard, *American Nervousness; Its Causes and Consequences, a Supplement to Nervous Exhaustion (Neurasthenia)* reprint (New York: Arno, 1972 [c. 1881]); Francis G. Gosling, *Before Freud: Neurasthenia and the American Medical Community, 1870–1910* (Urbana: University of Illinois Press, 1987).

9. California Constitutional Convention, 1878–1879 (Sacramento: State Printing Office, 1881), vol. III, 1517; E. B. Willis and P. K. Stockton, *Debates and Proceedings of the Constitutional Convention of the State of California* (Sacramento: State Printing Office, 1881), vol. III, 1523.

10. San Francisco *Chronicle*, March 20; April 1, 3, 6–9, 11, 17; May 6, 1879.

11. Lilley, "Early Career," 118–19, 123; Bancroft, *History of California*, vol. VII, 352; Burton J. Bledstein, *The Culture of Professionalism: The Middle Class and the Development of Higher Education in America* (New York: Norton, 1976), 122–23.

12. San Francisco *Chronicle*, January 1, February 10 (February 18 for the death of Clara Newlands), August 31, 1882; San Francisco *Call*, March 1–13, 1882; San Francisco *Bulletin*, March 1–13, 1882.

13. Newlands, *Spring Valley Water Works* v. *Board of Supervisors* 1881, 4–5, 3, Huntington Library, San Marino, California.

14. *California Reports*, 62:87.

15. *San Francisco Municipal Reports*, 1882–83, appendix, 151–58.

16. Newlands, *Spring Valley Water Works* v. *Board of Supervisors of the City and County of San Francisco* 1882, *California Reports*, 61:18–20, 36–40; Lilley, "Early Career," 146.

17. Bryce, *American Commonwealth*, vol. II, 539–40.

18. Newlands, *Spring Valley* v. *San Francisco* (November 1883), 26.

19. *United States Reports*, 110:354; George H. Morrison to George Bancroft, "Francis G. Newlands Memoir," Bancroft Library, 62; *United States Reports*, 110:355.

20. Newlands Memoir, Bancroft Library, 110.

4. THE "WRETCHED CASE"

1. Robert H. Kroninger, *Sarah & the Senator* (Berkeley: Howell-North, 1964), 15–21; *The Wasp*, XIV (January 24, 1885), 8–9, XII (February 16, 1884), 4. *The Wasp*, which did not have a popular audience, saw it as "the foulest, hardiest and most formidable conspiracy ever organized against the property of a man more wealthy than wise."
2. Chicago *Herald*, June 4, 1884, as quoted in Oscar Lewis and Carrol D. Hall, *Bonanza Inn* (New York: Knopf, 1939), 142–43.
3. Carl B. Swisher, *Stephen J. Field: Craftsman of the Law* (Washington, D.C.: 1930), 219, noted also by Lilley, "Early Career," 158–59; Newlands to Frederick W. Sharon, June 9, 1891, Sharon MSS; San Francisco *Chronicle*, October 24, November 25, 1878; San Francisco *Call*, October 7, 1884.
4. George H. Morrison to George Bancroft, Bancroft MSS of Newlands Biography for *Builders of the Commonwealth*, Bancroft Library, 68; Lilley, "Early Career," 161; Stephen J. Field to Edward Phelps, April 5, 1887, Newlands-Johnston Papers, Sterling Library, Yale University, New Haven, Connecticut; Edith Dobie, *The Political Career of Stephen Mallory White: Study of Party Activities under the Convention System*, Stanford University Publications Series History, Economics, and Political Science, vol. II, no. 1 (Palo Alto: Stanford University Press, 1921), 48; R. Hal Williams, *The Democratic Party and California Politics, 1880–1896* (Palo Alto: Stanford University Press, 1973), 49–50.
5. *The Wasp*, XIII (July 12, 1884), 8–9.
6. Ambrose Bierce, "Three Kinds of Rogue," in *Black Beetles in Amber* (San Francisco: Western Authors, 1892), 25.
7. Newlands to Betsy Moffat, July 10, 1885; Newlands to Betsy Moffat, February 9, 1883, Barland-Newlands MSS.
8. H. H. Bancroft, *Chronicles of the Builders of the Commonwealth*, IV (San Francisco: History Company, 1892), 78–79.
9. *California Reports*, vol. 75, 1–78; Newlands to F. W. Sharon, February 3, 1888, Sharon MSS.
10. Lilley, "Early Career," 171–72; Newlands, "Address to the Members of the Democratic Party of California," November 12, 1885, Newlands-Johnston MSS.
11. Richard Bayne to Newlands, November 21, 1885, Newlands-Johnston MSS; *Alta California*, March 12, 1886; Morrison and Bates, "Sketch of Francis G. Newlands," 24, Bancroft Library; *Alta California*, November 24, 1886.
12. Lilley, "Early Career," 182.
13. Lilley, "Early Career," 183; San Francisco *Bulletin*, March 25, 1887.
14. Lilley, "Early Career," based upon personal interview with Janet Newlands, Reno, Nevada, May 1963; Field to American Ambassador, April 5, 1887, Newlands MSS.
15. Lilley, "Early Career," 187; Newlands to F. W. Sharon, February 3, 1888, Sharon MSS.
16. Newlands to F. W. Sharon, February 3, 1888, Sharon MSS; *The Wasp*, January 3, 1885, 3, April 19, 1884, 5; Newlands to Sharon, December 17, 1887, Sharon MSS.
17. William M. Stewart to Newlands, December 20, 1887; Stewart to William

F. Herrin, March 11, 1888, William M. Stewart Papers, Nevada Historical Society, Reno, Nevada.

18. Stewart to Herrin, April 24, 1888; May 12, 1888, Stewart MSS.
19. Lilley, "Early Career," 190; Bancroft, *Builders of the Commonwealth*, 78–79.
20. J. O. Denny, ed., *The Bar Association of San Francisco: An Illustrated History from 1872 to 1924* (San Francisco: Arthur Wheeler, 1923), 21; Oscar T. Shuck, ed., *History of the Bench and Bar of California* (Los Angeles: Commercial Printing House, 1901), 417–21; Reno *Evening Gazette*, September 5, 1888.
21. Ward McAllister, *Society as I have Found It* (New York: Cassell, 1890); Douglas S. Watson, "The San Francisco McAllisters," *Quarterly of the California Historical Society*, 11 (June 1932), 127. Bierce, "To an Insolent Attorney," in *Black Beetles in Amber*, 176.
22. Brooks W. McCracken, "Althea and the Judges," *American Heritage* 18 (June 1967), 60–63, 75–79; Kruninger, *Sarah & the Senator*, 201, 202; Albert R. Buchanan, *David S. Terry of California: Dueling Judge* (San Marino, CA: Huntington Library, 1956).
23. Stewart to W. E. Sharon, December 12, 1888, Stewart MSS; Newlands to F. W. Sharon, January 7, 1889; Newlands to F. W. Sharon, January 10, 1889, Sharon MSS.
24. Carson City *Morning Appeal*, December 25, 1888; San Francisco *Examiner*, December 27, 1888; *Nevada State Journal*, December 29, 1888.

5. NEWLANDS AS A NEVADAN

1. Stewart to Newlands, January 15, 1889, Stewart MSS.
2. San Francisco *Bulletin*, March 26, 1887.
3. Stewart to Newlands, February 9, 1889, Stewart MSS.
4. Reno *Evening Gazette*, February 25, May 21, 1889; Stewart to Newlands, February 9, 1889, Stewart MSS.
5. Referred to as the "fortified monopoly" by Grace Dangberg, *Conflict on the Carson* (Minden, Nevada: Carson Valley Historical Society, 1975), 1–108.
6. Samuel P. Hays, *Conservation and the Gospel of Efficiency: The Progressive Conservation Movement 1890–1920* (New Haven: Yale University Press, 1959), 1.
7. Stewart to Newlands, May 25, 1889; July 17, 1889; July 18, 1889, Stewart MSS.
8. Reno *Evening Gazette*, October 7, 1889.
9. Ibid.
10. Reno *Evening Gazette*, September 30, 1889; Donald J. Pisani, *To Reclaim a Divided West: Water, Law, and Public Policy, 1848–1902* (Albuquerque: University of New Mexico Press, 1992), 196–98.
11. John W. Bird, "The End of the 'Monster' of Riparianism in Nevada," *Nevada Historical Society Quarterly*, 22 (Winter 1979), 271–72; John M. Townley, "Reclamation in Nevada, 1850–1904" (Ph.D. diss., University of Nevada, Reno, 1976), 208–209.
12. Townley, "Reclamation in Nevada," 140–47; William D. Rowley, "Opposition to Arid Land Irrigation in Nevada, 1890–1900," *Proceedings* of the West Coast Association of American Geographers (1981).
13. *Statutes of Nevada*, 1889, 102–107; Townley, "Reclamation in Nevada," 199, n.87.

14. Reno *Evening Gazette*, October 19, 1889; Dangberg, *Conflict on the Carson* condemns Newlands's representation of the "Fortified Monopoly," 1–108.
15. Townley, "Reclamation in Nevada," 200–201; William Lilley III, and Lewis L. Gould, "The Western Irrigation Movement, 1878–1902: A Reappraisal," in *The American West: A Reorientation*, ed. Gene M. Gressley, University of Wyoming Publications, XXXII (Laramie, 1966), 61–62.
16. Reno *Evening Gazette*, October 14, 1889, notes Newlands's purchase at Donner Lake totaled $18,000; Pisani, *To Reclaim a Divided West*, 198–202.
17. Barbara Richnak, *A River Flows: The Life of Robert Fulton* (Incline Village, NV: Comstock, 1983), 82; Reno *Evening Gazette*, October 21, 1889; Pisani, *To Reclaim a Divided West*, 203; Eric N. Moody, *Western Carpetbagger: The Extraordinary Memoirs of "Senator" Thomas Fitch* (Reno: University of Nevada Press, 1978).
18. Reno *Evening Gazette*, November 5, 1889.
19. Reno *Evening Gazette*, November 5, 1889; Stewart to Newlands, November 8, 1889, Stewart MSS.
20. Reno *Evening Gazette*, November 5, 1889; Stewart to Newlands, November 8, 1889, Stewart MSS.
21. *Public Papers of Francis G. Newlands*, ed. Arthur B. Darling (Washington, D.C.: W. F. Roberts, 1937), vol. I, 92.
22. Stewart to Newlands, November 8, 1889, Stewart MSS; Reno *Evening Gazette*, February 25, 1889.
23. Allen Weinstein, *Prelude to Populism: Origins of the Silver Issue, 1867–1878* (New Haven: Yale University Press, 1970), 53–54; Glass, *Silver and Politics*, 30.
24. Reno *Evening Gazette*, December 2, 1889.
25. William Hammond Hall to Newlands, May 10, 1891, Newlands MSS.
26. Carson City *Morning Appeal*, January 17, 1890.
27. Robert L. Fulton to William H. Mills, January 24, 1884; Fulton to Newlands, April 27, 1890, Robert L. Fulton Papers in possession of John Fulton, Tahoe City, California; "Storage and Reclamation: Mr. Newlands's Plans," a letter to the Nevada State Board of Trade, January 6, 1890, Nevada State Historical Society, Reno; Richnak, *A River Flows*.
28. Newlands to Fulton, December 24, 1889, Fulton MSS.
29. David B. Griffith, *Populism in the Western United States, 1890–1900*, 2 vols. (Lewiston, NY: Edwin Mellen, 1992), vol. 2, 529–88.

6. MORE THAN NOBLE WORDS

1. Oakland *Tribune*, January 25, 1890; Yerington to Newlands, February 22, 1890, Yerington MSS; Reno *Evening Gazette*, February 24, 1890; Austin *Reveille*, March 5, 1890; Yerington to H. F. Bartine, March 31, 1890, Yerington MSS.
2. Newlands to B. G. Leete, Washington *Post*, February 22, 1890, as published in the Reno *Evening Gazette*, April 28, 1890; Reno *Evening Gazette*, May 7, 19, 1890.
3. Carson City *Morning Appeal*, June 22, 1890; Reno *Evening Gazette*, June 25, 1890; Yerington to Stewart, June 21, 1890; Stewart to Newlands, July 18, 1890, Stewart MSS.
4. Reno *Evening Gazette*, August 15, 16, 1890.

5. Yerington to Stewart, August 17, 1890, Yerington MSS.
6. Reno *Evening Gazette*, August 18, 1890; Winnemucca *Silver State*, August 17, 1890; San Francisco *Post* as quoted in the Reno *Evening Gazette*, August 25, 1890.
7. "Black" Wallace, so named because of his staunch Republicanism after the Civil War, appeared in Nevada in 1863 and finally settled in Eureka. His election to county offices gained him access to local and state affairs. By the 1880s he was the strongest lobbyist with the legislature, representing primarily the interests of the Central Pacific Railroad. Many believed that he controlled legislation in Carson City and was the chief power in the state's Republican party. See Glass, *Silver and Politics*, 48–49; Reno *Evening Gazette*, September 6, 1890; Carson City *Morning Appeal*, September 9, 1890.
8. Stewart to Newlands, September 10, 1890, Stewart MSS.
9. Stewart to Newlands, September 13, 1890, Stewart MSS.
10. Yerington to A. C. Cleveland, September 17, 1890, Yerington MSS; Newlands to F. W. Sharon, September 25, Sharon MSS; Stewart to Newlands, October 2, 1890, Stewart MSS; Reno *Evening Gazette*, October 2, 1890.
11. Fulton to Newlands, November 12, 1890, Fulton MSS.
12. Carson City *Morning Appeal*, September 30, October 31, 1890; Fulton to Isaac Frohman, November 17, 1890, Fulton MSS.
13. Reno *Evening Gazette*, February 17, 1891.
14. Fulton to Newlands, February 24, 1891, Fulton MSS.
15. Reno *Evening Gazette*, March 4, 1891.
16. Fulton to Newlands, February 24, 1891, Fulton MSS; Carson City *Morning Appeal*, December 13, 1890, quoting the Eureka *Sentinel;* Peter Miraldo, Oral History, Oral History Collection, University of Nevada, Reno, Nevada, 57.
17. Isaac Frohman, secretary to Newlands, to Fulton, April 16, 1891, Fulton MSS; Reno *Evening Gazette*, June 12, 1891; Alan I. Marcus, *Agricultural Science and the Quest for Legitimacy: Farmers, Agricultural Colleges, and Experiment Stations, 1870–1890* (Ames: Iowa State University Press, 1985).
18. Reno *Evening Gazette*, December 24, 1891.
19. Newlands to Robert Fulton, March 15, 1892, Fulton MSS; Arthur B. Darling, ed., *Public Papers of Francis G. Newlands*, 2 vols. (Washington, D.C.: W. F. Roberts, 1937), I, 4.
20. Fulton to Sharon, April 5, 1892, Fulton MSS.
21. Reno *Evening Gazette*, July 11, 1892, quoting Carson City *Tribune;* Stewart to Newlands, July 7, 1892, Stewart MSS; Glass, *Silver and Politics*, 44; Newlands to F. W. Sharon, January 29, 1894, Sharon MSS.
22. Reno *Evening Gazette*, September 12, 1892; *Nevada State Journal*, September 12, 1892.
23. Glass, *Silver and Politics*, 60; Reno *Evening Gazette*, July 16, 1892; *Nevada State Journal*, "Reminiscences" by J. L. Considine, March 21, 1937; Nixon to Fulton, April 9, 1892, Fulton MSS; *Central Nevadan* (Battle Mountain) "Homes for Comstock Miners," March 19, 1892.
24. *Political History of Nevada*, ed. William D. Swackhamer, 6th edition (Carson City: State Printing Office, 1974), 84.
25. J. L. Considine, "Reminiscences," *Nevada State Journal*, March 21, 1937; Newlands to F. W. Sharon, January 29, 1894, Sharon MSS.

26. Yerington to D. O. Mills, December 14, 1892, Yerington MSS.
27. Newlands to Fulton, January 31, 1893, Fulton MSS.
28. Stewart to Newlands, February 28, 1893, Stewart MSS.
29. Reno *Evening Gazette*, March 23, 1893.
30. U.S. *Congressional Record*, 53rd Cong. 1st sess. vol. 25, part 1, August 22, 1893, 623; Yerington to Newlands, August 25, 1893, Yerington MSS; Glass, *Silver and Politics*, 79.
31. Reno *Evening Gazette*, October 27, 28, 1893.
32. Reno *Evening Gazette*, October 27, 28, 1893.
33. Newlands to F. W. Sharon, January 29, 1893, Sharon MSS.
34. Glass, *Silver and Politics*, 81–82.
35. Glass, *Silver and Politics*, 81–82; Reno *Evening Gazette*, September 15, 1894.
36. Yerington to Will Sharon, November 5, 1894, Yerington MSS.
37. Box 114, Newlands MSS.
38. *Political History of Nevada*, 184; Glass, *Silver and Politics*, 81–82; Yerington to D. J. Colton, October 4, 1894, Yerington, MSS; Reno *Evening Gazette*, November 10, 12, 1894.
39. Stewart to Newlands, July 4, 1895, Stewart MSS.
40. Lilley, "Early Career," 288.
41. *Nevada State Journal*, March 9, 15, 17, 21, 1895.

7. CHALLENGING THE OLD GUARD

1. Reno *Evening Gazette*, September 21, 1894, quoting interview in San Francisco *Examiner*.
2. Reno *Evening Gazette*, January 3, 1896; Winnemucca *Silver State*, January 9, 1896.
3. R. R. Bigelow to Fulton, January 4, 1896, Fulton MSS; San Francisco *Examiner*, January 5, 1896.
4. *Congressional Record*, 54th Cong., 1st sess., appendix, 341. (1895).
5. Lilley, "Early Career," 302–305; *St. Louis Republican*, April 28, 1897; *St. Louis Globe-Democrat*, June 4, 1896; William M. Stewart, interview in *Rocky Mountain News*, June 11, 1896; Marion Butler to Stewart, June 24, 1896, Stewart MSS; Elmer Ellis, *Henry Moore Teller: Defender of the West* (Caldwell, Idaho: Caxton, 1941), 256; Newlands to Henry M. Teller, July 8, 1896, Henry M. Teller Papers, Colorado Historical Society, Denver.
6. Francis G. Newlands, address to the convention of the National Silver Party, July 22, 1896, Newlands MSS; *Nevada State Journal*, July 22–23, 25–26, 1896; Russell R. Elliott, *Servant of Power: A Political Biography of Senator William M. Stewart* (Reno: University of Nevada Press, 1983), 182.
7. Glass, *Silver and Politics*, 111.
8. Reno *Evening Gazette*, December 24, 1896; Yerington to Newlands, January 13, 1897, refers to January 7, 1897, letter from Newlands supporting Nixon, Yerington MSS.
9. Yerington to Newlands, January 13, 1897, Yerington MSS.
10. Stewart to Wallace, February 9, 1897, Stewart MSS.
11. Yerington to Whitelaw Reid, January 12, 1897; Yerington to D. O. Mills, January 17, 1897; Yerington to Newlands, January 18, 1897; Yerington to D. O. Mills, January 20, 1897, Yerington MSS; Elliott, *Servant of Power*, 183.
12. Newlands statement on Tariff Bill, April 1, 1897, Newlands MSS.

13. Stewart to William F. Herrin, December 24, 1897, Stewart MSS; Yerington to D. O. Mills, December 21, 1897, Yerington MSS.
14. Will Sharon to Newlands, June 26, 1898, Newlands MSS.
15. Newlands to Will Sharon, June 6, 1898, Newlands MSS; Yerington to Sharon, July 8, 1898, Yerington MSS.
16. Stewart to John P. Jones, July 31, 1898; Stewart to Henry M. Teller, July 30, 1898, Stewart MSS.
17. Yerington to D. O. Mills, August 16, 1898, Yerington MSS.
18. Glass, *Silver and Politics*, 135–37; Carson City *Morning Appeal*, September 9, 1898.
19. Russell R. Elliott, "Nevada's Mining Heritage: Blessing and Burden," in *East of Eden, West of Zion: Essays on Nevada*, Wilbur S. Shepperson, ed. (Reno: University of Nevada Press, 1989), 47–48. Yerington to D. O. Mills, November 26, 1898, Yerington MSS.
20. Yerington to Mills, November 26, 1898; *Nevada State Journal*, December 4, 1898; *Silver State* (Winnemucca), December 3, 1898.
21. Wallace to Stewart, February 16, 1897; Isaac Frohman to Stewart, August 1, 1898, Stewart MSS.
22. Thomas Wren to Newlands in *Morning Appeal*, December 19, 1898; various Stewart letters in December 1898, Stewart MSS.
23. Carson City *Morning Appeal*, January 1899.
24. Carson City *Morning Appeal*, January 8, 1899; Glass, *Silver and Politics*, 150–51.
25. Glass, *Silver and Politics*, 150–55; this is the overriding theme of Glass's book.
26. Newlands to Carson City Opera House, January 17, 1898, Newlands MSS; *The Journals of Alfred Doten, 1849–1903*, ed. Walter Van Tilburg Clark, vol. III (Reno: University of Nevada Press, 1973), 2017.
27. *Nevada State Journal*, March 26, 1899; Glass, *Silver and Politics*, 159.
28. Newlands speech, January 23, 1899, Newlands MSS.
29. Stewart to E. B. Stahlman, February 10, 1899, Stewart MSS.
30. Newlands to Henry L. Wright, March 15, 1899, Sharon MSS; Yerington to D. O. Mills, February 9, 1899, Yerington MSS.
31. Nixon to Newlands, March 28, 1899, Newlands MSS.
32. Sally S. Zanjani, "The Election of 1890: The Last Hurrah for the Old Regime," *Nevada Historical Society Quarterly*, 20 (Spring 1977): 54–55.

8. WITH WATER ON HIS WHEEL

1. Nixon to Newlands, February 8, 1900, Newlands MSS.
2. Clarence D. Van Duzer to Newlands, January 5, 1900, Newlands MSS; Glass, *Silver and Politics*, 171.
3. Sharon to Newlands, March 20, 1900, Newlands MSS.
4. Sharon to Newlands, April 12, 13, 1900, Newlands MSS; Stewart to Charles H. Tweed, September 19, 1900, Stewart MSS.
5. Wallace to Stewart, May 26, 1900, Stewart MSS; Newlands to Sharon, January 2, 1900, Newlands MSS; Glass, *Silver and Politics*, 171.
6. Van Duzer to Newlands, May 29, 1900; Newlands to Sharon, June 1, 1900, Newlands MSS.
7. Newlands to W. F. Herrin, c. July 1900, and Newlands to Herrin, January 24, 1901, Newlands MSS; "Death Calls William F. Herrin, Chief Council," *Southern Pacific Bulletin*, 16 (April 1927), 5–6.

8. H. R. Cooke to Newlands, May 5, 1900, Newlands MSS; Stewart to Wallace, May 15, 1900, refers to the sacred 16-to-1 ratio that Newlands dismissed, Stewart MSS; Glass, *Silver and Politics*, 178; *Nevada State Journal*, July 17, 1900. Kirk H. Porter and Donald Bruce Johnson, *National Party Platforms, 1840–1856* (Urbana: University of Illinois Press, 1956), 115, 123.

9. Glass, *Silver and Politics*, 180–81; *Territorial Enterprise*, September 7, 1900; Carson City *Morning Appeal*, September 7, 1900.

10. E. L. Bingham of the Tuscarora *Times-Review* to Newlands, November 11, 1900, Newlands MSS; Yerington to D. O. Mills, November 8, 1900, Yerington MSS.

11. Stewart to Joseph R. DeLamar, November 17, 1900; December 4, 18, 1900, Stewart MSS.

12. Ralph M. Easely, secretary of the Civic Federation of Chicago to Newlands, August 3, 1899; Newlands to E. Rosewater, July 10, 1899; Franklin H. Head, president of the Civic Federation of Chicago, August 9, 1899; Newlands to Easley, September 28, 1899, Newlands MSS; Martin J. Sklar, *The Corporate Reconstruction of American Capitalism, 1890–1916: The Market, the Law, and Politics* (Cambridge, MA: Cambridge University Press, 1988), 207; R. I. Holaind, "The Chicago Trust Conference," *Annals* 15 (January 1900), 69–80; *Congressional Record*, 33rd sess., appendix, 675; Hans B. Thorelli, *The Federal Anti-Trust Policy: Origination of an American Tradition* (Baltimore: Johns Hopkins University Press, 1955), 522.

13. Newlands to House of Representatives, "Storage Reservoirs—The Arid Land Question," January 9, 1901; James G. Scrugham, ed., *Nevada: A Narrative of the Conquest of a Frontier Land*, vol. 1 (Chicago: American Historical Society, 1935), 323.

14. Donald J. Pisani, *From the Family Farm to Agribusiness: The Irrigation Crusade in California and the West, 1850–1931* (Berkeley: University of California Press, 1984), 291–92; Hiram Martin Chittenden, *Preliminary Report on Examination of Reservoir Sites in Wyoming and Colorado*, 55th Cong., 2nd sess., 1897, H. Ex. Doc. 141.

15. Stewart to Herrin, February 14, 1901; Herrin to Stewart, February 20, 1901, Stewart MSS; Yerington to D. O. Mills, February 12, 1901, Yerington MSS.

16. D. Jerome Tweton, "Theodore Roosevelt and the Arid Lands," *North Dakota Quarterly*, 36 (Spring 1968), 21–28; William Lilley III and Lewis L. Gould, "The Western Irrigation Movement, 1878–1902: A Reappraisal," in *The American West: A Reorientation*, ed. Gene M. Gressley (Laramie, WY: n.p., 1966), 71; Pisani, *To Reclaim a Divided West*, 312–15.

17. *Congressional Record*, 56th Cong., 2nd sess., part 2 (January 30, 1901), 1701–02; Lilley and Gould, "Western Irrigation Movement," 59, 73.

18. *Congressional Record*, 56th Cong., 2nd sess., February 19, 1901, vol. 34, part 3, 2666; *Congressional Record*, 56th Cong., 2nd sess., March 1, 1901, vol. 34, part 4, in U.S. Senate, 3289; Ray Palmer Teele, *Irrigation in the United States: Discussion of Its Legal, Economic and Financial Aspects* (New York: Appleton, 1915), 242; Marc Reisner, *Cadillac Desert: The American West and Its Disappearing Water* (New York: Viking Penguin, 1986); Donald Worster, *Rivers of Empire: Water, Aridity, and the Growth of the American West* (New York: Pantheon, 1985).

19. Washington *Times*, December 29, 1901.

20. Darling, ed., *Newlands*, 72–75; Pisani, *To Reclaim a Divided West*, 313; Lilley and Gould, "Western Irrigation," 73.

21. Newlands, "National Irrigation Works," *Forestry and Irrigation*, 8 (February 1902), 65 (63–66); Elting E. Morison, ed., *The Letters of Theodore Roosevelt*, 8 vols. (Cambridge: Harvard University Press, 1951), II, 317; San Francisco *Chronicle*, February 7, 1902.

22. *Nevada State Journal*, June 19, 1902.

23. Reno *Evening Gazette*, June 16, 1902; *Nevada State Journal*, June 18, 1902.

24. *Statutes at Large of the United States of America, 1901–1903*, vol. XXXII, part 1 (Washington, D.C.: Government Printing Office, 1903), 390; William Cronon, "Landscapes of Abundance and Scarcity," in *The Oxford History of the American West*, ed. Clyde A. Milner III, Carol A. O'Connor, and Martha A. Sandweiss (New York: Oxford University Press, 1994), 618; Lawrence B. Lee, *Reclaiming the American West: An Historiography and Guide* (Santa Barbara, CA. ABC-Clio Press, 1980); Pisani, *To Reclaim a Divided West,* calls it "the boldest piece of legislation ever enacted pertaining to the trans-Mississippi West," 322.

25. Reno *Evening Gazette*, June 4, 1902; Newlands to M. F. Michael, December 7, 1904, Newlands MSS.

26. *Statutes at Large 1901–1903*, 389; Reno *Evening Gazette*, June 4, 1902; Russell R. Elliott, *Nevada's Twentieth-Century Mining Boom: Tonopah-Goldfield-Ely* (Reno: University of Nevada Press, 1966); Sally Zanjani, "A Theory of Critical Realignment: The Nevada Example, 1892–1908," *Pacific Historical Review* 48 (May 1979).

27. Yerington to Newlands, January 31, 1902, vol. 21, 187; Yerington to Newlands, March 8, 1902, vol. 26, 323, Yerington MSS.

28. Carson City *News*, c. July 26, 1902; Yerington to D. O. Mills, July 28 and August 16, 1902, Yerington MSS; see also James W. Hulse, "Making Law in the Great Basin: The Evolution of the Federal Court in Nevada, 1855–1905," *Western Legal History*, 1 (Summer/Fall 1988), 160–61.

29. Horace F. Bartine to Newlands, December 31, 1903; Newlands to J. Roff, August 14, 1904; Newlands to Marion S. Wilson, February 10, 1903, Newlands MSS; Yerington to D. O. Mills, January 18, 1903, Yerington MSS; *The Morning Appeal*, January 28, 1903.

9. NEWLANDS

1. Scrugham, *Conquest of a Frontier Land*, vol. 1, 413.

2. Darling, ed., *Newlands*, 77–80; *Statutes of the State of Nevada, Twenty-First Session of the Legislature, 1903* (Carson City: State Printing Office, 1906), 25.

3. Newlands to J. H. Dennis, August 4, 1903, Newlands MSS.

4. Newlands to F. W. Sharon, February 10, 1904, Sharon MSS.

5. Robert W. Cherny, *A Righteous Cause: The Life of William Jennings Bryan* (Boston: Little, Brown, 1985), 72–90.

6. Thomas J. Osborne, "Empire Can Wait," in *American Opposition to Hawaiian Annexation, 1893–1898* (Kent, OH: Kent State University Press, 1981), 109, 120, 133; Merze Tate, *Hawaii: Reciprocity or Annexation* (East Lansing: Michigan State University Press, 1968), 254; Joseph A. Fry, "Strange Bedfellows: Newlands, Morgan, and Hawaii," *Halcyon* (1989), 105–23; Newlands to William F. Sheehan, National Democratic Committee, September 17, 1904, Newlands MSS.

7. Newlands to Alton B. Parker, July 20, 1904, Newlands MSS.

8. Newlands to Parker, July 30, 1904, Newlands MSS.

9. Newlands to Maxwell, July 27, 1904, Newlands MSS.
10. Newlands to F. W. Sharon, May 25, 1904, Sharon MSS; Newlands to Will F. Sheehan, September 17, 1904, outlines his support of Sparks to a Democratic national committeeman but at the same time points out Spark's huge indebtedness, possibly $300,000, but emphasizes that, "he is an acute, adroit politician. . . ." Ostrander, *Rotten Borough*, misses the hidden meaning in this letter, but in other correspondence it is clear that the Newlands and Nixon camps were cooperating. See Nixon to Newlands, February 3, 1904; Newlands to J. Roff, September 14, 1904; Newlands to W. Taggart, August 23, 1904; At the opening of the legislature in January 1905, Sparks wrote Newlands that he heard Nixon was restless about the upcoming election and that he looked for "a little fun before he [Nixon] was elected," Sparks to Newlands, January 9, 1905; W. E. Sharon writes to Newlands that when he tried to explain the situation to Mrs. Sparks he made "no impression upon her and left her at Carson raising her wrath for both of us," January 1905, Newlands MSS; *Miner-Transcript* (Nevada City), June 30, 1905; *Reese River Reveille*, August 2, 1905; *Nevada State Herald* (Wells), August 11, 1905.
11. Newlands to William F. Sheehan, September 17, 1904, Newlands MSS.
12. Newlands to E. L. Bingham, January 23, 1905, Newlands MSS.
13. Ibid.
14. Smythe to Newlands, December 14, 1905; Newlands to Bartine, Bingham, Nate Roff and James C. Sweeney, March 1905; Newlands to Roff, December, 14, 1904, Newlands MSS.
15. Nate W. Roff to Newlands, March 24, 1905; E. L. Bingham to Newlands, March 30, 1905; James G. Sweeney to Newlands, April 12, 1905, Newlands MSS.
16. *Nevada State Journal*, March 1905.
17. William F. Herrin to Newlands, January 23, 1905, Newlands MSS; Newlands, "Common Sense of the Railroad Question," *North American Review*, 180 (April 1905), 579 (576–85); Newlands to David J. Lewis, January 19, 1905, Newlands MSS.
18. Ian Bell, *The Dominican Republic* (Boulder, CO: Westview, 1981), 61; Sumner Wells, *Naboth's Vineyard* (Mamaroneck, NY: Appel, reprint of 1926 edition), vol. II, 621–28.
19. Newlands, "The San Domingo Question," *North American Review*, 180 (June 1905), 897–98 (885–98).
20. Reno *Evening Gazette*, June 17, 1905; M. M. Gardwood (letter), "The Big Stick and the Big Ditch," *Progressive West*, 1 (June 1905), 1–2; Newlands, Banquet Address to the Irrigation Committee of the House and Senate, Sheridan, Wyoming, June 30, 1905, Special Collections, Library, University of Nevada, Reno, Newlands MSS.
21. Alice Roosevelt Longworth, *Crowded Hours: Reminiscences of Alice Roosevelt Longworth* (New York: Scribner's, 1933), 70–72; Carol Felsenthal, *Alice Roosevelt Longworth* (New York: Putnam's, 1988), 78–81.
22. Alice Roosevelt Longworth, *Crowded Hours*, 73, 78.
23. Ibid., 86, 96, 107.
24. Newlands to F. W. Sharon, November 1, 1905, Sharon MSS; Cherny, *A Righteous Cause*, 102.

25. Newlands, "Democrat in the Philippines," *North American Review*, 181 (December 1905), 933, 943; Newlands, "The Right Way to Help the Filipinos," *The Independent*, 60 (March 8, 1906), 560–64; Newlands to David Monroe of the *North American Review* (October 1905); Newlands to William Howard Taft, December 30, 1905, Newlands MSS.
26. Newlands to E. L. Bingham, November 29, 1905, Newlands MSS; Robert Laxalt, *Nevada: A Bicentennial History* (New York: Norton, 1977), 67; C. Elizabeth Raymond, *George Wingfield: Owner and Operator of Nevada* (Reno: University of Nevada Press, 1992) sees Wingfield's grip on Nevada politics as equally uncertain, but this view is controversial and revisionist; Jerome E. Edwards, *McCarran: Political Boss of Nevada* (Reno: University of Nevada Press, 1982) sees his subject possessing a vice-like grip on the state's politics.
27. Smythe to Newlands, December 14, 1905, Newlands MSS.
28. Newlands to E. L. Bingham, December 27, 1905, Newlands MSS.

10. THE ROAD AHEAD

1. David Sarashon, *The Party of Reform: Democrats in the Progressive Era* (Jackson: University of Mississippi Press, 1989), 26.
2. Newlands to Roosevelt, January 3, 1906, Newlands MSS; Newlands, "Common Sense of the Railroad Question," *North American Review*, 180 (April 1905), 577 (576–85).
3. Newlands, "Common Sense on the Railroad Question," 582–84; John Morton Blum, *The Republican Roosevelt* (Cambridge, MA: Harvard University Press, 1977, second edition), 73, 87, 105; *Congressional Record*, Senate, March 2, 1906, 6874.
4. Newlands to Leslie M. Shaw, secretary of the treasury, January 20, 1906, Newlands MSS.
5. Nate Roff to Newlands, January 28, 1906; Newlands to Roff, February 17, 1906; James G. Sweeney to Newlands, March 12, 1906, Newlands MSS.
6. Newlands, "The New San Francisco," *The Independent*, 60 (May 10, 1906), 1093–96; Yerington to Newlands, May 16, 1906, Yerington MSS.
7. Yerington to D. O. Mills, August 17, 1906, Yerington MSS.
8. Newlands to James T. Boyd, January 1907, Newlands MSS.
9. Yerington to D. O. Mills, June 22, 1907, Yerington MSS.
10. John M. Townley, "Reclamation and the Red Man: Relationships on the Truckee-Carson Project, Nevada," *The Indian Historian*, 11, no. 1 (1978), 21–28.
11. Roosevelt to Newlands, March 14, 1907; Newlands to Hudson, dated Cairo, Ill., May 15, 1907; Newlands to editor of Washington *Post*, from Reno, June 4, 1907, Newlands MSS.
12. Elliott, *Nevada's Twentieth-Century Mining Boom*, 378.
13. Newlands to W. E. Sharon, December 16, 27, 1907, Newlands MSS; Sally Zanjani, *Goldfield: The Last Gold Rush on the Western Frontier* (Athens, OH: Swallow Press/Ohio University Press, 1992).
14. Commission Report, House Document No. 607, 22; Elliott, *Twentieth-Century Mining Boom*, 384; Raymond, *George Wingfield*, 79–80.
15. Newlands to W. E. Sharon, December 16, 1907, Newlands MSS.

16. Newlands to Sparks, December 28, 1907, Newlands MSS; *Nevada State Journal,* February 13, 1908.
17. J. D. Finch to Newlands, February 7, 1908; J. S. Dunnigan to Newlands, February 10, 1908; W. H. Husky to Newlands, March 2, 1908, Newlands MSS; Elliott, *History of Nevada,* 223.
18. James T. Boyd to Newlands, February 27, 1908, Newlands MSS.
19. Boyd to Newlands, February 27, 1908; William A. Douglass and Robert A. Nylen, *Letters from the Nevada Frontier, Correspondence of Tasker L. Oddie, 1898–1902* (Norman: University of Oklahoma Press, 1992), xi–xxii; Loren B. Chan, *Sagebrush Statesman: Tasker L. Oddie of Nevada* (Reno: University of Nevada Press, 1973), 37–46.
20. Rhyolite *Herald,* March 7, 1908.
21. *Nevada State Journal,* June 6, 22, 1908; Carson City *News,* July 11, 1908.
22. Carson City *News,* July 4, 1908; Scrugham, *History of Nevada,* 73–74; Goldfield *Chronicle,* August 21, 1908; Newlands to Flanigan, August 17, 1908.
23. Sparks *Forum,* September 2, 1908; San Francisco *Examiner,* September 4, 1908.
24. "Disbursements to Newspapers," folder name Election of 1908, Financial, Newlands MSS.
25. "Summary of Remarks: Election 1908," September 28 to November 3, 1908, Newlands MSS; Goldfield *Chronicle,* August 23, 1908; Elko *Independent,* October 23, 1908, quoting from an article in the San Francisco *Examiner;* White Pine *News,* August 12, 1923.
26. Reno *Gazette,* October 22, 1908.
27. Summary of Remarks: Election 1908, Newlands MSS.
28. Newlands, "The Development of American Waterways," *North American Review,* 187 (June 1908), 875–79 (873–79); Newlands speech to Traffic Club of Chicago banquet, January 30, 1908, "The Coordination of Railroad and Water Transportation," Newlands MSS.
29. H. A. Dunn to Newlands, October 20, 1908; P. S. Triplett to Newlands, October 30, 1908, Newlands MSS.
30. H. A. Dunn to Newlands, October 29, 1908, Newlands MSS; Goldfield *Chronicle,* October 29, 1908; Father Dermody to Newlands, October 31, 1908, Newlands MSS; *Nevada Political History,* ed. John Koontz (Carson City: State Printing Office, 1959), 66.
31. *Nevada Recorder* (Ramsey, Nevada), October 25, 1908; *Nevada State Journal,* October 28, 1908.
32. Election file, 1908, Newlands MSS.

11. RACISM AND REFORM

1. Newlands to Professor J. Lawrence Laughlin of the University of Chicago (August 21, 1911), Newlands MSS; William D. Rowley, "Senator Newlands and the Modernization of the Democratic Party," *Nevada Historical Society Quarterly,* 15 (Summer 1972), 24–34; Mark H. Haller, *Eugenics: Hereditarian Attitudes in American Thought* (New Brunswick: Rutgers University Press, 1963), 5; John R. Commons, *Race and Immigrants in America* (New York: Macmillan, 1908); R. W. Shufeldt, *The Negro: A Menace to American Civilization* (Boston: Richard G. Badger, 1907); Alfred Holt Stone,

Studies in the American Race Problem (New York: Doubleday, Page, 1908), are examples of the spate of studies appearing on the subject during the Progressive era; Newlands, "A Western View of the Race Question," *Annals of the American Academy of Political and Social Science*, 24 (September 1909), 49–51; Rowley, "Francis G. Newlands: A Westerner's Search for a Progressive and White America," *Nevada Historical Society Quarterly*, 17 (Summer 1974), 69–79.

2. Darling, ed., *Newlands*, vol. 1, 296–99; New York *Times*, June 17, 1912. *Congressional Record*, 56th Cong., 1st sess., part 1, vol. 33, 674; Ray Stannard Baker, *Following the Color Line: American Negro Citizenship in the Progressive Era* (Harper & Row, ed. of original Doubleday, Page, 1918), 256–57; Newlands to Nevada Governor Denver Dickerson, February 3, 1909, Newlands MSS.

3. Newlands, "A Western View of the Race Question," 49–51.

4. Newlands to J. H. Patten, July 8, 1912, Newlands MSS; Darling, *The Public Papers*, 297; Newlands to Franklin K. Lane, July 11, 1911, Newlands MSS; for a typically argued view supporting racial homogeneity as an essential foundation for a democratic society, see Miles C. Everett, "Chester Harvey Rowell, Pragmatic Humanist and California Progressive" (Ph.D. diss., University of California, Berkeley, 1965); Frank W. Van Nuys, "A Progressive Confronts the Race Question: Chester Rowell, the California Alien Land Act of 1913, and the Contradictions of Early Twentieth-Century Racial Thought," *California History*, 123 (Spring 1994), 213; John Higham, *Strangers in the Land: Patterns of American Nativism, 1860–1925* (New Brunswick, NJ: Rutgers University Press, 2nd ed., 1988), 174; for a discussion of Newlands's anti-Oriental views, see Harlan H. Hague, "The Racial Attitudes of Francis G. Newlands," *The Pacific Historian*, 15 (Fall 1971), 11–30.

5. Washington *Herald*, December 17, 1907.

6. Atlanta *Constitution*, December 27, 1907; New York *Evening Post*, February 8, 1909; *Nevada State Journal*, February 4, 1909.

7. Darling, *The Public Papers*, 296–99; the letter also appears in the *Nevada State Journal*, February 4, 1909; *Annals of American Academy* (May–June 1909).

8. Macon *Telegraph*, February 12, 1909; Santa Cruz *Sentinel*, February 11, 1909; Newlands to James A MacKnight, July 16, 1912, Newlands MSS; Washington *Bee*, August 1912.

9. New York *Evening Journal*, August 6, 1912.

10. As quoted in the *Nevada State Journal* (Reno), July 26, 1913, from the San Francisco *Bulletin;* Newlands to A. R. White and enclosed statement on Booker T. Washington, January 4, 1916, Newlands MSS.

11. George M. Fredrickson, *The Black Image in the White Mind: The Debate on Afro-American Character and Destiny* (New York: Harper & Row, 1971), 320.

12. Carson City *Daily News*, January 19, 1909.

13. Newlands to Denver Dickerson, Governor of Nevada, January 5, 1909, Newlands MSS.

14. *Nevada State Journal*, April, 19, 1909; Newlands to James T. Boyd of Reno, March 25, 1909, Newlands MSS; *Reese River Reveille*, April 1, 1905; *Nevada State Journal*, March 1905; Fallon *Standard*, March 19, 1913.

15. By 1908 he addressed such groups as the American Institute of Architects and a City Planning Conference in Washington, D.C. on what had been accomplished in planning for the city. Before an Art Federation Conference in Washington, D.C. (May 11, 1909), he proposed federal support of the arts or a "Government Bureau of the Fine Arts" to promote the appreciation of beauty and artistic achievement in American life. This he had suggested the year before at the University of Nevada when he tied the efficient use of resources of the West to the cultivation of beauty through the fine arts and support of them through national appropriations. He concluded that "demands not only for comfort, but for the beautiful will require that training in the fine arts shall be added to the national domain of education." Address to American Institute of Architects, December 17, 1908, Newlands MSS; Address to Art Federation Convention, May 11, 1909, Washington, D.C., Newlands MSS; Address to City Planning Conference, "What has been accomplished in City Planning in Washington, D.C.," May 22, 1909, Newlands MSS; Newlands speech at the dedication of the Mackay Memorial Statue, June 9, 1908, Newlands MSS.
16. Michael G. McCarthy, *Hour of Trial: the Conservation Conflict in Colorado and the West, 1891–1907*, (Norman: University of Oklahoma Press, 1977); "Pinchot Land Leasing Policies," 1908, Newlands MSS; Henry S. Graves to Newlands containing "Answer to Protest of Adams and McGill against Extension of the Nevada National Forest," March 19, 1910, Newlands MSS; *Report of the National Conservation Commission*, 60th Cong., 2nd sess., Sen. Doc. 676, vol. 3 (Washington, D.C.: GPO), 360.
17. Newlands to W. F. Marrs, February 24, 1910, Newlands MSS; G. L. Shumway, Executive Chairman American Irrigation Federation, "Give Settlers a Free Hand," *The Irrigation Age*, 22 (March 1907), 145; F. H. Newell, "Reclamation and Homemaking: Review of General Conditions in Reclamation Service," *Scientific American* (August 12, 1911); F. H. Newell to Newlands, January 25, 1910, Newlands MSS.
18. Truckee-Carson Farmers' Association to Newlands, March 10, 1910; Newlands to William Howard Taft, August 14, 1909, Newlands MSS.
19. Newlands speech on Nevada Progressivism, 1910, Box 85, Newlands MSS; Newlands to the *Nevada State Journal*, September 10, 1910; Newlands to Tallman, February 8, 1911; R. P. Dunlap to Newlands, May 12, 1910, Newlands MSS.
20. Newlands to *Nevada State Journal*, June 22, 1910; Newlands to August Belmont, February 14, 1910, Newlands MSS.
21. Charles S. Thomas, "Autobiography," typescript copy, Charles S. Thomas Papers, Colorado Historical Society, Denver, 175–79.
22. Millard F. Hudson to Newlands, February 11, 1910, Newlands MSS.
23. Newlands to Charles W. Bryan, December 20, 1910, Newlands MSS.
24. Newlands to H. F. Bartine, April 25, 1910; New York *Evening Post*, May 30, 1910; William C. Liller to Newlands, June 25, 1910; Newlands to Liller, July 2, 1910; Newlands to Franklin K. Lane, July 11, 1911; Newlands to Walter H. Page, July 12, 1911; Newlands to Clay Tallman, July 29, 1911, Newlands MSS.
25. *The Outlook*, "The Decade's Work in Saving Watersheds," 95 (June 25, 1910), 358–59; Newlands to *Outlook* editors, June 1910, Newlands MSS; Pinchot to Newlands, January 23, 1911, Newlands MSS.

26. Franklin K. Lane to Newlands, October 7, 1911, Newlands MSS.
27. Newlands to Wilson, July 1, 1912, Newlands MSS; Wingfield to Oddie, June 13, 1912, Oddie Papers, Huntington Library, San Marino, California; "News Item for Sir Francis," in Eureka *Sentinel*, March 16, 1912, notes the presence of Wingfield at a recent Republican State Central Committee. It noted that this "was the first time that Mr. Wingfield openly affiliated with either political party," and suggested this portended trouble for "Sir Francis Newlands, now-and-then of Nevada"; Raymond, *George Wingfield*, 103–104.
28. James D. Finch to Millard F. Hudson, January 29, 1912; Finch to Newlands, February 14, 1912; Wilson to Newlands, April 1, 1912; Wilson to Newlands, May 20, 29, 1912; Newlands to Wilson, July 1, 1912; Newlands biographical sketch by Millard F. Hudson, July 1, 1912; Newlands to Wilson, July 5, 1912, Newlands MSS.
29. Kirk H. Porter and Donald Bruce Johnson, *National Party Platforms, 1840–1956* (Urbana: University of Illinois Press, 1956), 169, 178, 184.
30. Box 104, Newlands MSS.
31. *Nevada State Journal*, July 3, 1912; Tonopah *Bonanza*, June 27, 1912; *Western Nevada Miner* (Tonopah); the *News*, Calinga, California, July 5, 1912; Clippings File, "Race Problems," Milwaukee, Wisconsin, June 27, 1912, Newlands MSS; Sacramento *Bee*, June 29, 1912.
32. Newlands to James T. Boyd, July 10, 1912, Newlands MSS.
33. Newlands to Wilson, September 24, 1912, Newlands MSS; Reno *Evening Gazette*, September 30, 1912.
34. Newlands speech 1912, Box 85, Newlands MSS.
35. *Nevada State Journal*, November 14, 15, 1912; Progressive Legislation: Retrenchment and Tax Reforms by Francis G. Newlands, Newlands MSS; William D. Rowley, "The Wisconsin Idea in Nevada," *Nevada Historical Society Quarterly*, 34 (Summer 1991), 350–59; Ramonzo Adams, *Taxation in Nevada: A History* (Reno: Nevada State Historical Society, 1918); *Lyon County Wasp*, December 19, 1912.

12. VISIONS WON AND LOST

1. Darling, ed., *Newlands*, 269, 329; Department of Commerce, press release, September 19, 1917, RG 1115, Records of the Bureau of Reclamation (Records of the National Reclamation Association), Box 25, file "Special Correspondence with Presidents, Senators, etc." National Archives, Washington, D.C.; Newlands to Wilson, September 24, 1912: in the presidential campaign of 1912 Newlands related what he saw as "encouraging words regarding the irrigation movement and its enlargement into a general river regulation movement." He noted George Maxwell had asked him to call "the enlarged policy" to the attention of Wilson; see also Newlands to Wilson, October 17, 1917, Newlands MSS; George Maxwell to Newton D. Baker (secretary of war), June 19, 1918, RG 115, Records of the Bureau of Reclamation (Records of the National Reclamation Association), Box 25, file "Special Correspondence with Presidents Senators, etc." National Archives.
2. *Silver State* (Winnemucca), June 28, 1913; Newlands, "Possibilities of a Democratic Administration," *The Independent*, 73 (October 3, 1912), 758; San Francisco *Bulletin*, April 28, 1913.

3. Alfred Chartz to Newlands, May 25, 1913, Newlands MSS; Reno *Evening Gazette,* June 28, 1913, quoting from the National *Miner* (National, Nevada).
4. Wingfield to Newlands, May 17, 1913; Wingfield to Newlands, June 10, 1913, Newlands MSS; Wingfield to Newlands, April 30, 1913, Newlands MSS; Newlands to Wingfield, April 29, 1913; Newlands to William F. Herrin, May 24, 1913; Reno *Evening Gazette,* July 1, 1913; James Boyd to Newlands, May 24, 1913, Newlands MSS; W. E. Sharon to Newlands, May 30, 1913, Newlands MSS.
5. Bryan to Newlands, September 11, 1913, Newlands MSS; Newlands to Bryan, September 18, 1913; "Notes on the Tariff Question and Democratic Politics, 1914," Box 89, Newlands MSS.
6. Newlands, "Possibilities of a Democratic Administration," *The Independent,* 73 (October 3, 1912), 759; Reno *Evening Gazette,* June 28, 1913.
7. *Congressional Record,* vol. 51, 11089; Thomas C. Blaisdell, Jr., *The Federal Trade Commission: An Experiment in the Control of Business* (New York: Columbia University Press, 1932), 10; E. D. Durand, "Creation of a Federal Trade Commission," *Quarterly Journal of Economics,* 29 (November 1914), 90–97; Darling, *Newlands,* 350–51.
8. The *Morning Appeal,* September 8, 1914; Newlands to Wilson, c. September 1914, Box 73; introduction to Col. House and Wilson to Newlands on Mexican policy 1914, Newlands MSS.
9. Newlands Speech at Fallon, October 5, 1914, Box 110, Newlands MSS; John Koontz, ed., *Political History of Nevada* (Carson City: State Printing Office, 1960), 68; *Statutes of the State of Nevada, Twenty-Sixth Session of the Legislature, 1913* (Carson City: State Printing Office, 1913), 194.
10. Newlands to Martin, March 14, 1913; Mrs. Jewett W. Adams and Mrs. Fred Stadtmuller to Newlands, July 3, 1914; Newlands to Mrs. Jewett W. Adams, July 26, 1914, Newlands MSS; Newlands to Martin, April 10, 1914; Ann Bail Howard, *The Long Campaign: A Biography of Anne Martin* (Reno: University of Nevada Press, 1985); Austin E. Hutcheson, ed., "The Story of the Nevada Equal Suffrage Campaign: Memoirs of Anne Martin," University of Nevada *Bulletin,* 24 (August 1948); Mrs. Fred H. Tucker, "The Newlands Bill: Senate Bill 2739: What It Is and What Women Can Do About It," pamphlet from General Federation of Women's Clubs, January 1914, Newlands MSS.
11. Clay Tallman to Newlands, April 20, 1914, Newlands MSS.
12. Lloyd B. Patrick to Newlands, February 15, 1914; James G. Sweeney to Newlands, July 13, 1914; Newlands to Sweeney, July 26, 1914; George B. Thatcher to Newlands, August 4, 1914; J. F. Shaugnessy to Newlands, August 25, 1914; George B. Thatcher to Newlands, August 4, 1914, Newlands MSS.
13. Newlands to F. H. Newell, September 13, 1914; *Las Vegas Age,* November 1, 1913; Church to Newlands, November 29, 1913; Newlands to Church, December 9, 1913, Newlands MSS; Bernard Mergen, "Seeking Snow: James E. Church and the Beginnings of Snow Science," *Nevada Historical Society Quarterly,* 35 (Summer 1992), 75–104.
14. James T. Boyd to Newlands, September 29, 1914, Newlands MSS.

15. William D. Rowley, *Reno: Hub of the Washoe Country* (Woodland Hills, CA: Windsor Press, 1985); Anne Martin to Newlands, June 12, 1914; Wingfield to Newlands, May 6, 1914, Newlands MSS.
16. "Is Newell Trying to Make Serfs Out of the Water Users," *Irrigation Age*, 29 (February 1914), 110–11, 119; F. G. Hough to James Finch, November 11, 1914; F. G. Hough to Newlands, November 22, 1914, Newlands MSS.
17. Newlands to Wilson, November 11, 1914; *The Socialist*, c. September 1914; Reno *Evening Gazette*, October 1, 1914.
18. *The Commoner*, September 1914; Newlands to Bryan, September 24, 1914, Newlands MSS.
19. Koontz, *Political History of Nevada*, 69; Franklin K. Lane to Newlands, November 5, 1914; Key Pittman to Newlands, November 4, 1914; Newlands to Pittman, November 11, 1914; Tumulty to Newlands, November 4, 1914, Newlands MSS.
20. Newlands to Wilson, November 11, 1914, Newlands MSS.
21. Newlands to Thomas, November 11, 1914; Newlands to J. F. Kunz, November 14, 1914; Disbursements to Newspaper Advertisement, 1914; Newlands to Henry S. Pritchett, November 20, 1914; Newlands to Martin, November 19, 1914; Newlands to Charles Bryan, November 20, 1914, Newlands MSS.
22. James D. Finch to Newlands, September 26, 1916, Newlands MSS.
23. Carson City *News*, March 18, 1913.
24. *The University of Nevada Sagebrush*, October 12, 1915.
25. *Nevada State Journal*, November 14, 1915.
26. Newlands to Hall McAllister, June 15, 1915, Newlands MSS; speech at Verdi, Nevada, reprinted in the Carson City *Appeal*, October 1916.
27. Newlands speech to the Reno Commercial Club, October 25, 1917, Newlands MSS.
28. Herbert Croly, *The Promise of American Life* (New York: Macmillan, 1909); journalists still appealed to the didacticism and tenets of the New Nationalism in the late twentieth century. See John B. Judis and Michael Lind, "For a New Nationalism," *New Republic* 212 (March 27, 1995), 19–27.
29. Frederick Jackson Turner, "Social Forces in American History," *American Historical Review* 16 (January 1911), 223.
30. "About People We Know," *Town and Country* (October 20, 1916), 17.
31. Martin J. Sklar, *The United States as a Developing Country: Studies in U.S. History in the Progressive Era and the 1920s* (New York: Cambridge University Press, 1992). "A rich culmination of classical social theory, centered upon defining 'modern civilization,' or 'modern society,' emerged around the turn of the century, and many of its basic elements can be found, empirically, in the thought of leading personae dramatis of American intellect and politics in the period," 47.
32. Speech to Reno Commercial Club (October 25, 1917), Newlands MSS; *Nevada State Journal*, December 25, 28, 1917.
33. Rowley, "Francis G. Newlands and the Promises of American Life," *Nevada Historical Society Quarterly*, 32 (Fall 1989), 169–80.

INDEX

WILLIAM D. ROWLEY is Professor of History at the University of Nevada at Reno. He has served as Executive Secretary of the Western History Association and is a longtime student of western resource history. He is author of *M. L. Wilson and the Campaign for the Domestic Allotment Plan, U.S. Forest Service Grazing and Rangelands: A History*, and *Reno: Hub of the Washoe Country*. Rowley serves on the governing board of the Forest History Society, is Editor-in-Chief of the *Nevada Historical Society Quarterly*, and is a frequent consultant to resource management agencies.